SPORTS NUTRITION

SPORTS NUTRITION

S.L.ARORA
SURESH GOPAPALNI

CYBER TECH PUBLICATIONS
4264/3, Ansari Road, Daryaganj, New Delhi-110002 (India)
Ph.: 011-23244078, 011-43559448 Fax: 011-23280028
E-Mail: cyberpublicationsdelhi@yahoo.com
Website: www.cybertechpublications.com

SPORTS NUTRITION

S.L.ARORA SURESH GOPALANI

First Edition 2011

Published by :

G.S. Rawat for **Cyber Tech Publications**
4264/3, Ansari Road, Daryaganj, New Delhi-110002 (India)
Ph.: 011-23244078, 011-43559448 Fax: 011-23280028
E-Mail: cyberpublicationsdelhi@yahoo.com
Website: www.cybertechpublications.com

CONTENTS

Preface

The argument has been made that regular exercise, particularly in elite athletes with highly demanding training regimens, increases protein requirements over those for sedentary individuals. This argument is often based on nitrogen balance. Several well-controlled studies have shown that nitrogen balance in athletes is greater than in inactive controls. Increased protein needs may come from increased amino acid oxidation during exercise or growth and repair of muscle tissue. Muscle protein synthesis (MPS) is increased after resistance and endurance exercise, suggesting that additional protein would be necessary to provide amino acids for the increased protein synthesis. Increased synthesis is ostensibly necessary for production of new myofibrillar proteins for muscle growth during resistance training and for mitochondrial biogenesis during endurance training.

In contrast, it has been extensively argued that exercise, even extensive, prolonged, and intense exercise, does not increase the dietary requirement for protein. The argument is often based on the fact that exercise has been shown to increase the efficiency of use of amino acids from ingested protein. Butterfield and others demonstrated this concept in a series of classic experiments showing that even at relatively low protein intakes and negative energy balance, nitrogen balance was improved when exercise was performed.

More recently, it has been shown that exercise training increases muscle protein balance, suggesting that the reuse of amino acids from muscle protein breakdown is more efficient. This notion was investigated in a prospective, longitudinal study on the whole-body protein level using stable isotopic tracers. Whole-body protein balance was reduced in novice weightlifters after training, suggesting that protein requirements would be less with regular exercise training.

A common criticism of the studies that show increased use of amino acids with exercise is that the intensity or duration of exercise is not as great as that practiced by top sport athletes, and the requirements would be underestimated. Many studies have shown that amino acid oxidation is elevated during exercise. Animal studies have shown that exercise of sufficient intensity and duration may result in a catabolic state after exercise. MPS is decreased after exercise at high intensities and long duration. It also has been reported that low-intensity endurance and resistance exercise does not stimulate MPS.

These results, together with the data indicating that higher intensity exercise increases MPS, suggest that there may be a continuum of exercise intensity in which the response of muscle protein metabolism changes. At lower intensities, there is no response, but as intensity increases, MPS is stimulated. At the highest levels of exercise intensity and duration, however, the impact of the exercise reduces the response of MPS. Protein requirements may be related to the intensity and duration of the exercise that is practiced.

– Author

1

Introduction

Studies related to fundamental hydration issues have required clinicians to re-examine certain practices and concepts. The ingestion of substances such as creatine, caffeine, and glycerol has been questioned in regards to safety and hydration status. Reports of overdrinking (hyponatremia) also have brought into question the practices of drinking appropriate fluid amounts and the role that fluid-electrolyte balance has in the etiology of heat illnesses such as heat cramps. This article offers a fresh perspective on timely topics related to hydration, fluid balance, and exercise in the heat.

CORE TEMPERATURE AND HYDRATION

Proper hydration is important for optimal sport performance and may play a role in the prevention of heat illnesses. Dehydration increases cardiovascular strain and increases core temperature (T_c) to levels higher than in a state of euhydration. These increases, independently and in combination, impair performance and put an individual at risk for heat illness. Exercise in the heat in which dehydration occurs before or during exercise results in T_c that is directly correlated (r ¼ 0.98) with degree of dehydration. The link between dehydration and hyperthermia has shown that independently and additively they result in cardiovascular instability that puts individuals at risk for heat exhaustion.

Despite laboratory evidence linking dehydration with increased T_c, some authors argue that this physiologic phenomenon does not occur in field settings. This may be because field studies fail to control exercise intensity. T_c is driven by metabolic rate, and when the same subject is tested in a controlled laboratory environment, a higher metabolic rate produces a higher T_c. Without controlling or measuring relative exercise intensity, a hydrated individual could exercise at a higher metabolic rate and drive his or her T_c to the same level as a dehydrated individual working at a lower intensity. Without a randomized crossover experimental design that controls exercise intensity, field studies cannot validly conclude that hydration is not linked to T_c.

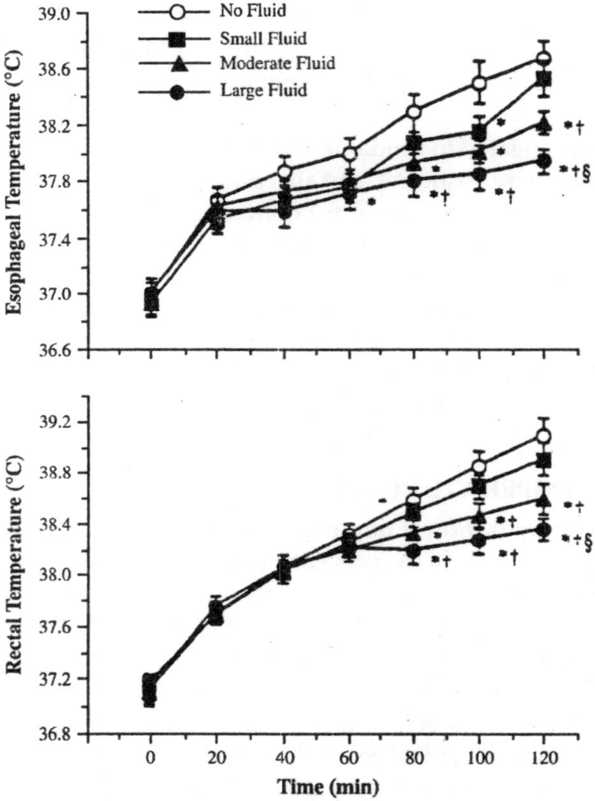

Fig. 1. The degree of dehydration that occurs during exercise is correlated with the increase in esophageal (top graph) *and rectal* (bottom graph) *temperatures. Subjects cycled for 120 minutes in a 33°C environment at approximately 65% $VO2_max$ while replacing 0% (No Fluid), 20% (Small Fluid), 48% (Moderate Fluid), or 81% (Large Fluid) of the fluid lost in sweat. Subjects lost 4.2%, 3.4%, 2.3%, and 1.1% body weight in the conditions.* (From *Montain SJ, Coyle EF. Influence of graded dehydration on hyperthermia and cardiovascular drift during exercise. J Appl Physiol 1992;73(4):1340-50; with permission.)*

Field studies disputing relationships between T_c and dehydration also cite that laboratory studies use environments that are too hot, and that the physiologic relationship does not exist in temperate environments (approximately 23°C) often associated with field studies. Laboratory studies have shown that the increase of T_c with dehydration is exacerbated in hot environments, but still observed in cold environments (8°C). Dehydration impairs thermoregulation independent of ambient conditions, but the effect is seen especially at high ambient temperatures when the thermoregulatory system is more heavily stressed. Laboratory-based studies have clearly shown that when exercise intensity and hydration state are controlled, T_c increases at a faster rate when subjects are dehydrated.

CAFFEINE

Caffeine and its related compounds, theophylline and theobromine, have long been recognized as diuretic molecules, which encourage excretion of urine via increased blood flow to the kidneys. The recommendation that caffeine be avoided by athletes because hydration status would be compromised is based on several studies examining the acute effects of high levels (>300 mg) of caffeine. More recent studies have tested the credibility of this recommendation by re-examining hydration status in varying settings after short-term caffeine intake and, for the first time, after long-term intake.

Using increased urine output as an indicator of diuresis and dehydration, early studies showed that the threshold for an increase of urine output was 250 to 300 mg of caffeine intake. Urine output was greater for the first 3 hours after in-gestion, but when urine was collected for 4 hours, the difference in urine output between caffeineand placebo was negated. When double the caffeine was ingested (612 mg or 8.5 mg/kg), urine volume increased over the next 4 hours. The molecular properties of caffeine do not refute the fact that it may act as an acute diuretic, but when observations span a short time (<24 hours), it is difficult to understand long-term changes in hydration.

When 24-hour urine volume is examined, the ingestion of caffeine at levels of 1.4 to 3.1 mg/kg does not increase urine output or change hydration status. When large amounts of caffeine are ingested (8.2–10.2 mg/kg), the increases in urine excretion vary from person to person, but may be 41% greater than control levels. It cannot be concluded from these studies that "caffeine causes dehydration" because acute increases in urine volume with large caffeine intake (>300 mg) may be offset later by decreased urine output and result in no change in long-term hydration status.

Acute ingestion of caffeine before exercise (1–2 hours) at levels up to 8.7 mg/kg does not alter urine output and fluid balance when subjects exercise at 60% to 85% VO_{2max} for 0.5 to 3 hours. The possible mechanism for a lack of a diuretic effect with caffeine during exercise is most likely due to an increase in catecholamines and diminished renal blood flow. There is little evidence to suggest that short-term use of caffeine alters hydration status at rest or during exercise.

Because most Americans consume caffeine on a regular basis, it is surprising that few studies have examined the effects of controlled caffeine intake over several days. In 2004, the authors' research team conducted a field study involving a crossover design in which subjects exercised for 2 hours, twice a day, for 3 consecutive days. Subjects rehydrated ad libitum and consumed a volume equal to 7 cans daily of either caffeinated or decaffeinated soda. Throughout the 3 days, no differences of urine volume, body weight, plasma volume, and urine specific gravity were observed between the two conditions.

The authors reported similar results in an investigation in which subjects consumed 3 mg caffeine/kg/d for 6 days; during the following 5 days, 20 subjects decreased their intake to 0 mg/kg/d, 20 maintained intake at 3 mg/kg/d, and 20 doubled their intake to 6 mg/kg/d. Urine volume and other markers of hydration status showed that, regardless of caffeine inges-tion, hydration status did not change throughout the 11 days (Fig. 2). Heat tolerance and thermoregulation examined on the 12th day during exercise in a hot environment did not differ between conditions.

Acute ingestion of moderate to low levels of caffeine (<300 mg) does not promote dehydration at rest or during exercise. Long-term ingestion of low to high levels of caffeine does not compromise hydration status and thermoregulation at rest and during exercise. Varying one's level of caffeine ingestion (either increasing or decreasing) also does not seem to change hydration status. There is no evidence to support caffeine restriction on the basis of impaired thermoregulation or changes of hydration status at levels less than 300-400 mg/d.

HYPONATREMIA

Hyponatremia has received attention in the media as a result of its occurrence in popular road running races. Hyponatremia is a serious complication of low plasma sodium levels (<130 mEq/L). The exact cause is likely multi-faceted and circumstantial. Hyponatremia has been observed in exercising individuals who became dehydrated, maintained hydration, and became overhydrated. Asymptomatic hyponatremia is the most common type of hyponatremia and is defined as a decrease in sodium level (<130 mEq/L) that occurs in the absence of life-threatening symptoms. Asymptomatic hyponatremia per se is not harmful or detrimental to performance. When plasma sodium decreases to less than 125 mEq/L, hypona-tremic illness may occur. Hyponatremic illness is a medical emergency that is symptomatic and requires immediate medical treatment.

Overdrinking, identified as an increase in body mass, significantly increases one's risk for developing hyponatremia and should be avoided. Some observational studies have found that increased dehydration results in higher sodium levels, but this does not mean that dehydration prevents hyponatremia. The increased risk of heat illnesses associated with dehydration does not warrant dehydration as a method for preventing hyponatremia. High sweat rates or sodium-concentrated sweat may lead to large losses of sodium and put one at risk for hyponatremia, especially in events lasting more than 3 hours. It is recommended that one should ingest fluid at a rate that closely matches fluid loss (ie, <2% body weight loss).

Replacing large fluid losses with equal amounts of pure water may dilute the plasma sodium level, so it has been suggested that replacement of electrolytes can be achieved through sports drinks or salt tablets. Mathematical modeling has shown that in a variety of conditions the ingestion of sodium may attenuate the decline of serum sodium over time (Fig. 3). However, recent studies involving consumption of sodium through sports drinks and salt tablets have confirmed and refuted this relationship. Some of these differences in results may lie in methodologic differences, assumptions, and conflicting conclusions.

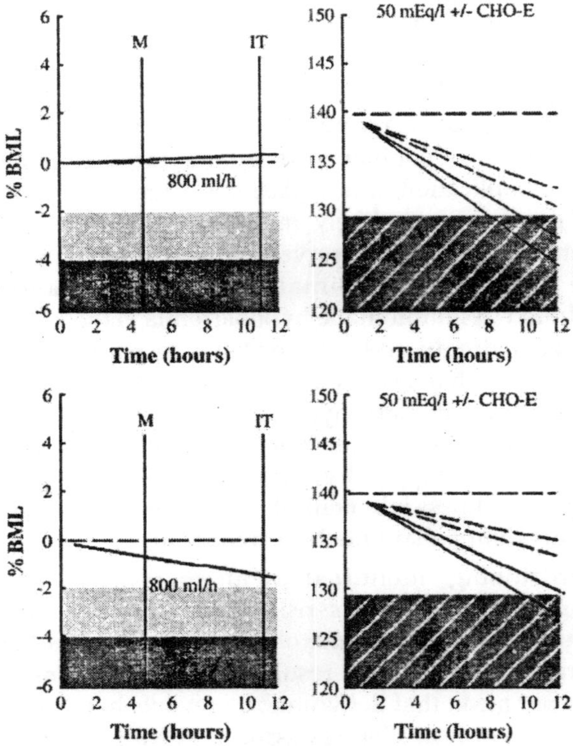

Fig. 3. Predicted effectiveness of a carbohydrate-electrolyte sports drink (CHO-E) containing 17 mEq/L of sodium and 5 mEq/L of potassium for attenuating the decline in plasma sodium concentration (mEq/L) expected for a 70-kg person drinking water at 800 mL/h when running 10 km/h in cool (18°C; upper panel) *and warm (28°C;* lower panel) *environments. The solid shaded areas depict water loss that would be sufficient to diminish performance modestly and substantially. The hatched shaded area indicates the presence of hyponatremia.* M *indicates the finishing time for the marathon run.* IT *indicates the approximate finishing time for an iron-man triathlon. For the sodium figures, the solid lines reflect the effect of drinking water only, and hatched lines illustrate the effect of consuming the same volume of a sports drink. The pair of lines of similar type represent the predicated outcomes when total body water accounts for 50% and 63% of body mass. BML, body mass loss.* (From *Montain SJ, Cheuvront SN, Sawka MN. Exercise associated hyponatraemia: quantitative analysis to understand the etiology. Br J Sports Med 2006;40(2):98-105; with permission.)*

Understanding the etiology and cause of hyponatremia may help to understand its prevention better. It is well agreed that overconsumption of fluids is the primary, but not the only, cause. Whether replacement of sweat losses with equal volumes of sodium-containing beverages would prevent or attenuate hyponatremia is still debated.

More studies that look at varying environmental conditions, sweat rates, and body masses may help shed light on this complex picture. Some authorities have suggested that allowing dehydration would prevent hyponatremia because the contraction of extracellular fluid would increase sodium concentration. Until further studies are conducted, promoting dehydration (ie, >2% of pre-exercise weight) is not warranted and may put some individuals at greater risk for exertional heat illnesses and could compromise performance.

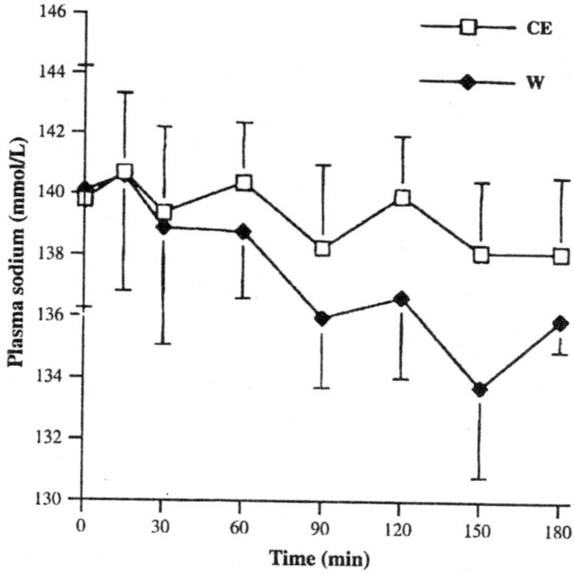

Fig. 4. Ingestion of a carbohydrate-electrolyte beverage (CE) slightly attenuated the decline of plasma sodium observed with ingestion of plain water (W) over 180 minutes of exercise at a moderate intensity in a hot environment (34°C). (Adapted from *Vrijens DM, Rehrer NJ. Sodium-free fluid ingestion decreases plasma sodium during exercise in the heat. J Appl Physiol 1999;86(6):1847-51; with permission.)*

CREATINE

Creatine is one of the most popular nutritional supplements on the market. Athletes of all levels and varieties of sports are using it in hopes of gaining a competitive edge. During creatine supplementation, 90% of the increase in body weight (0.7–2.0 kg) is accounted for by increases of total body water (TBW). The increase of TBW during the "loading phase" results from increases of intracellular water stores, but prolonged use of creatine results in TBW increases in all body fluid compartments. Some authors speculate that creatine use while exercising in the heat impairs heat tolerance and may be a contributing factor for heatstroke. Those authors propose that creatine increases one's risk for heat injury because the increases of intracellular water stores deplete intravascular volume. Before any published conclusive studies concerning creatine's effect on hydration status and use in the heat, the American College of Sports Medicine published a consensus statement stating that "high-dose creatine supplementation should be avoided during periods of increased thermal stress... there are concerns about the possibility of altered fluid balance, and impaired sweating and thermoregulation...".

Paradoxically, studies using short-term and long-term creatine supplementation have shown that subjects exercising in the heat (30-37°C) for 80 minutes have either no change or an advantageous lower heart rate and T_c. Work from our laboratory also has shown that creatine supplementation does not alter exercise heat tolerance, even when subjects begin exercise in a dehydrated state. One study that found lower T_c with creatine use during exercise in heat suggests that the increases of TBW with supplementation may hyperhydrate the body and lower T_c. Despite early concerns about creatine supplementation and exercise in the heat, more recent studies have shown conclusively that heat storage does not increase as a result of creatine use. There is no evidence to support restriction of creatine use during exercise in the heat.

EXERCISE-ASSOCIATED CRAMPS

Although the exact mechanism is unknown, skeletal muscle cramps are associated with numerous congenital and acquired conditions, including hereditary disorders of carbohydrate and lipid metabolism, diseases of neuromuscular and endocrine origins, fluid and electrolyte deficits (ie, owing to diarrhea or vomiting), pharmacologic agents (ie, b-agonists, ethanol, diuretics), and toxins. The medical treatments for these various forms of muscle cramps are as varied as their etiologies. McGee specifically classified leg muscle cramps as con-tractures (ie, electrically silent cramps caused by myopathy or disease), tetany (ie, sensory plus motor unit hyperactivity), dystonia (ie, simultaneous contraction of agonist and antagonist muscles), or true cramps (ie, motor unit hyper-activity). The last category includes skeletal muscle cramps that are due to heat, fluid-electrolyte disturbances, hemodialysis, and medications.

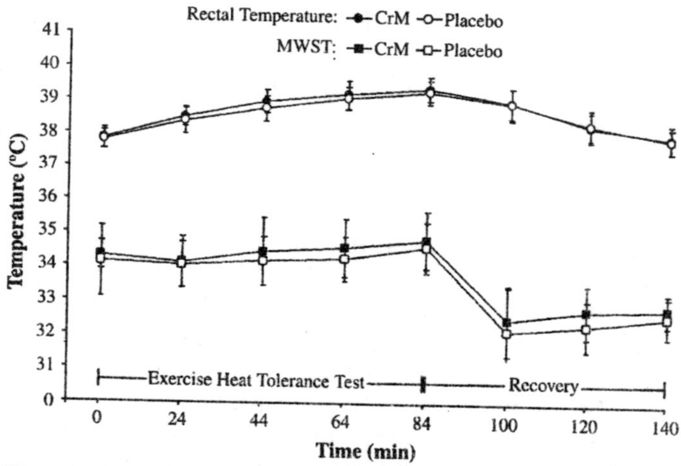

Fig. 5. The use of creatine monohydrate (CrM) does not compromise exercise heat tolerance. After becoming dehydrated, rectal temperature and mean weighted skin temperature (MWST) had similar responses in CrM and placebo treatments when subjects exercised in the heat and recovered in a cool environment. (From Watson G, Casa D, Fiala KA, et al. Creatine use and exercise heat tolerance in dehydrated men. J Athl Train 2006;41(1):18–29; with permission.)

The International Classification of Diseases defines heat cramps, a form of motor unit hyperactivity, as painful involuntary contractions that are associated with large sweat (ie, water and sodium) losses. Heat cramps occur most often in active muscles (ie, thigh, calf, and abdominal) that have been challenged by a single prolonged event (ie, >2–4 hours) or during consecutive days of physical exertion. A high incidence of heat cramps occurs among tennis players, American football players, steel mill workers, and soldiers who deploy to hot environments. These activities result in a large sweat loss, consumption of hypotonic fluid or pure water, and a whole-body sodium and water imbalance. The distinctions between heat cramps and other forms of exercise-associated cramps are subtle, but sodium replacement usually resolves heat cramps effectively; successful treatment via sodium administration confirms a preliminary diagnosis of heat cramps.

Bergeron described a tennis player who was plagued by recurring heat cramps. This athlete secreted sweat at a rate of 2.5 L/h and had a sweat sodium (Naþ) concentration of 83 mEq/L. This sweat Naþ concentration is high, in that most heat-acclimatized athletes exhibit 20 to 40 mEq Naþ/L of sweat (ie, heat acclimatization reduces sweat Naþ concentration), but occurs naturally in a small percentage of humans. During 4 hours of tennis match play, this young athlete lost 10 L of sweat and a large quantity of electrolytes (ie, 830 mEq of Naþ; 19,090 mg of Naþ; 48.6 g of sodium chloride). Given that the average sodium chloride intake of adults in the United States is 8.7 g (3.4 g Naþ) per day, it is not difficult to see how this athlete could experience a whole-body Naþ deficit. To offset his 4-hour sodium chloride loss in sweat, this athlete would require 1.6 L of normal saline, 7.8 to 9.8 cans of canned soup (85–107 mEq per can), 12.6 servings of tomato juice (66 mEq of Naþ per serving), or 39.5 to 127.7 L of a sport drink (6.5–21 mEq Naþ/L). These options are unreasonable. A long history of heat cramps ended when this tennis player began consuming supplemental salt during meals. Other tennis players have been successfully treated using a similar course of action.

In 2004, the authors' research team evaluated a female varsity basketball player (body mass 78.5 kg, height 187 cm) who experienced exercise-induced cramps during the winter months in New England, with signs and symptoms identical to heat cramps. The authors measured her sweat rate as 1.16 L/h, her sweat sodium concentration (ie, via whole-body washdown) as 42 mEq/L, and her daily consumption of sodium. These values were normal and typical of winter sport athletes. Three days of observations indicated that her dietary intake of Na^+ per day was similar to her daily sweat Na^+ loss (ie, both 3200-3600 mg). Because she did not train or compete in a hot environment, the authors hesitated to diagnose her malady as heat cramps. When she began ingesting supplemental sodium (ie, by liberally salting each meal at midseason), however, the skeletal muscle cramps resolved permanently. This case suggests that a history of skeletal muscle cramps, with a large daily Na^+ turnover owing to a high sweat rate, indicates the need for an evaluation of whole-body Na balance. It further suggests that heat cramps may have been named because they usually occur in hot environments, but they also may occur in mild environments when sweat Na^+ concentration and sweat losses are large.

A study by Stofan and colleagues examined the link between sweat sodium losses and heat cramps. Sweat rate, sodium content, and percent body weight loss were measured on a single day of a "two-a-day" practice in subjects who had a history (episode within the last year) of severe heat cramps. Although heat cramps were not observed, football players with a history of heat cramps had sweat sodium losses two times greater than matched controls. Although the exact etiology of heat cramps may be unknown, sodium deficits seem to contribute to their development. In most cases, restoration and compensation of sodium losses seems to prevent further heat cramps.

FLUID NEEDS AND HYDRATION PLAN

Water losses during exercise should be replaced at a rate equal to (not greater than) the sweat rate. Loss of sweat during exercise needs to be replaced after exercise, but dehydration (>2% body weight) during exercise can be detrimental to performance in part by increases in T_c. It is difficult to replace 100% of fluid loss during exercise, especially if it occurs in hot environments for long durations or if sweat loss is great. Authorities have suggested that a minimal amount of dehydration (<2% body weight) may be tolerated without compromising performance. Regardless, knowledge of sweat rate is necessary to develop a hydration plan (Table 1), but without this it has been recommended to ingest 200 to 300 mL every 10 to 20 minutes. Thirst lags behind changes in hydration (termed *voluntary dehydration*). When individuals have high sweat rates, and large volumes of fluid cause gastrointestinal stress, it may be advantageous for them to train themselves to tolerate consumption of fluids at a rate similar to their sweat losses.

In attempts to optimize endurance performance in the heat, glycerol has been used to increase TBW. It is an osmotically active molecule that acutely (<4 hours) increases TBW stores. Although using glycerol plus water is an effective prehydration strategy, it does not increase sweat rate or reduce performance time or T_c in a race setting. Using glycerol as a part of a rehydration strategy between exercise bouts increases exercise time to exhaustion in the heat (37°C). The increase is likely due to increases of plasma volume, not because of cardiovascular effects, thermoregulatory effects, or differences in fluid-regulating hormones. It is generally accepted that glycerol, although a hyperhydrating agent, is not an ergogenic aid in most situations. Future research should examine the importance of timing in glycerol ingestion for performance benefits.

When multiple, dehydrating exercise sessions are occurring over a short time (ie, two workouts per day in football or track and field), athletes must re-hydrate immediately and quickly between bouts. Intravenous rehydration has been used in the belief that direct administration of fluid into the central circulation optimally replaces lost fluid. Contrary to this belief, when hydrating with equal amounts of intravenous and oral fluid ingestion, intravenous is not superior to restore plasma volume after dehydration. Oral rehydration results in better cardiovascular stability, lower T_c, rating of perceived exertion, thirst, and thermal sensation than intravenous rehydration. However, these changes do not translate into improved exercise time to exhaustion. Regardless, oral hydration is preferred (versus intravenous) for individuals who would be exercising subsequently in the heat. An exception occurs when large amounts of fluid must be replaced in a short time, and gastric emptying and intestinal absorption rates may limit the ingestion of fluids orally. In such cases, a combination of intravenous and oral rehydration may be warranted so that fluid requirements are met, and the oropharyngeal reflex is stimulated.

Athletes often supplement with glycerol or choose to use intravenous rehydration because of the difficulty of matching fluid intake with fluid losses during intense exercise in the heat. This makes theoretical sense given the possibility of large sweat rates (ie, >1.5 L/h) and the likelihood that fluid consumption could not match the sweat rate given gastric emptying and intestinal absorption rates, especially when the ingestion must occur when the exercise is intense. An individualized rehydration plan that considers sweat rate, the semantics of the actual competition parameters, and personal preferences and tolerance is recommended to ensure that rehydration is optimized in these circumstances. When the individualized rehydration plan is practiced and rehearsed in practices and preliminary competitions, the need for glycerol and intravenous rehydration will likely be eliminated because of the benefits associated with the "rehydration training," and ultimately the degree of dehydration would be minimized.

SUMMARY

Hydration status affects exercise performance in the heat and may influence the development of exertional heat illnesses. However, numerous factors that influence hydration state are not understood by the public. Field-based studies may lead athletes to believe that T_c is not influenced by hydration, but these studies contradict well-controlled laboratory experiments. For many years, recommendations have been published that active individuals should avoid caffeinated beverages with little supporting scientific evidence. Research from the authors' laboratory shows that long-term intake of moderate levels of caffeine does not compromise hydration status. Hyponatremia also has received a lot of attention, but until more is known about its etiology and prevention, it isrecommended that athletes drink an amount of fluid to minimize dehydration (but not overdrink).

The use of creatine as an ergogenic aid initially was overshadowed by questions regarding its safety during exercise in the heat. Research shows no reason for these concerns. Although the mechanism of heat cramps is still not fully understood, it seems that deficits in sodium from sweating and/or diet is a predisposing factor. The reader is encouraged to read thorough review articles on these topics. Ultimately, clinical practice should be dictated by evidence in the literature and not perpetuate unproven myths.

2

Protein Requirements and Recommendations for Athletes

Protein nutrition for athletes has long been a topic of interest. From the legendary Greek wrestler Milo – purported to eat copious amounts of beef during his five successive Olympic titles – to modern athletes consuming huge amounts of supplements, protein intake has been considered paramount. Recommendations for protein intake for athletes has not been without controversy, however. In general, scientific opinion on this controversy seems to divide itself into two camps – those who believe participation in exercise and sport increases the nutritional requirement for protein and those who believe protein requirements for athletes and exercising individuals are no different from the requirements for sedentary individuals.

There seems to be evidence for both arguments. Although this issue may be scientifically relevant, from a practical perspective, the requirement for protein – as most often defined – may not be applicable to most athletes.

The argument over protein requirements for athletes and active individuals often takes a general form; requirements for athletes are compared with the requirements set for sedentary individuals. Often, the athletic population participates in either endurance exercise or resistance exercise. Even this division does not take into account, however, the myriad physiologic and metabolic demands of training that inevitably vary for athletes involved in different sports. The demands of training may vary within a particular sport or in individuals. In this article, the authors argue that the controversy over protein requirements that is expressed often in the literature – although interesting from a scientific standpoint—is irrelevant for athletes, coaches, and nutrition practitioners.

Contributing to the controversy is the perception of the definition of protein requirement. Athletes define their dietary requirement for protein differently than scientists. Typically, the definition for the requirement of protein is based on nitrogen balance (ie, the minimum amount of protein necessary to balance all nitrogen losses and maintain nitrogen balance). This approach, or something similar, has been used to determine the estimates of protein intake necessary for athletes. More complex models of protein requirements include consideration for the metabolic demands of the body. The obligatory and adaptive demands for amino nitrogen are included in this model. Although these models have been used to set requirements for sedentary populations and to estimate requirements for athletes, it is unlikely that athletes consider them to be the appropriate measuring stick to make recommendations of protein intake that would be of maximum benefit.

This article addresses the issue of protein intake for athletes from a practical standpoint. The background information from previous studies has been presented in many excellent reviews that have examined the issue extensively, so this information is presented only briefly here. The focus instead is on how—in the authors' view—various factors involved in protein nutrition may influence the adaptations that result from training and nutritional intake, and how this information may be used by practitioners, coaches, and athletes to determine appropriate protein intakes during training for optimal competitive results.

CONTROVERSY

The argument has been made that regular exercise, particularly in elite athletes with highly demanding training regimens, increases protein requirements over those for sedentary individuals. This argument is often based on nitrogen balance. Several well-controlled studies have shown that nitrogen balance in athletes is greater than in inactive controls. Increased protein needs may come from increased amino acid oxidation during exercise or growth and repair of muscle tissue. Muscle protein synthesis (MPS) is increased after resistance and endurance exercise, suggesting that additional protein would be necessary to provide amino acids for the increased protein synthesis. Increased synthesis is ostensibly necessary for production of new myofibrillar proteins for muscle growth during resistance training and for mitochondrial biogenesis during endurance training.

In contrast, it has been extensively argued that exercise, even extensive, prolonged, and intense exercise, does not increase the dietary requirement for protein. The argument is often based on the fact that exercise has been shown to increase the efficiency of use of amino acids from ingested protein. Butterfield and others demonstrated this concept in a series of classic experiments showing that even at relatively low protein intakes and negative energy balance, nitrogen balance was improved when exercise was performed. More recently, it has been shown that exercise training increases muscle protein balance, suggesting that the reuse of amino acids from muscle protein breakdown is more efficient. This notion was investigated in a prospective, longitudinal study on the whole-body protein level using stable isotopic tracers. Whole-body protein balance was reduced in novice weightlifters after training, suggesting that protein requirements would be less with regular exercise training.

A common criticism of the studies that show increased use of amino acids with exercise is that the intensity or duration of exercise is not as great as that practiced by top sport athletes, and the requirements would be underestimated. Many studies have shown that amino acid oxidation is elevated during exercise. Animal studies have shown that exercise of sufficient intensity and duration may result in a catabolic state after exercise. MPS is decreased after exercise at high intensities and long duration. It also has been reported that low-intensity endurance and resistance exercise does not stimulate MPS. These results, together with the data indicating that higher intensity exercise increases MPS, suggest that there may be a continuum of exercise intensity in which the response of muscle protein metabolism changes. At lower intensities, there is no response, but as intensity increases, MPS is stimulated. At the highest levels of exercise intensity and duration, however, the impact of the exercise reduces the response of MPS. Protein requirements may be related to the intensity and duration of the exercise that is practiced.

Arguments against protein requirements often are based on difficulties showing increased muscle mass at higher levels of protein intake. At best, studies are equivocal. Although studies have shown gains in muscle mass at higher protein intakes, a meta-analysis concluded that protein supplements had no impact on lean body mass during training. When the apparent increases in nitrogen balance are extrapolated to gains in lean body mass, the calculations suggest gains that are physiologically impossible—on the order of 200 to 500 g/d. These results show the tendency for nitrogen balance methods to overestimate nitrogen balance at high intakes, perhaps owing to increases in the urea pool size. Suffice to say that there are studies providing evidence for increased protein requirements for athletes and the opposite. These arguments are described in detail in other articles.

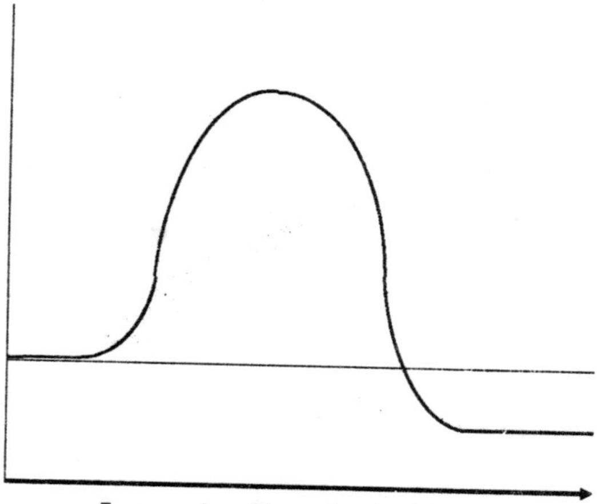

Fig. 1. Proposed response of muscle protein synthesis (PS) after exercise as exercise intensity increases.

METHODOLOGIC CONSIDERATIONS

Methodologic inadequacies remain partly responsible for current difficulties in assessing protein requirements of the human diet for exercise. In terms of experimental design, most studies involve measurements of nitrogen losses or tracer-labeled amino acid oxidation rates.

Nitrogen balance techniques are used most often to estimate protein requirements by quantification of all protein that is consumed and all nitrogen that is excreted. Positive nitrogen balance indicates an anabolic situation, and negative balance indicates protein catabolism. Healthy adults who are not growing should be in nitrogen balance over a given period of time; however, for a short period, balance may be positive or negative. Nitrogen balance is indirectly reflective of a complex series of ongoing metabolic changes in (1) whole-body protein turnover, (2) amino acid oxidation, (3) urea production, and (4) nitrogen excretion during fasting, fed, postprandial, and postabsorptive periods of the day.

Nitrogen balance data are not without inherent problems. Limitations of nitrogen balance have been well covered previously. Suffice to say that criticisms of nitrogen balance are multiple and include a lack of sensitivity because it involves only gross measures of nitrogen intake and excretion ; difficulties in precisely quantifying nitrogen losses, which may be particularly important for active individuals ; changes in size of the body urea pool ; mismatches between nitrogen balance and measurable changes in protein mass, especially at high intakes ; poor reproducibility ; and accommodation by limitation of other processes at nitrogen balance with low protein intakes.

Application of nitrogen balance measurements to athletes may be especially unsuitable. For a strength athlete, whose goal is to increase lean body mass and ultimately muscle strength and size, protein requirements set to attain nitrogen balance are inappropriate; rather, the athlete aims to consume enough dietary protein to induce a positive nitrogen balance. It may be more appropriate to discuss protein requirements with respect to the strength athlete as the effect of dietary protein on protein synthesis and breakdown. Similarly, consideration of nitrogen balance only may not be appropriate for an endurance athlete; balance may be attained, but with a compromise in some physiologically relevant processes, such as upregulation of enzyme activity, capillarization, or mitochondrial biogenesis after endurance training. The nitrogen balance approach underlies the establishment of dietary reference intake for protein in sedentary individuals, so comparison of like with like makes feasible the argument that nitrogen balance should be used for determination of protein requirements for athletic populations.

Other methods for determining protein requirements include use of stable isotopic tracers and functional indicators of protein adequacy. Use of these methods has been the source of a great deal of controversy over the years for athletic and nonathletic populations.

PROTEIN AND PERFORMANCE

Although nitrogen balance and stable isotope studies are of great interest in building an experimental database to support, refute, or challenge official published levels of requirements, from a practical standpoint, coaches, athletes, and individuals involved in daily exercise regimens are not usually interested in the scientific debate over the issue of protein requirements. Performance is ultimately the only outcome that is important for athletes. Many authors have made this point, yet the studies that have attempted to investigate the influence of protein intake on performance have been scarce. Millward stated, "Thus, the key test of adequacy of either protein or amino acid intake must be the long-term response in terms of the specific function of interest." This key test would vary for each type of exercise training performed, each sport, each position within a particular sport, and even among individuals participating in any given event or sharing a position (eg, an American football quarterback compared with a running back). Energy balance, intake of other nutrients, and individual genetic makeup all contribute to the response to training and nutrient intake, and the influence of the amount of protein ingested per day on performance for an athlete varies and often is difficult to determine.

There are ample limitations for determination of optimal protein intake by measurement of performance. These limitations have been articulated previously and include difficulty, if not impossibility, in controlling innumerable physiologic variables (eg, training status, training details, energy balance, and standardization of life aspects such as sleep, work, and emotional upheavals) and inherent difficulty in defining the appropriate end points to be measured and the insensitivity of performance and end point measures.

Determination of appropriate protein intake to optimize performance, by any method, is limited by the definition of the population to be targeted. Generally, studies broadly divide athletes into strength or power athletes and endurance athletes. These broad distinctions may not be specific enough to provide appropriate protein intake information for many athletes. There have been attempts to categorize various athletic groups further. Tarnopolsky considered that endurance athletes may be divided into three broad categories and estimated protein needs for these groups. Delineations such as these provide more information for practitioners, but as is pointed out in Tarnopol-sky's article, there are individuals who do not fit the broad categorizations. It seems clear that, at this juncture, there are ample gaps in knowledge that do not allow general recommendations that may be meaningful to all athletes. Football and rugby players incorporate a great deal of power and endurance training. A decathlete, by definition, participates in quite varied training. Gender is an important factor to consider, but few data exist on performance measures on different protein intakes for men and women. To recommend a specific number of grams of protein to all participants in a broad category of athletes seems nonsensical. Protein recommendations are best made based on the individual circumstances of each athlete.

HABITUAL INTAKES OF PROTEIN FOR ATHLETES

Within the limitations available, determination of protein requirements in studies to date often suggests that protein intake should be greater for athletes than for sedentary individuals. Generally, the range given is 1.2 to about 2.0 g protein/kg body weight per day. As mentioned, many authors dispute these higher estimates and maintain that exercise does not increase requirements, even among highly trained athletes expending large amounts of energy. An often noted point is that even if the highest of estimates are the true requirement, it is likely that for most athletes, the point is moot. More recently published articles have provided summaries of protein intake for endurance and strength-based athletes. It is clear from these studies that reported dietary protein intakes are normally greater than even the increased estimates proposed. Such athletes are at little risk of protein deficiency, provided that a net energy balance is achieved to maintain body weight, and sound nutritional practices are adhered to. Supplemental protein seems to be unnecessary for most athletes who consume a varied diet that contains complete protein foods and meets energy needs.

As Tarnopolsky pointed out, however, the range of protein intakes indicates that there are numerous individuals, perhaps 20%, who may consume levels of protein below some estimates of requirements for sedentary individuals. Perhaps individuals at greatest risk of consuming insufficient protein are those whose lifestyle combines other factors known to increase protein needs with intense training and competition, including individuals with insufficient energy intake, vegetarians, athletes competing in weight-class competitions, athletes participating in a suddenly increased level of training (eg, training camps), and individuals undergoing weight-loss programs. Generally, the evidence available indicates that most athletes who could be considered at risk tend to eat ample protein. The ranges indicate, however, that certain individuals may be at risk of insufficient protein intake, assuming that protein requirements fall in the elevated ranges.

Coaches, trainers, and athletes are apt to question whether a vegetarian diet can provide adequate protein to meet the increased dietary needs of highly trained athletes. Concerns may stem from the ability of a vegetarian diet to provide all essential amino acids (EAA) in the diet. Because a vegetarian diet is a plant-based diet, the quality of the ingested protein may be questioned. All EAA and nonessential amino acids can be supplied by plant food sources alone, provided that a variety of foods are consumed, and energy intake remains adequate to meet these needs. Of particular concern, however, are individuals who avoid all animal protein sources (ie, vegans) because plant proteins may be limited in amino acids containing lysine, threonine, tryptophan, or sulfur. If the diet is too restricted, suboptimal mineral and protein intake is possible.

Although most vegetarian diets meet or exceed dietary recommendations for protein, they often provide less protein than do nonvegetarian diets. Vegetarian athletes are likely to consume protein of lower quality that may increase the amount of protein required to meet needs. Perhaps more importantly, use of ingested amino acids, particularly by muscle, and nitrogen balance may be less with plant protein sources. These concerns suggest that it is possible that some vegetarian athletes may need to consider carefully the amount of protein intake necessary to accomplish the same training and competitive goals. In studies to date, well-planned, appropriately supplemented vegetarian diets seem to support effectively parameters that would affect athletic performance, albeit data on athletic populations are scarce. Similar increases in muscle strength and cross-sectional area in older men eating primarily meat protein or soy protein were noted during

12 weeks of resistance exercise training, suggesting that dependence on predominantly plant protein sources does not influence the response to training when dietary energy and protein intakes are matched. The issue of protein quality is recognized as a potential concern for individuals who avoid all animal protein sources (ie, vegans); however it is unlikely that concerns would apply to every vegan athlete.

INFLUENCE OF ENERGY INTAKE ON PROTEIN USE

In any discussion of protein requirements and recommendations, the influence of energy intake must be considered. Energy intake is likely to have as much influence on protein requirements as does protein intake itself. It is impossible to maintain positive nitrogen balance in the face of energy deficits; even given high protein intakes. It has been estimated that approximately one third of the variation in nitrogen balance among individuals may be accounted for by energy intake. Early work showed that athletes gain strength and maintain muscle mass even during periods of low protein intake, provided that energy intake is sufficient. During resistance exercise training, it has been shown that positive energy balance is more important than increased protein to elicit gains in lean body mass. Energy intake must be carefully considered before making any recommendation for protein intake to a given individual.

The influence of energy balance on protein metabolism and balance suggests another area of potential concern for some athletes. Athletes who restrict energy intake may need to be especially conscious of protein intake. Athletes involved in weight-class sports (eg, boxing and wrestling), esthetic sports (eg, figure skating, gymnastics, and diving), and sports in which excess weight may be deemed to impair performance (eg, horse-racing [jockeys], rowing, or distance running) may need to be particularly vigilant. Even so, there is no reason to suspect that all or even many of these athletes need to ingest protein in excess of their current diet. It is often thought that a prominent example of a population that may need special attention is female, particularly young, gymnasts. It is possible that protein needs are greater because nutritional assessments of female gymnasts indicate that many have an energy intake lower than energy expenditure. Female gymnasts have been shown to consume less protein than female controls, and this intake is related to lower whole-body protein balance. If female gymnasts are examined in more detail, it seems that most of even this potentially vulnerable population of athletes consume enough protein. In Table 1, calculations are shown for the protein intake for a small, approximately 45-kg athlete and a possible range of energy and protein intakes. For all but the lowest energy and protein intakes, sufficient protein would be ingested. Although most gymnasts, similar to other athletes, likely habitually consume ample protein to support their training and competition, these data suggest that some individuals within this population may be in need of particular attention when recommending protein intakes. Other athletes with similar training and psychological issues also may be at risk.

Many athletes desire to decrease body mass with as small a reduction of lean mass as possible. Numerous studies support a role for high-protein diets in promoting greater body weight and fat loss while maintaining lean mass compared with diets low in protein composition. These studies investigated weight loss in obese or overweight populations, so the applicability of these findings to athletes is questionable. Nevertheless, it is possible that increased dietary protein intake may have relevance to some athletes who desire loss of body mass with minimal reductions of lean mass and perhaps performance.

The leucine content of the diet has been hypothesized to be a potential mechanism important in maintaining lean mass and promoting fat loss. Leucine is a key regulator of MPS, and maintenance of MPS during hypo-caloric conditions may mediate maintenance of lean body mass. Support for this idea is found in a study by Harber and colleagues. MPS was increased after a period of high protein intake compared with higher carbohydrate intake. Although this concept provides a rationale for use of higher protein intakes for athletes desiring to reduce body mass, it has never been tested in exercising individuals over a period of training and may not apply. Bolster and coworkers showed that MPS was reduced after exercise in runners on a very high protein diet compared with more moderate protein intakes. Studies in exercising

humans from Wolfe's laboratory (Elliot et al, unpublished data) and others fail to show that extra leucine provides additional stimulation of MPS.

There are potential drawbacks of higher protein intakes during hypocaloric situations—and possibly during energy balance—that must be avoided if performance is not to suffer. Performance of well-trained cyclists was impaired on a diet in which protein intake was elevated in place of carbohydrates. If carbohydrate intake is compromised to increase protein intake, glycogen stores may be reduced, and training intensity for some athletes (ie, athletes whose training involves high-intensity or prolonged workouts) could suffer. Another possible problem with ingestion of high-protein diets is the potential for instigating negative nitrogen balance if the high protein intake is curtailed. Quevedo and coworkers showed that nitrogen balance was reduced for a time after a reduction in protein intake, but that nitrogen balance slowly returns to zero balance at the lower intakes. The likely explanation for this decrease in nitrogen balance after a reduction in protein intake lies in the pathways of protein and amino acid degradation. It is likely that degradative pathways are upregu-lated during times of high protein intake, and the decreased intake level is insufficient to replenish losses. These studies were conducted at rest during energy balance. It is possible that this loss of nitrogen would be even greater in athletes during hypocaloric situations, even given the known upregu-lation of protein use owing to exercise. The applicability of this model to well-trained athletes at high levels of exercise is unknown. Nevertheless, careful consideration of training and competitive demands for each athlete must precede recommendations for increased protein intakes.

FACTORS THAT AFFECT USE OF INGESTED PROTEIN

Estimates of protein requirements for athletes and all other populations are based on the concept that the adaptations owing to protein ingestion depend solely on the amount of protein ingested on a daily basis given the training demands for a given group (eg, endurance or resistance-trained athletes). The influence that other dietary factors, such as type of protein being consumed, and that other nutrients in the diet and timing of protein ingestion may have on the use of the ingested protein and the adaptations stemming from intake of the protein is not taken into account. In recent years, a growing body of evidence based on acute metabolic studies suggests that the metabolic response to protein and amino acid ingestion, particularly in muscle, is far more complex than is implied simply by consideration of the amount of protein ingested on a daily basis. For any given protein intake, the metabolic response—and presumably the adaptations in the muscle—would vary and depend on a variety of factors involved in the form and process of nutrient intake.

The composition of the ingested protein would influence the response to a given diet. The impact of protein quality on protein requirements has long been recognized as an important consideration for making nutritional recommendations. On a whole-body level, studies suggest that although vegetarian diets may be sufficient for positive nitrogen balance, reliance on animal proteins results in superior balance. The purported superiority of animal proteins may not be as clear, however, as some studies indicate.

Whole-body studies may not give a clear picture of the importance of protein intake to other tissues, particularly muscle. In a series of experiments involving modeling based on stable isotopes, the complexities of use of amino acids from meals including different types of proteins has been examined. In general, use of amino acids from animal proteins (eg, milk) is greater than plant proteins (eg, wheat), but differences exist even among different plant proteins. These data suggest that amino acids from different protein sources may be preferentially used by different tissues. Amino acids ingested as milk proteins are taken up in greater amounts by peripheral (ie, muscle) rather than splanchnic tissues. There is an interaction of protein type and the amount of protein ingested, such that use of amino acids from ingested animal proteins is diminished less than plant proteins at higher protein intake levels. Although these investigations were performed in resting subjects, and the relevancy to athletes may be questioned, these data make it clear that use of amino acids from ingested proteins may be handled differently depending on the type of protein that is ingested. These results may be interpreted to support the idea that adaptations to diets with different types of proteins during training may be different even if similar amounts of proteins are ingested.

Data on amino acid use from various proteins after exercise are limited. Consistent with the data based on modeling in resting adults, Phillips and colleagues reported that uptake of amino acids from milk proteins into muscle is greater than from soy protein after resistance exercise. In resting volunteers, casein may provide a superior anabolic response compared with whey proteins on a whole-body level. On a muscle level after resistance exercise, however, the differences in amino acid uptake between casein and whey proteins are less clear.

Other nutrients ingested concurrently with protein also influence use of the ingested amino acids. At rest, whole-body amino acid retention is increased when proteins are consumed with carbohydrates. Although the total retention of ingested amino acids is greater with carbohydrate than fat ingestion, the uptake into body regions seems to be differentially affected. Concurrent fat ingestion resulted in greater retention of ingested amino acids in peripheral tissues than did sucrose ingestion. Consistent with these results in resting subjects, it has been shown that carbohydrate ingestion increases the use of amino acids ingested concomitantly after resistance exercise, an effect likely mediated by the insulin response. Preliminary evidence suggests that lipid increases amino acid use of milk proteins ingested during recovery from resistance exercise. The mechanism for this effect remains to be elucidated. The results from several studies examining use of ingested proteins after exercise are summarized in Fig. 2. Taken together, these results show that ingestion of a particular amount of protein stimulates metabolic processes that are influenced by the nutrients ingested concurrently. These acute responses suggest that adaptations in athletes could be independent of the amount of protein ingested.

In addition to other nutrients and the type of protein, the metabolic response of muscle may be affected by the timing of the ingestion of amino acids or protein in relation to the exercise bout. Timing of ingestion of a mixture of carbohydrate, fat, and protein; carbohydrates alone; and EAA plus carbohydrates would influence the anabolic response to resistance exercise. It seems that different sources of amino acids do not engender the same response to varied timing of ingestion. In a previous study, the anabolic response to ingestion of a solution of EAA and carbohydrates immediately before exercise was approximately three times that of the response when the solution was ingested after exercise. In a more recent study using an identical protocol, however, the response to ingestion of whey proteins immediately before exercise was similar to that after exercise. It seems that not only timing of ingestion, but also the interaction of the type of protein with the timing determines the anabolic response in muscle.

Taken together, the anabolic response of muscle depends not only on the form of the ingested amino acids, but also on the nutrients ingested in association with the amino acids and the timing of the ingestion in relation to exercise—not to mention the interaction of all these factors. The complexity involved in assessing the relationship of the anabolic response to exercise and nutrition is readily apparent. Consideration of only the amount of protein ingested on a daily basis does not provide a complete picture of the metabolic situation that would influence the adaptations to training and nutrition. Broad recommendations for a particular amount of protein for all athletes or even subgroups of those involved in various types of sport without consideration of many other factors seems nonsensical.

IMPLICATIONS OF SHORT-TERM STUDIES FOR LONG-TERM ADAPTATIONS

The conclusion that use of amino acids from ingested protein varies depending on the factors discussed previously is based on studies that acutely measure changes in net muscle protein balance (NBAL). These investigations often make use of stable isotopic tracers, arteriovenous balance, or muscle biopsy samples to examine the changes in muscle metabolism resulting from an intervention. The assumption is made that changes in metabolism observed during short-term measurement periods represent the potential for long-term changes that may affect adaptations to protein ingestion.

In Wolfe's laboratory in Galveston, Texas, the potential for acute studies to represent long-term changes has been investigated. Results from these studies are consistent with the notion that determinations of protein use based on results from acute studies are representative of those that may occur over longer periods of training. Stable isotopic tracers were used to measure MPS and NBAL in volunteers over a 24-hour period under two conditions: (1) while resting and (2) during a 24-hour period when they performed resistance exercise and ingested EAA. Comparison of the results during a 3-hour period after exercise (ie, comparable to the time typically used in acute studies) were made with results obtained over 24 hours. Exercise plus EAA ingestion increased the rate of MPS measured over 24 hours and improved NBAL compared with rest. The difference between rest and exercise plus amino acid ingestion was similar whether determined over 3 hours or a full 24-hour period, suggesting that acute changes in NBAL represent those that occur over longer periods.

If the acute response of muscle to exercise and nutrient intake is to be deemed representative of long-term changes, the response of NBAL before and after resistance exercise training must be constant. In other words, changes in the acute response over a period of training and dietary manipulation would mean that measurement of the acute response before training could not be extrapolated to estimate the entire response to training. In a recent study, we determined the acute response of NBAL to resistance exercise during ingestion of EAA in untrained volunteers before and after a period of resistance training (Tipton et al., unpublished results). The response of NBAL to resistance exercise and EAA was similar before and after 16 weeks of training consistent with the notion that extrapolation of results from the acute study could be used to determine the use of amino acids from protein ingestion over longer periods. Similarly, Phillips and colleagues reported that the anabolic response of muscle NBAL to ingestion of milk and soy protein after exercise successfully predicted the accumulation of muscle mass in healthy young volunteers over a 12-week period. Another study in which NBAL was measured before and after 28 days of bed rest with and without EAA supplementation offers further support for the efficacy of short-term studies. Positive NBAL resulted from ingestion of EAA before and after bed rest, although the response was attenuated after the extended inactivity. Comparison of muscle mass lost during bed rest from dual-energy x-ray absorptiometry measures with estimates based on extrapolation from the acute NBAL measurement was quite similar.

Finally, molecular data indicate that an acute bout of exercise impacts gene expression, primarily through the transcriptional and translational signaling pathways. The ability of researchers to examine the molecular mechanisms behind training-induced changes has increased in recent years. These types of studies have provided information suggesting that many long-term training-induced adaptations are the result of the cumulative effect of the acute, transient changes that occur during recovery from each individual exercise bout. It seems that the type of nutrients consumed after exercise affects the regulation of metabolic gene expression and the adaptations to training. The transient nature of the response to exercise and feeding on the metabolic and molecular levels is consistent with the notion that adaptation to exercise training depends on the accumulation of the responses to each individual exercise bout. All of these results support the use of acute studies for determination of the impact of various nutritional and exercise regimens on protein use and providing information on the potential for long-term adaptations.

SUMMARY AND RECOMMENDATIONS

The debate concerning protein requirements is interesting from a scientific standpoint, but is likely to be ignored by athletes in favor of articulating protein recommendations for each athlete. Most athletes seem to ingest sufficient protein. Some individual athletes, particularly within certain populations (vegetarians, athletes involved in weight-class sports, female endurance runners, and individuals involved in weight-loss regimens), are potentially at risk of not consuming sufficient high-quality protein, however, and perhaps extra attention may be warranted for these types of athletes. Broad, generalized recommendations do not seem to offer much use other than as an overall guide. Many factors must be considered for each individual athlete before a recommended protein intake should be determined. It is possible that some athletes may need to consider increasing protein intakes, especially if energy balance is an issue. If protein is increased at the expense of carbohydrates, however, the performance of some athletes may suffer. If glycogen status is not imperative for training demands, higher amounts of protein may be well tolerated. Careful consideration of the competitive goals and training demands should be an important aspect of any nutritional recommendation.

Protein intake is fundamental aspect of an athlete's diet. There can be little doubt that higher protein intakes would not be a problem for many athletes, and there are situations where it may be warranted. Careful examination of the energetic and metabolic demands of the training is crucial for determination of optimal protein intake. A "first, do no harm" approach is likely to be the optimal strategy. As such, risk/benefit analysis would be prudent. There seems to be little health risk of higher protein intakes until very high levels. Many believe that there is no risk until intakes reach approximately 40% of energy intakes, and it would be unusual for athletes to ingest protein at that level. A male athlete consuming 3000 kcal/d would have to eat 300 g of protein (ie, 3.75 g/kg/d for an 80-kg athlete) to reach these levels. There is no evidence that ingestion of protein at that level is beneficial, but the likelihood of a health risk is slight.

Increasing habitual protein intake is unnecessary and provides little benefit for most athletes who consume a well-balanced diet that meets energy demands and includes varied sources of high-quality protein. There are situations in which a particular athlete may benefit from higher protein intakes. Increasingly, studies suggest that increasing protein may be beneficial for some, perhaps especially so for individuals in weight-loss situations. Much more work needs to be done in this area. There also are athletes for whom high protein intakes may be unnecessary, but do have possible utility that has yet to be determined. If it is determined that protein intake at these levels is not detrimental for optimal training and competition, there may be no reason to limit protein intake.

Finally, it seems that a simple approach to determining appropriate intake may be best. Determination of the optimal energy intake to balance training demands is crucial. Careful consideration of ample carbohydrate intake should be a priority, particularly for athletes engaged in repeated, high-intensity training sessions. Protein intake can be set at a level that is not harmful and may be beneficial. Fat intake should not be so low that deficiencies of essential fatty acids are an issue. Fat intake is associated with a more enjoyable diet, and so overly restricting fats may lead to compliance issues. There is no reason to incorporate dietary regimens that would not be followed.

In the authors' view, much of the protein requirement controversy is really much ado about nothing. It is an interesting, ivory-tower debate that has yet to be resolved. From a practical standpoint, however, habitual protein intakes are fine for most athletes. There are individual athletes for whom increased protein intake may be warranted so long as the coach, physician, and nutritionist have carefully weighed the risks and benefits. There is no reason to recommend protein supplements per se because there is no evidence that supplements work better than foods. The amount of protein necessary to increase muscle mass by 5 kg for an 80-kg male athlete is estimated in Table 2. Even considering the broad assumptions made, it is clear from these calculations that very little additional protein is necessary to support gains in muscle mass, and that it is not difficult to obtain any extra protein from foods.

For athletes who are best served staying at energy balance, consuming a well-balanced diet that includes sufficient carbohydrates to fuel training and ensure performance and protein from a variety of sources should be key. For athletes interested in gaining muscle mass, an increase in energy intake, including a relatively high proportion of protein, is likely to be the primary objective. For athletes interested in losing mass and experiencing negative energy balance, a relatively high protein intake may be warranted within the context of preserving intake of other essential nutrients. Particular care must be taken to ensure sufficient carbohydrate intake as well.

3

Body Composition in Athletes: Assessment and Estimated Fatness

The study of body composition attempts to partition and quantify body weight or mass into its basic components. Body weight is a gross measure of the mass of the body, which can be studied at several levels from basic chemical elements and specific tissues to the entire body. Body composition is a factor that can influence athletic performance and as such is of considerable interest to athletes and coaches. This article provides an overview of models and methods used for studying body composition, changes in body composition during adolescence and the transition into adulthood, and applications to adolescent and young adult athletes.

LEVELS OF BODY COMPOSITION

The study of body composition historically has been driven by the availability of methods to measure or, more appropriately, to estimate it. Since the early 1980s, considerable progress has been made in the development and refinement of tech-niquesto estimate the composition of the body, so that virtually all components of the body can now be measured. This progress has resulted in the modification of the models that provide the framework for studying body composition.

Body composition can be approached at a variety of levels. The five-level approach provides a sound guide: atomic, molecular, cellular, tissue, and whole body. The multilevel view provides a framework within which the lure and difficulty inherent in the study of body composition can be appreciated. Basic chemical elements compose the atomic level. There are 106 elements in nature. About 50 are found in the human body, and with more recent technologic advances, all 50 can be measured in vivo. Oxygen, carbon, hydrogen, and nitrogen account for greater than 95% of body mass, and the addition of seven other elements—sodium, potassium, phosphorus, chloride, calcium, magnesium, and sulfur—accounts for 99.5% of body mass.

The molecular level of body composition focuses on four of five components: water, lipid (fat), protein, minerals, and carbohydrate. The last component, carbohydrate, occurs in small amounts in the form of glycogen, largely in the liver and skeletal muscle, and is not usually considered in estimates of body composition. The following equation is used:

Body mass ¼ water þ protein þ mineral þ fat

Most mineral is located in bone with a small fraction in other tissues. Historically, the relative contribution of each of the four components to body mass was derived from chemical analyses of human cadavers, although each can now be measured in vivo.

At the cellular level, body mass is viewed as composed of cells and substances outside of cells. The body cell mass (BCM) is defined by intracellular fluids and intracellular solids and is the metabolically active component of the body. Presently available methods do not permit measurement of cell solids in vivo. Extracellular fluids (ECF) and extracellular solids (ECS) compose the substances outside of the cells. The primary ECF are bone minerals and other components of connective tissues. Adipocytes are fat cells; they store lipids and comprise fat mass (FM). The equation is as follows:

Body mass ¼ BCM þ ECF þ ECS þ FM

At the tissue level, the study of body composition focuses on the contribution of specific tissues to body mass: skeletal muscle, adipose, bone, blood, viscera, and brain. Skeletal muscle, adipose, and bone tissues historically have been a primary focus in studies using traditional technologies, such as anthropometry and radiography. New technologies permit more refined assessment of these primary tissues (eg, the mineral content of bone tissue or subcutaneous versus internal adipose tissue). The fifth level of body composition is the whole body, its size, shape, physique, and proportions. Anthropometry is the basic tool for estimating body size and configuration, although photographic techniques also have been used, especially for the study of shape and physique.

The body mass index (BMI) (weight [kg]/height^2 [m]) and skinfold thicknesses are perhaps the most widely used anthropometric indicators at this level of body composition. Two other properties of the whole body are crucial in the study of body composition—volume and density.

MODELS OF BODY COMPOSITION

The two-component model historically has been the model of choice for partitioning body mass into meaningful components or compartments. This traditional approach has evolved into more complex models that include three, four, or more compartments.

Two Components

The two-component model partitions body mass into its lean (fat-free mass

[FFM]) and fat (FM) compartments. The equation follows:

Body mass ¼ FFM þ FM

The term lean body mass is occasionally used, but FFM is more appropriate. Lean body mass is a more anatomic concept that includes some essential lipids, whereas FFM is a biochemical concept. This model has had the widest application in the study of body composition, including many studies of athletes. FM is the more labile of the two compartments; it is readily influenced by diet and training. A shortcoming of the two-component model is the heterogeneous composition of FFM; it includes water, protein, mineral (bone and soft tissue mineral), and glycogen.

Three Components

The three-component model includes FM and partitions FFM into total body water (TBW) and fat-free dry mass (FFDM). The equation is as follows:

Body mass ¼ TBW þ FFDM þ FM

Water is the largest component of body mass, and most is located in lean tissues. FFDM includes protein, glycogen, and mineral in bone and soft tissues.

Four Components

With the development of techniques to measure bone mineral, the four-component model is a logical extension of the preceding model. FFDM is partitioned in bone mineral (BM) and the residual. The following equation is used:

Body mass ¼ TBW þ BM þ FM þ residual

Overview

All models include FM. It is the aspect of body composition that has received and continues to receive most attention. Excess FM can have a negative influence on physical performance and is often viewed by coaches and trainers as a major limiting factor in athletic achievements. Excessive fatness also is a major independent risk factor for several degenerative diseases.

FM, although often treated as a singular component of body composition, is heterogeneous. Fat, or more appropriately lipid, is physiologically divided into essential and nonessential lipids. Essential lipids are vital components of cells and are basic for a variety of physiologic functions; they constitute about 10% of total lipids in the body. The remaining lipids, 90% of total body lipids, are nonessential. They are triglycerides, which provide a storage form of available energy and perhaps thermal insulation. The small amount of essential lipids in the body usually are not considered in estimates of body composition and usually are grouped with the residual component or with FM, depending on the model and method of assessment.

FFM is highly correlated with overall body size. Partitioning FFM into fractions has several problems. Error is inherent in the measurement of each component, and the more components included in a model increases the chances of error. The techniques available for the measurement of TBW, potassium, calcium, and sodium each have associated error. When measured, these properties must be converted to the body composition component of interest. The transformation of the measured property to the component is essentially mathematical and includes a variety of assumptions.

Multicomponent models are additive; it is assumed that the separately measured properties can be summed to provide an estimate of the whole. Thus, the measurement of body composition is essentially an estimate of body composition.

The different models of body composition have been largely developed on adults. They also assume that during periods of stable body mass, the various components exist in a steady state, which means that they are constant, or the relationships among components are constant. The assumption of constant relationships has permitted the development of procedures to estimate the different fractions of body mass in adults. The application of these procedures to children and adolescents, to adults in different stages of the life cycle, and to elite athletes requires care in interpretation of various estimates. The proportions of each component and the relationships among components change during growth and maturation and with aging. Systematic training for sport is an additional factor that influences body composition.

METHODS FOR ESTIMATING BODY COMPOSITION

Methods of estimating body composition in vivo are numerous and often quite complex (Table 1). The methods are sufficiently different in technique that one may inquire whether they provide reasonably similar estimates of body composition. The formulas for estimating FFM or FM, or components of FFM, and the assumptions underlying the procedures are based primarily on adults in the general population (ie, nonathletes). Their application to growing and maturing children and adolescents and to athletes may result in spuriously high or low estimates.

Several commonly used methods are briefly described. Three have been used regularly for some time—the measurement of body density (Db), TBW, and potassium concentration. Two more recent methods—dual-energy x-ray absorptiometry (DXA) and bioelectrical impediance analysis (BIA)—also are described. The specific protocols for each of these methods and their limitations are discussed in detail in Roche et al and Heymsfield et al. Anthropomet-ric approaches also are briefly summarized.

Body Density—Densitometry

Density is mass per unit volume. The density of specific body tissues varies. The density of lean tissues (>1.100 g/cm) is greater than the density of water (1 g/cm) and fat (0.9007 g/cm). Density is inversely related to body fat content: The greater the proportion of fat, the lower the Db. A measure of Db permits an estimate of the percentage of body mass that is fat (% Fat). The most common method for measuring Db is underwater (hydrostatic) weighing, but air or helium displacement techniques also are used. Two formulas are used most often to convert Db to % Fat:

% Fat – 4:570/Db – 4:142

% Fat – 4:950/Db – 4:500

The formulas and their underlying assumptions are derived from adults. The two equations give reasonably similar estimates of % Fat except for the very lean and very obese.

The estimate of % Fat is based on the assumption that the densities of the fat and fat-free components are known and are constant, and that adults are identical in composition except for variability in the proportion of fat. The proportions and chemical composition of the various components of FFM change with growth and maturation, in addition to interindividual differences in composition of FFM.

An estimate of FM is derived by multiplication and subtraction: FM – body mass x % Fat FFM – body mass – FM

Total Body Water—Hydrometry

Water is the largest component of the body, varying between 55% and 65% of body mass in normally hydrated young men, with lower values for women. The TBW of 70-kg young men can range from 38 to 45 kg of water. Emphasis is on normal hydration. TBW varies during the course of a day, depending on fluid intake and physical activity level, especially strenuous exercise. It also varies with severe protein-energy undernutrition and extreme obesity.

Most of the water in the body is in lean tissues. Water constitutes approximately 72% to 74% of FFM in normally hydrated adults, although the estimated water content of FFM has been reported to vary between 67% and 74%. In contrast, adipose tissue is relatively nonaqueous and contains a small proportion of water, about 20%.

The measurement of TBW provides an estimate of FFM. The process is based on two principles of isotope dilution: Certain substances distribute themselves evenly throughout a fluid space or compartment of the body, and the dilution of a known amount of substance, an isotope tracer, administered into an unknown volume or mass enables the calculation of the unknown volume or mass. The protocol consists of administering a known amount of a stable isotope tracer, allowing it sufficient time to dilute or mix, and then measuring its concentration after dilution and after correcting for the amount of the tracer lost from the body by excretion or exhalation. Three isotopes generally are used to measure TBW: deuterated water (H, deuterium), tritiated water (H, tritium), and O-labeled water (heavy isotope of oxygen).

TBW usually is measured in the morning after an overnight fast. The isotope is administered to the subject based on body mass. Time is permitted for its equilibration with body water, usually 2 to 4 hours depending on the isotope. The concentration of the isotope in serum, urine, or saliva is measured. Assuming that the percentage of water in FFM is constant in adults, FFM is estimated as follows:

FFM – TBW/0.732

FM – body mass – FFM

TBW can be subdivided into water that is intracellular (ICW) and extracellular (ECW). Estimates of ICW and ECW in young men are 57% and 43%.

ECW usually is measured with the same isotope dilution principles as TBW with either chloride or bromide as the isotope. ECW is composed mainly of water in support and transport tissues: plasma, dense connective tissue (tendon, cartilage, bone), interstitial lymph, and transcellular fluids (cerebrospinal fluid, joint fluids). ICW corresponds closely to skeletal muscle mass, the work-producing tissue of the body, but is not exclusively composed of it. After estimating ECW, ICW usually is derived by subtraction:

ICW – TBW – ECW

Body Potassium—Whole Body Counting

Potassium occurs primarily in cells and especially in skeletal muscle tissue. Measurement of the concentration of potassium in the body can provide an es-timate of FFM. This is done by measuring the amount of potassium-40 (K), a naturally occurring isotope of potassium that accounts for 0.0118% of the naturally occurring potassium in the human body. The concentration of K is measured with highly sensitive detection instruments, whole body counters, which count the gamma emissions of the naturally occurring potassium. A constant proportion of potassium in FFM is assumed, but there is a sex difference. FFM is estimated as follows:

FFM – mEqK/68.1 in males

FFM – mEq K/64.2 in females

FM – body mass – FFM

More recent studies indicate variation in the potassium content of FFM, specifically values lower than the proportions indicated here. Most of the available data for estimating body composition from measures of total body potassium use the constants reported by Forbes. Total body potassium per unit FFM tends to decline with age in adulthood and shows differences between American blacks and whites.

Dual-Energy X-Ray Absorptiometry

DXA is used to measure bone mineral and soft tissue composition of the body. It provides estimates for the total body and of specific regions in the form of bone mineral, fat-free soft tissues (sometimes called bone-free lean tissue), and fat. The method requires a low radiation exposure, 0.05 to 1.5 mrem, depending on the machine and how quickly the total body scan is done. The DXA unit measures the attenuation of the low-dose x-ray beam as it passes through different tissues of the body. How much of each photon beam is absorbed by the atoms in bone mineral and soft tissues of the body is recorded during the scan and converted to estimates of bone mineral and soft tissues. The DXA instrument must be linked with appropriate computer algorithms to derive estimates of bone mineral, fat-free soft tissue, and fat tissue content of the total body. The algorithms also permit division of the body into anatomic segments—arms, legs, trunk, and head—to permit estimates of regional body composition.

The derivation of fat and fat-free soft tissue from DXA scans is based on the ratio of soft tissue attenuation of the low-energy and high-energy photon beams as they pass through the body. The attenuation of the low-energy and high-energy soft tissues is known based on scans of pure fat and fat-free soft tissues and theoretical calculations. It is assumed that the attenuation of fat and fat-free soft tissues is constant. The attenuation for fat is lower than that for fat-free soft tissues. Using these constants and the scans from the DXA unit, the amount of fat and fat-free soft tissue is calculated.

The derivation of bone mineral requires adjustment for the soft tissue overlying bone. DXA technology provides an estimate of total body bone mineral content (g) and total bone area (cm^3). The ratio of total body bone mineral to total bone area is used to estimate bone mineral density (g/cm^3). DXA basically measures the cross-sectional area of a scan (total bone area) and not bone volume; expressing bone mineral relative to bone area is only an approximation of bone mineral density.

Several types of commercially available DXA instruments are presently in use. Each type of unit has its own computer algorithms for deriving estimates of body composition, and there are inter-instrument differences. There is concern for the comparability of measurements, especially of soft tissue, from machines produced by different manufacturers. All of them assume that the attenuation characteristics of bone, fat-free soft tissue, and fat are known and constant.

Bioelectrical Impedance Analysis

The method of estimating body composition from BIA is based on the fact that lean tissue has a greater electrolyte and water content than fat. This difference in electrolyte content permits an estimate of FFM from the magnitude of the body's electrical conductivity or from the body's impedance to an electrical current as it flows from the source (usually the ankle) to the sink (usually the wrist) electrodes. FFM has low impedance and high conductivity, whereas FM, which has a relatively low water and electrolyte content, has high impedance and low conductivity.

BIA uses an imperceptible electrical current, which is introduced into the body via electrodes placed on the ankle. The injected current passes through the body, and the voltage that is produced is measured in voltage-sensing electrodes placed on the wrist. The ratio of voltage to the current is impedance. Impedance to the flow of the current is related to the shape, volume, and length of the body, which is the conductor of the current. Because impedance is proportional to the geometry of the conductor, variation in body shape may be a factor in the application of BIA.

BIA measures the voltage for the path from the ankle to the wrist. It yields a measure of resistance, which is the major component of impedance. Resistance usually is converted to TBW, which is transformed into an estimate of FFM as described earlier.

The equation used to convert resistance to TBW usually includes stature.

Several types of commercially available BIA units are presently in use, and there are differences among the units. They are portable (the size of a briefcase) and relatively inexpensive. BIA also is convenient, rapid, and noninvasive. As such, it is finding increased application for estimates of body composition. As with other methods, BIA has many underlying assumptions, which need to be verified.

Anthropometry

The use of anthropometric dimensions to estimate body composition has a long history. Skinfold measurements are used most often to predict Db, which is converted to an estimate of % Fat. A variety of prediction equations incorporating skinfold measurements and other dimensions (height, limb and trunk circumferences, skeletal widths) are available. Most are based on samples of nonathlete adults, and several are based on children and adolescents, although equations for athletes also are available. Prediction equations are sample specific and should be cross-validated. "Generalized" equations that adjust for age and the curvilinear relationship between skinfold thicknesses and Db also have been developed. Equations based on advances in body composition methodology and multicomponent models also are available for the general population and for female athletes.

Some degree of error is inherent in the measurement of body dimensions and body composition. Error associated with the measurements per se and with prediction equations should be noted. The standard error of estimate associated with available equations to predict body density generally ranges between 2% and 5%. For a discussion of error associated with anthropometry and the accuracy of body composition prediction equations, see Malina and Sun and Chumlea.

More recently, the BMI has found increasing use as an alternative method for rapid assessment of body composition of athletes. The BMI is widely used in epi-demiologic surveys of the weight status in adults: underweight (BMI <18.5 kg/m), overweight (BMI >25 < 30 kg/m), and obesity (BMI >30 kg/m). It also is used as a screening device of overweight and obesity in children and adolescents. The BMI is reasonably well correlated with total and percentage body fat in large and heterogeneous samples, although it has limitations especially with youth. Correlations between the BMI and FFM and FM are reasonably similar among youth, which would suggest that the BMI is an indicator of heaviness and indirectly of body fatness. At the extremes of heaviness, the BMI is probably a reasonable indicator of fatness in the general population. Given the relatively large body size (height and mass) and relative leanness of athletes, the BMI has limitations with athletes.

Applications

The methods described provide an estimate of FFM and FM. Db is converted to % Fat; TBW, ^{40}K, and BIA (resistance) yield estimates of FFM. The other half of the two-component model is derived by subtraction. The three-component model involves the simultaneous measurement of Db and TBW to derive an estimate of % Fat, whereas the four-component model includes Db, TBW, and total body bone mineral to estimate % Fat. Multicomponent models provide the advantage of greater accuracy of estimates. The cost and technical constraints of the required methodology often limit their applicability outside of the clinical or laboratory setting, however.

Most of the available body composition data for athletes are derived from the two-component model using Db. Data are less extensive for estimates derived from TBW, ^{40}K, multicomponent models, DXA, and BIA. The assumptions underlying the methods are based on nonathletic adults, and limitations of applications to youth and adult athletes need to be recognized. Fat estimates from densitometry are based on the assumption that the density of fat and lean tissues is constant. FFM estimates from TBW and ^{40}K are based on the assumption that the water and potassium contents of the FFM are constant. They also assume that the density of fat and lean tissues and the water and potassium contents of the FFM are the same in children, adolescents, and adults, which is not the case. An important issue in growing and maturing individuals is the age at which adult density, water concentration, and potassium concentration of FFM are achieved.

BIA is finding increased application. The method is useful to describe the body composition of groups, but estimates have large errors within individuals, which limits its application. BIA is influenced by nutritional and hydration status and is not sensitive to acute changes in electrolytes and fluids. There also is significant variation between BIA machines produced by different manufacturers. The resistance (R) function of impedance is used most often with stature (length of the conductor) to estimate FFM, but there is uncertainty about the appropriate hydration factor to use in converting R to FFM. Other equations use R and stature, in conjunction with body mass, circumferences, and skin fold measurements to estimate FFM.

DXA is used most often to estimate bone mineral content and density. DXA measures of total body bone mineral content also are used in the four-component model to increase the accuracy of body composition estimates. The procedures require the measurement of Db, TBW, and bone mineral, and it is unclear whether the time and expense involved markedly improve the accuracy of the body composition estimates.

DXA also is being used more often to estimate FFM, FM, and % Fat. The accuracy of these estimates needs further verification relative to estimates derived from the more established methods of body composition assessment, specifically densitometry and hydrometry.

An important issue in all body composition studies is validation. How accurately does a given technique estimate the specific components of body composition? What is the appropriate criterion against which to compare estimates of body composition derived from the different methods and models? Do the different methods and models provide the same estimates of FFM, FM, and % Fat? The assessment of bone mineral content increases the accuracy of the four-component model over the three-component model. The instrument to measure bone mineral content is expensive, however: Is this expense justifiable given the small increase in the accuracy of the body composition estimates? These and other questions need to be considered in evaluating the application of new technologies and multicomponent models.

CHEMICAL MATURITY

If the principles and methods for estimating body composition are to be accurately applied to youth, including young athletes, it is important to determine when during growth are adult values for the primary components of FFM attained. When adult values are reached, chemical maturity is said to be attained. The concept of chemical maturity was introduced by Moulton : "The point at which the concentration of water, proteins, and salts [minerals] becomes comparatively constant in the fat-free cell is named the point of chemical maturity of the cell."

During the interval of growth and maturation, approximately the first 2 decades of life, the relative contribution of water to body mass decreases, and corresponding contributions of solids—protein, mineral, and fat—to body mass increase. Growth is an accretive process, adding or accumulating solids at the expense of fluids. The relative contributions of protein and mineral to FFM also increase, whereas the relative contribution of water to FFM decreases.

The estimated composition of FFM from late childhood through adolescence into young adulthood is summarized in Table 2. With growth and maturation during adolescence, the relative contribution of solids (protein and mineral) to FFM increases, and that of water decreases. Sex differences are apparent. FFM in males contains relatively less water and relatively more protein and mineral compared with females. The sex difference also is reflected in the estimated potassium content and density of the FFM, which are greater in males than in females. The difference reflects the sex difference in muscle mass and bone mineral and persists into young adulthood. The gain in bone mineral between age 10 years and young adulthood reflects, to a large extent, the growth and maturation of the skeleton during the adolescent growth spurt. The relative mineral content of FFM in males increases from 5.4% at about 10 years to 6.6% at 17 to 20 years, a small increment (1.2%) that is, however, about 22% of the initial value at age 10. The corresponding increase in the relative mineral content of FFM in females is less, 5.2% to 6.1%, a relative increase of about 16% of the initial value in late childhood. It is apparent that chemical maturity of FFM is not attained until after the adolescent growth spurt, probably about 16 to 18 years in girls and 18 to 20 years in boys.

The information summarized in Table 2 represents estimates of the chemical composition of the FFM. The estimates are derived in part from limited biochemical cadaver analyses and from in vivo estimates of TBW, potassium, nitrogen, calcium, and bone mineral. Estimates also vary from laboratory to laboratory, which is not unexpected because different data, assumptions, and methods are used in their derivation. There are continued effortsto arrive at the more accurate estimates of the chemical composition of the FFM. Nevertheless, an important conclusion to be derived from these estimates and ongoing studies is that the chemical maturity of FFM changes during growth and maturation and is not attained until late adolescence or young adulthood. The equations and constants based on adult values and earlier studies are often adjusted for the chemical immaturity of the FFM in growing and maturing individuals.

CHANGES IN BODY DENSITY, TOTAL BODY WATER, AND TOTAL BODY POTASSIUM DURING GROWTH

The basic properties used for estimating body composition change with growth and maturation. TBW and total body potassium, both of which are found primarily in lean tissue, follow a growth pattern similar to that of height and body mass with a clear adolescent spurt during which growth in TBW and total body potassium is greater in males than in females. Both reach a plateau at about 15 to 17 years in females and increase into the early 20s in males. Db has a different growth pattern. It declines in males from about 8 to 10 years, but then increases more or less linearly to about 16 to 17 years of age. In females, Db decreases from about 8 to 11 years, then increases only slightly, and finally reaches a plateau by about 14 years. Both sexes also show a slight decline in Db in late adolescence and young adulthood. Db is inversely related to body fat content, although not linearly. Males have greater Db than females at all ages and have a correspondingly lower % Fat.

GROWTH IN FAT-FREE MASS, FAT MASS, AND FAT PERCENTAGE OF BODY MASS

The growth patterns of FFM, FM, and % Fat from late childhood through adolescence into young adulthood have been described. FFM follows a growth pattern similar to that of height and weight. Sex differences are small during childhood and become established during the adolescent growth spurt. Young adult values of FFM are reached earlier in females, about 15 to 16 years, compared with 19 to 20 years in males. In late adolescence and young adulthood, males have, on average, an FFM that is about 1.5 times larger than that of females. The average FFM of young women is about 70% of the mean value for men. The difference reflects the male adolescent spurt in muscle mass and the sex difference in adult height.

When FFM is expressed per unit height (kg/cm), the sex difference is relatively small in late childhood and early adolescence, but after 14 years of age, males have more FFM for the same height as females. The sex difference increases with age so that young men have an estimated 0.36 kg FFM/cm height, whereas young women have an estimated 0.26 kg FFM/cm height.

Estimated FM increases more rapidly in females than in males from late childhood through adolescence, but seems to reach a plateau or to change only slightly near the time of the adolescent growth spurt in boys (about 13– 15 years). In contrast to FFM, females have, on average, about 1.5 times the FM of males in late adolescence and young adulthood.

Estimated % Fat is greater in females than in males from late childhood through adolescence into young adulthood. Percent Fat increases gradually through adolescence in the same manner as FM in females; it also increases gradually in males until just before the adolescent spurt (about 11–12 years) and then gradually declines. Percent Fat reaches its lowest point at about 16 to 17 years in males and then gradually increases into young adulthood. In contrast to estimates of FM, % Fat declines during male adolescence. The decline is due to the rapid growth of FFM and slower accumulation of FM at this time. As such, fat contributes a lesser percentage to body mass in male adolescence.

To illustrate the impact of adolescence on body composition, differences in estimates of body composition between early and late adolescence are summarized in Table 3. Corresponding data for a mixed-longitudinal sample of youth from the Fels Longitudinal Study are included for comparison.

The Fels data are derived from subjects who had at least six serial measurements of Db between 8 and 23 years. A multicomponent model that included age-specific and sex-specific estimates of the density and major components of FFM was used to derive % Fat, FM, and FFM. Allowing for methodologic variation, the estimates are reasonably similar. Males gain almost twice as much FFM as females over adolescence, and females gain about twice as much FM as males. The net result is a decline in relative fatness in males and an increase in relative fatness in females.

A major portion of changes in body composition over adolescence is concentrated in the interval of rapid growth in height. Peak height velocity (PHV) occurs, on average, at 12 and 14 years of age in a sample of North American and European girls and boys. Assuming 1 year each side of PHV, the interval between 11 and 13 years in girls and 13 and 15 years in boys provides an estimate of changes in body composition at this time (Table 4). The interval of maximal growth in height accounts for about 40% of the total adolescent gain in FFM and FM. Although these estimates are based on cross-sectional data from the literature, they correspond reasonably well with limited data from longitudinal studies. Czech boys, many of whom were athletes, gained about 7.5 kg/y in FFM and 0.8 kg/y in FM and declined about 0.4%/y in % Fat near the time of PHV. The decline in relative fatness is an effect of the larger increase in FFM, so that FM, although increasing slightly, contributes a small percentage of body mass at this time. In the mixed-longitudinal sample from the Fels study (see Table 2), peak gain in FFM was about 7 kg/y in boys, whereas no clear spurt in FFM was evident in girls. In a separate analysis of adolescent changes in total body bone mineral content, peak gains occurred, on average, a bit more than one half of a year after PHV in both sexes. Estimated peak gain in BMC was, on average, greater in boys, 407 ± 93 g/y, than in girls, 325 ± 67 g/y. Peak gain in bone mineral content occurred closer to the age of menarche, suggesting that adolescent growth in bone mineral is closely related to sexual maturation in girls.

BODY COMPOSITION OF ATHLETES

Why Estimate the Body Composition of Athletes?

It is important to know how the different components of body composition vary with age, sex, and maturity status, especially during adolescence. Likewise, it is important to understand the influence of systematic training for sport on body composition. Many discussions of body composition in athletes focus on relative fatness because of the potentially negative influence of excessive fatness on performance. Focus of such discussions is often on female athletes, usually in the context of low levels of fatness, late sexual maturation, menstrual irregularities, and disordered eating.

Weight control and in many instances reduction are issues with many athletes. Associated concerns are potential metabolic complications with long-term weight reduction and weight control behaviors that may lead to complications of disordered eating, particularly among female athletes. Among male athletes, there is concern for low levels of fatness of males in weight category sports, specifically wrestling.

Youth Athletes

The body composition of young athletes is influenced by their growth and maturity status. With few exceptions, young athletes of both sexes tend to be at or above median reference values in height and mass; exceptions are gymnasts of both sexes and female figure skaters. Elite young male athletes tend to be, on average, advanced in maturity status, although there is variation among sports. Earlier maturation in males is associated with larger size and FFM, greater strength and power, and a lower % Fat compared with average ("on time") and later maturing peers of the same chronologic age. The size, strength, and power associated with earlier maturation in males are an advantage in many sports. Elite young female athletes tend to be, on average, average and later in maturity status compared with peers of the same chronologic age. Later maturation in females is associated with smaller body size, a more linear physique, lower % Fat, and generally better performances compared with early maturing peers. Discussions of the body composition of young athletes should consider individual differences in maturity status; studies rarely consider maturity-association variation among young athletes. Variation associated with individual differences in biologic maturation is a potential confounding factor in evaluating the body composition of young athletes.

Because FFM follows a growth pattern similar to that for height and mass, and FFM is highly correlated with height and mass, most studies of body composition of young athletes emphasize % Fat. As noted, excessive fatness tends to exert a negative influence on performances, especially performances that require the movement or projection of the body through space (ie, running, jumping, vaulting), in contrast to those that require projection of objects (ie, shot put, discus throw). Coaches of young athletes often focus on weight control and relative fatness. Middle school, high school, and collegiate wrestling currently set minimum weight or % Fat requirements (see later).

Estimates of the relative fatness of adolescent athletes in a variety of sports are shown relative to data for nonathletes in Fig. 1. The estimates are means based on densitometry with one exception; data for a sample of female gymnasts based on DXA also are included. Allowing for variation among samples and in methodology, athletes as a rule have a lower % Fat than nonathletes of the same chronologic age. Male athletes and nonathletes show a decrease in % Fat during adolescence; athletes have less relative fatness at most ages, but there is considerable overlap (Fig. 1A). In contrast, % Fat in female athletes tends to be reasonably stable across adolescence, whereas that for nonathletes increases with age (Fig. 1B). The difference in % Fat between female athletes and nonathletes is greater than that between male athletes and nonathletes. Allowing for the sports represented, there seems to be more variation in % Fat among female than male athletes 14 to 18 years old.

Young Adult Athletes

Estimated % Fat in young adult male and female athletes in numerous sports is summarized in Tables 5 and 6. Most data are based on body density derived from hydrostatic weighing; estimates based on other methods are limited. Data for youth and adult track and field athletes by discipline are considered separately (see later).

The data summarized in Tables 5 and 6 provide an overview of estimated relative fatness and associated variation in young adult athletes in a variety of sports. Samples sizes are generally small, and many sports are not well represented. Corresponding estimates for % Fat predicted from skinfold measurements in national-level Polish athletes and American intercollegiate female athletes in numerous sports are summarized in Tables 7 and 8, respectively. Within corresponding sports, % Fat of female athletes is, on average, greater than that of male athletes. Variation in % Fat by position or event within a sport is apparent for American football players, but is not marked among female basketball, volleyball, and track and field athletes, with the exception of the throwing events. The ethnic composition of samples of athletes is not usually reported; this is relevant given ethnic variation in body proportions and composition. Ethnic variation in bone mineral content between American blacks and whites has been long documented and influences estimates of Db via hydrostatic weighing. Observations using more recent technology indicate that black women have a larger appendicular skeletal muscle mass than white women matched for age, body size, and menstrual status. The ethnic difference is more marked in the upper than the lower extremity. Limited data for American black and white males show less ethnic variation in limb musculature, but after adjustment for age, height, and mass, skeletal muscle mass of the legs is significantly larger in American blacks of both sexes. The ethnic difference also persists after adjusting for variation in relative leg length. Arm skeletal muscle mass also is significantly larger in American blacks of both sexes after adjusting for age and mass and for relative arm length.

The preceding observations on ethnic variation are based on nonathletes. Corresponding body composition data for athletes are limited. Estimated fatness (hydrostatic weighing) of collegiate football players is lower in black (14.7 ± 5.6%, n = 55) than white (19.0 ± 7.1%, n = 35) players. Relative fatness estimated from skinfold measurements gives similar estimates, but BIA tends to overestimate % Fat based on Db, and near-infrared spectrophotometry tends to underestimate % Fat based on Db in black and white players. Among female collegiate athletes, differences in estimated % Fat predicted from skinfold measurements between black and white athletes are, on average, quite small (see Table 8) and within the range of error associated with the prediction equation.

Adolescent and Young Adult Track and Field Athletes

Data on the size, physique, and body composition of track and field athletes in specific events within the sport are more extensive compared with other sports and span early adolescence through young adulthood. The literature dealing with track and field athletes is diverse and can be summarized in the framework of four general themes: (1) talent identification and selection; (2) interest in the growth, body composition, and functional characteristics of elite young athletes in a variety of sports; (3) increased popularity of distance running for children and adolescents; and (4) interest in the comparative morphology of athletes in general. The data often include estimates of % Fat based primarily on measured Db and predicted Db based on skinfold measurements; estimates based on other methods are limited. The data permit evaluation of variation in % Fat by event. Estimates of mean % Fat are summarized in Figs. 2, 3, and 4 for sprinters and hurdlers, middle and long distance runners, and jumpers and throwers. Corresponding estimates for specific jumping and throwing disciplines, pole vaulters, race walkers, and decathletes are not extensive. Data for adolescents and young adults from the general population are included for comparison.

Most samples of male sprinters and hurdlers tend to be below the reference in % Fat from early adolescence into young adulthood, although there is some overlap during adolescence (Fig. 2A). In contrast, % Fat of female sprinters and hurdlers is well below the reference.

Estimates of % Fat among middle and long distance runners show considerable overlap within sex, although there seems to be more variation among females than males (Fig. 3). Most estimates for males are below the reference during adolescence into young adulthood (Fig. 3A). The reported estimate for a sample of 17-year-old male distance runners (2.6%)is spuriously low. As noted, % Fat of female middle distance and distance runners varies (Fig. 3B). Most values are below the reference value, but several approach the reference in later adolescence. In young adulthood, however, estimates of % Fat are considerably lower, especially in distance runners.

Estimated % Fat of field athletes in jumping and throwing events shows two distributions with little overlap (Fig. 4). The relative fatness of male jumpers is consistently below the reference from adolescence into adulthood. In contrast, % Fat of male adolescent throwers is consistently above the reference, reflecting in part their massiveness. Percent Fat tends to decline with age, however, among samples of throwers. Among young adult throwers, estimates for several samples are lower than corresponding values for adolescent throwers and fluctuate above and below the reference values.

Female jumpers have relative fatness levels consistently below the reference, and % Fat in young adult jumpers tends to be lower than that for adolescents. Percent Fat of female throwers varies above and below the reference in adolescence and young adulthood, which is in contrast to the trend in male throwers. In female jumpers and throwers, variation in % Fat is greater among young adults than among adolescents.

Estimates of % Fat in male track and field athletes except for throwers are generally below the reference. There is considerable overlap among mean estimates for sprinters and hurdlers, middle distance and distance runners, and jumpers, and all have % Fat that is generally lower than in samples of throwers. Trends in % Fat among adolescent track and field athletes should be viewed in two contexts: first, the decline in % Fat that accompanies the growth spurt and sexual maturation in males, and second, the decline in % Fat associated with systematic training.

In female track and field athletes, there is considerable overlap in mean estimates of % Fat among for runners of all disciplines and jumpers, and all are, on average, generally below the reference. Relative fatness of female throwers tends to be higher, but estimates fall above and below the reference.

Comparison of % Fat of male and female athletes within the same track and field events suggests several trends: (1) Percent Fat in male sprinters and hurdlers is only slightly lower than and overlaps the male reference, whereas corresponding estimates of % Fat in female athletes in these events are well below the female reference. (2) Percent Fat varies from early adolescence through adolescence into young adulthood in male and female middle distance and distance runners; it is considerably lower than the reference among female runners, whereas % Fat in male runners approximates the male reference at many ages (3). The same general trend is apparent in jumpers and throwers. Percent Fat in female jumpers is well below the female reference, whereas it is quite close to the reference in male jumpers. Percent Fat in female throwers straddles the reference, but is above the reference in male throwers, especially in adolescence. Relative fatness tends to be lower in young adult compared with adolescent male throwers; such variation with age is lacking in female throwers.

Wrestling

Weight management and specifically weight reduction are concerns in wrestling. Organizations associated with the sport have developed guidelines for minimum weight, defined as the lowest weight that an individual can maintain without comprising health. Wrestling rules of the National Federation of State High School Associations mandates the following:

Each state association shall develop and use a weight-management program that includes a specific gravity not to exceed 1.025; a body fat assess no lower than seven percent for males/ 12 percent for females; and a monitored weekly weight loss plan not to exceed 1.5 percent a week.

The American College of Sports Medicine suggests the following for young wrestlers: Assess the body composition of each wrestler before the season using valid methods for this population. Males 16 years old and younger with body fat below 7 percent or those over 16 with a body fat below 5 percent need medical clearance before being allowed to compete. Female wrestlers need minimal body fat of 12–14 percent.

The National Collegiate Athletic Association uses 5% Fat as the minimum allowable in weight certification formulas for wrestlers; however, body composition guidelines emphasize that estimates of body composition focus on a range of variation.

A key issue in putting the proposed guidelines into action relates to methods of estimating body composition and associated errors. Estimates derived from different methods may not be directly comparable. Some high school associations and school districts specify the type of estimate (DXA, BIA, skin-fold measurements) at times with associated costs.

In one of the few detailed studies, body composition was assessed via hydrostatic weighing in the preseason, late season, and postseason in a sample of 9 male wrestlers 15.4 ± 0.3 years old. Percent Fat at the three measuring points was 9.9 ± 0.5%, 8.0 ± 0.7% and 12.3 ± 0.8%. Corresponding estimates of FFM were 54.3 ± 3.1 kg, 53.2 ± 3 kg, and 56.2 ± 3.1 kg. The changes are relatively small and need to be viewed in the context of growth and maturation. Although body mass declined from the preseason to late season and increased into the postseason, linear growth, skeletal maturation, and growth-related hormones were not affected.

Among collegiate wrestlers competing at national tournaments (top 5-10% of wrestlers within each division), % Fat based on skinfold measurements was compared from the preseason to the competition. Body mass and % Fat declined from the preseason to the tournament, 74.0 ± 11.1 kg to 71.5 ± 10.4 kg for mass and 12.3 ± 3.4% to 9.5 ± 1.8%. Mean minimal weights established for each wrestler in the preseason did not differ at the tournament.

TRAINING AND BODY COMPOSITION

Body composition is responsive to the demands of systematic training, as is evident in the observations on wrestlers. It is essential to consider separately observations in growing and maturing youth and in mature adults. Of relevance, are changes in body composition associated with training greater than those associated with normal growth and maturation? The increase in FFM (hydrostatic weighing) observed in youth regularly active in sport from 11 to 17 years old would seem to suggest an increase greater than that expected with normal growth and maturation. This group of boys was larger in size and advanced in biologic maturation, however, compared with their age peers not engaged in sport. Similarly, among boys 11 to 13 years old undergoing a 5-month endurance training program, larger FFM (K) were observed in boys advanced in sexual maturation, suggesting perhaps that the boys were in their growth spurts. The two studies highlight the difficulties in attempting to partition changes in body composition associated with training from 11 to 17 years old or with a short-term training program from the changes that accompany normal growth and maturation during male adolescence. Much of the variation in body composition in both studies was associated with a reduction in fatness.

Corresponding observations for girls are limited. A program of 30 minutes of high-impact aerobic and strength training activities three times per week for10 months was associated with increases in FFM (2.2 ± 1.1 kg) and FM (0.5 ± 0.8 kg) in 9- to 10-year-old girls. Girls of the same age, body size, composition, and stage of sexual maturity who followed their normal pattern of activity for 10 months also increased in FFM (1.4 ± 1.4 kg) and FM (1.0 ± 0.8 kg). Both groups gained in FFM and FM, and there was, on average, no decrease in fatness. There also was considerable overlap between the trained and normal activity groups. Although the results are suggestive, they indicate difficulties inherent in attempting to partition growth-related from training-related changes in estimated body composition in adolescents. Studies comparing changes in body composition associated with training in young adults generally compare pretraining and post-training means for FFM and % Fat, but duration of training programs and frequency of training vary. In addition, the samples do not comprise athletes. Using data reported by Wil-more, differences between pretraining and post-training means in nine studies of males 18 to 23 years old range from −0.2 kg to +1.4 kg for FFM (overall mean +0.8 kg) and −0.4% to −3.0% for relative fatness (overall mean − 1.7%). Corresponding differences for 10 studies of females 18 to 22 years old range from −1.7 kg to +1.5 kg for FFM (overall mean +0.3 kg) and −2.1% to +3.1% for relative fatness (overall mean −0.4%). The persistence of changes associated with training are not usually considered; a relevant question is the following: How much training is needed to maintain changes in body composition induced by systematic training?

SEASONAL VARIATION IN BODY COMPOSITION IN ATHLETES

An issue related to the influence of training on body composition is changes in body composition of athletes during the course of a season. Studies commonly compare the body composition of athletes before and at the close of a competitive season. Of potential relevance is variation in body composition associated with preseason or early season and in-season training protocols. This variation was considered in a sample of 15 elite university-level female swimmers who had their body composition estimated via densitometry at three points during a competitive season: October, December, and March. Weight training with emphasis on high-repetition and low-resistance activities typically preceded swim training early in the season. Decreases in body mass (−1.3 ± 1.8 kg), FM (−2.4 ± 1.2 kg) and % Fat (−3.8 ± 1.9%) and an increase in FFM (1.1 ± 1.8 kg) characterized the early part of the season between October and December. These changes were generally maintained during the second part of the season, December to March, as the swimmers tapered in preparation for the national championships. Over this interval, changes in body mass (0.8 ± 1.2 kg), FM (0.8 ± 1.5 kg) and % Fat (1.2 ± 2%) were small, and FFM, on average, did not change (0 ± 1.1 kg). The results suggest that changes in body composition over the course of a season were concentrated primarily in the early part of the season. Corresponding changes in estimated body composition using anthropometric indicators have been described for female collegiate distance runners and basketball players.

BODY MASS INDEX AND ATHLETES

Many programs monitor the heights and weights of athletes in the form of the BMI. As noted, the BMI is reasonably well correlated with FM and % Fat in large and heterogeneous samples, but correlations between the BMI and FFM and FM are reasonably similar among youth. A question of interest is the association between the BMI and indicators of body composition at the extremes of the BMI distribution. This was addressed in a large sample of female athletes using anthropometric indicators of body composition. Although numbers of athletes with low (<18.5 kg/ m) and high (>25 kg/m) BMI are small, the trends in correlations suggest variable relationships. Among athletes with a BMI in the normal range (18.5 < 25 kg/m), correlations between estimates of fatness and muscularity are moderate and reasonably similar, ranging from 0.37 to 0.57. Correlations for % Fat and arm muscle are similar for nonathlete female college students with a BMI in the normal range, 0.44 and 0.34, although that for estimated calf muscle is lower, 0.15. Among those with a low BMI, correlations for fatness are higher and similar in athletes and nonathletes, 0.61 to 0.68. Correlations for estimated limb musculature and the BMI are low in athletes, −0.08 to 0.10, however, and higher in nonathletes, 0.27 and 0.39. Among those with a high BMI, correlations for fatness and estimated limb muscle circumferences are higher in athletes, 0.52 to 0.88, compared with athletes in the other two BMI categories. A similar high correlation, 0.88, is evident for % Fat in nonathletes with a high BMI, but correlations for limb musculature in nonathletes are negative. Overall, the data suggest variation in the association of the BMI and indirect estimates of fatness and muscularity at the extremes of the BMI distribution and indicate a need for further evaluation of the relationship between the BMI and body composition in athletes and nonathletes.

4

Female Athlete Triad Update

The passage of Title IX legislation in 1972 provided enormous opportunities for women to reap the benefits of sports participation. For most female athletes, sports participation is a positive experience, providing improved physical fitness, enhanced self-esteem, and better physical and mental health. Nonetheless, for a few female athletes, the desire for athletic success combined with the pressure to achieve a prescribed body weight may lead to the development of a triad of medical disorders including disordered eating, menstrual dysfunction, and low bone mineral density (BMD)—known collectively as the female athlete triad. Alone or in combination, the disorders of the triad can have a negative impact on health and impair athletic performance.

HISTORY OF THE TRIAD

In 1992, a special American College of Sports Medicine (ACSM) Task Force on Women's Issues convened a consensus conference to discuss the incidence of three distinct, yet seemingly interrelated disorders—disordered eating, amen-orrhea, and osteoporosis—seen in female athletes with increasing frequency. This combination of disorders was subsequently given the formal name of the female athlete triad (subsequently referred to in this article as the triad). Five years later, the ACSM published a position stand that not only documented the prevalence and consequences of the individual disorders of the triad, but also called for further research into the prevalence, causes, prevention, and treatment of the triad as a whole.

In the 9 years since the first Triad Position Stand was published, a significant amount of research has been completed. As a result, in 2003, the ACSM assembled a writing team of researchers and practitioners well versed in the area of the triad to develop a revised position stand, which is currently in its second set of reviews, but should be completed by the time this article is published. In addition to renaming the components of the triad, the new position stand proposes to emphasize many new concepts related to the triad, including the following :

- New research related to the mechanisms involved in the pathogenesis of the triad disorders
- Low energy availability as the key disorder underlying the other components of the triad
- The spectrum that exists for each of the disorders – energy availability, menstrual function, and bone strength – ranging from health to disease as opposed to focusing only on the extreme end point of each disorder – clinical eating disorders, amenorrhea, and osteoporosis.

PREVALENCE OF THE TRIAD

Despite allegations that the triad is just a "myth" and that researchers have grossly overestimated the extent of the problem, scientific data and anecdotal evidence indicate that the triad does exist and can have devastating consequences for female athletes. Perhaps one of the reasons for the contradictory opinions regarding the magnitude of the problem stems from the dearth of solid data documenting the prevalence of the triad among female athletes. To date, only three studies have examined all three disorders of the triad using direct measures of BMD (ie, dual-energy x-ray absorptiome-try [DXA]) in female athletes.

Beals and Hill examined the prevalence of disordered eating, menstrual dysfunction, and low BMD among 112 US collegiate athletes representing seven different sports. Disordered eating and menstrual dysfunction were assessed by a validated health, weight, dieting, eating disorder, and menstrual history questionnaire, and BMD was determined via DXA. Although only one athlete met the criteria for all three disorders of the triad (using a Z-score <-2.0), two additional athletes qualified when using a less conservative and more frequently used criterion for low BMD (ie, a Z-score <-1.0). In addition, 28 athletes met the criteria for disordered eating, 29 athletes met the criteria for menstrual dysfunction, and 2 athletes had low BMD (using a Z-score <−2.0). Ten athletes met the criteria for two disorders of the triad using the more conservative BMD criterion, and this prevalence was increased to 13 athletes when the less conservative BMD criterion was used.

In a similar study, Nichols and colleagues examined the prevalence of the triad of disorders among 170 high school athletes representing eight different sports. Disordered eating behaviors and attitudes were measured via the Eating Disorder Examination Questionnaire (Fairburn and Belgin, 1994), menstrual dysfunction was determined from a preparticipation examination questionnaire, and BMD was assessed via DXA (with a Z-score of <−1 or <−2 indicative of low BMD). Although only 2 athletes met the criteria for all three components of the triad, 10 girls met the criteria for two components; 18.2%, 23.5%, and 21.8% of the athletes met the criteria for disordered eating, menstrual dysfunction, and low BMD.

Using the entire population of elite Nowegian female athletes, Torstveit and Sundgot-Borgen compared the prevalence of the triad among athletes with that of a nonathletic control group in a three-phase study design. In phase one, all athletes (n ¼ 930) and all controls (n ¼ 900) completed a detailed menstrual, weight, diet history, eating, and activity patterns questionnaire, which also included body dissatisfaction and drive for thinness subscalesof the Eating Disorder Inventory (Garner etal, 1983). Based on data from phase one, a random sample of 300 athletes and 300 controls was selected and invited to complete a BMD test (phase two) and a clinical interview to ascertain eating disorder and disordered eating prevalence (phase three). A totalof 186 athletes and 145 controls completed all three phases of the study, and of these, just 3 athletes and 3 controls presented with the full-blown triad. Compared with controls, a significantly greater percentage of athletes showed disordered eating and menstrual dysfunction (3.4% versus 10.8%; P <.01), whereas the opposite was found for menstrual dysfunction combined with low BMD (2.2% athletes versus 6.9% controls; P <.05).

These prevalence studies indicate that the number of athletes with all three disorders of the triad simultaneously is relatively small. Nonetheless, from a health and performance perspective, any occurrence, no matter how small, deserves attention. The percentage of athletes in all three studies with disordered eating and menstrual dysfunction was substantial and warrants concern. The finding that fewer female athletes have low BMD should not be surprising. First, as described in greater detail later, exercise, particularly that of a high-impact or bone-loading nature, has been shown to provide a protective effect on bone even under conditions of menstrual dysfunction or disordered eating. Second, declines in BMD, particularly in the age groups of the female athletes routinely studied (ie, 13–25 years), can take a substantial amount of time to become apparent.

Finally, research suggests that BMD may not be the best measure of bone "health," thus, currently available research may not accurately reflect the impact of disordered eating or menstrual dysfunction on bone health.

ETIOLOGY OF THE TRIAD

It is generally hypothesized that the development of the triad follows a typical progressive pattern. The female athlete, believing that a lower body weight would enhance athletic success, begins to diet. For numerous reasons, the athlete's diet becomes increasingly restrictive, her eating behaviors increasingly unhealthful. The resulting energy restriction and pathogenic weight control behaviors predispose her to menstrual dysfunction and subsequent decreased BMD. According to this hypothesized scenario, the triad disorders are interrelated, such that the existence of one disorder is linked, directly or indirectly, to the others.

ENERGY AVAILABILITY

Spectrum of Energy Availability

As previously indicated, the revised ACSM Triad Position Stand will likely place a greater emphasis on the spectrum of behaviors and conditions within a given disorder category as opposed to the original version, which focused more on the extreme end point of each disorder category. The category of disordered eating is meant to convey a continuum of abnormal eating behaviors, ranging from failing to meet the energy demands of exercise (ie, low energy availability) to the clinical eating disorders, anorexia nervosa, bulimia nervosa, and eating disorders not otherwise specified. Each one of the major categories contained within the spectrum of disordered eating is briefly described.

Clinical Eating Disorders

The clinical eating disorders include anorexia nervosa, bulimia nervosa, and eating disorders not otherwise specified. To be diagnosed with a clinical eating disorder, an individual must meet a standard set of criteria outlined in the Diagnostic and Statistical Manual of Mental Disorders, 4th edition (DSM-IV). Clinical eating disorders are psychiatric conditions and go beyond simple body weight/shape dissatisfaction and involve more than just abnormal eating patterns or pathogenic weight control behaviors. Individuals with clinical eating disorders often display severe feelings of insecurity and worthlessness, have trouble identifying and displaying emotions, and experience difficulty forming close relationships with others. In addition, clinical eating disorders are often accompanied by comorbid psychological conditions, such as obsessive-compulsive disorder, depression, and anxiety disorder.

Subclinical Eating Disorders

The term subclinical eating disorder is frequently used to describe individuals, athletes and nonathletes, who have considerable eating pathology and body weight concerns, but do not show significant psychopathology or fail to meet all of the DSM-IV criteria for anorexia nervosa, bulimia nervosa, or eating disorders not otherwise specified. Many athletes who report using pathogenic weight control methods (eg, laxatives, diet pills, and excessive exercise) do not technically meet the criteria for a clinical eating disorder.

Low Energy Availability

Energy availability has been defined as the amount of dietary energy remaining for all other physiologic functions after energy has been expended in exercise. Low energy availability results from consuming fewer calories than necessary to cover the additional energy demands of exercise. Although low energy availability can and often does result from disordered eating, it also can occur in the absence of disordered eating. An athlete unwittingly or unknowingly may fail to meet her exercise energy requirements because of time constraints, food availability issues, or lack of appropriate nutritional knowledge.

Prevalence of Low Energy Availability and Disordered Eating in Athletes To date, no published studies have examined the prevalence of low energy availability among female athletes. Such research likely would prove difficult to conduct because it would necessitate accurately assessing energy intake and exercise energy expenditure. The limitations inherent in self-reported energy intake (eg, food records) and energy expenditure (eg, activity records) are well documented, and the expense or lack of generalizability involved in more direct measures (eg, metabolic feeding studies, doubly labeled water, whole room cal-orimetry) render such assessments impractical. Nonetheless, if it is assumed that most female athletes with disordered eating also are experiencing low energy availability, one can garner an estimate, albeit indirect, of prevalence.

Current estimates of the prevalence of disordered eating, including pathogenic weight control behaviors and subclinical and clinical eating disorders, range from less than 1% to 62% in female athletes and 0% to 57% in male athletes. These wide-ranging estimates are due to differences in screening instruments and assessment tools (eg, self-report questionnaires versus in-depth interviews), definitions of "eating disorders" employed (eg, few have used the DSM-IV criteria), and athletic populations studied (eg, collegiate versus high school athletes, elite athletes versus recreational athletes versus physically active people). Only four studies have used large (N > 400) heterogeneous samples of athletes and employed validated measures of disordered eating. The remainder employed inadequate sample sizes, examined single sports, or used inappropriate measures of disordered eating, all of which can bias prevalence estimates.

Research suggests that the prevalence of disordered eating is higher in sports that emphasize a lean physique or a low body weight (ie, thin-build sports). It has been hypothesized that the body weight demands of these sports, and the pressure to achieve an ideal body weight, whether real or perceived, causes a female athlete to become overly concerned with her body weight and develop disordered eating behaviors.

Etiology of Disordered Eating in Athletes

Most eating disorder experts agree that there is no single "cause" of eating disorders among athletes, but rather that the etiology is multifactorial and encompasses a complex interaction between sociocultural, demographic, environmental, biologic, psychological, and behavioral factors. Controversy currently exists whether athletes are at a greater risk for developing eating disorders than their nonathletic counterparts; some research suggests that the prevalence of disordered eating is greater among athletes, whereas other research does not. The current controversy notwithstanding, evidence does suggest that certain inherent pressures in the sport setting may trigger the development of an eating disorder in psychologically vulnerable athletes.

Sundgot-Borgen examined the etiology of disordered eating behaviors in 522 elite Norwegian female athletes and found that an early start of sport-specific training and dieting at an early age were frequently associated with the development of eating disorders. In addition, prolonged periods of dieting, frequent weight fluctuations, sudden increases in training volume, or traumatic life events (eg, an injury or a change of coach) tended to trigger the development of eating disorders.

Effects of Disordered Eating on Health and Performance

The effects of disordered eating on an athlete's performance vary, but largely depend on the severity and chronicity of the disordered eating behaviors and the physiologic demands of the sport. An athlete who engages in severe energy restriction or who has been bingeing and purging for a long time is likely to experience a greater decrease in performance than one who has engaged in milder weight control behaviors for a shorter time. Likewise, athletes involved in endurance sports and other physical activities with high energy demands (eg, distance running, swimming, cycling, basketball, field hockey, and ice hockey) are likely to be more negatively affected than athletes involved in sports with lower energy demands (eg, diving, gymnastics, weightlifting). The potential consequences of disordered eating on health and performance are presented in Table below.

MENSTRUAL DYSFUNCTION

Spectrum of Menstrual Function

The 1997 Triad Position Stand included only the extreme end point of menstrual dysfunction (ie, amenorrhea). The proposed revised triad uses the term menstrual dysfunction to depict more accurately the spectrum of menstrual irregularities that can plague female athletes, including luteal suppression (or shortened luteal phase), anovulation, oligomenorrhea, primary amenorrhea, and secondary amenorrhea. In contrast to disordered eating and bone strength, menstrual irregularities do not exist on a continuum. An athlete may or may not progress through subclinical menstrual disturbances before developing amenorrhea. Conversely, an athlete may experience subclinical menstrual disturbances for years without ever experiencing a complete cessation of menstruation. A brief description of the major categories of menstrual dysfunction is presented.

Luteal suppression

Also called luteal phase deficiency or shortened luteal phase, luteal suppression is generally an asymptomatic (ie, no overt symptoms) condition, characterized by a shortened luteal phase of the menstrual cycle (between ovulation and menstruation), which may be accompanied by a prolonged follicular phase (between menstruation and ovulation); the total cycle length remains relatively unchanged. Because there are no overt symptoms, luteal suppression can be diagnosed only by measuring ovarian steroid hormone concentrations in the blood or urine over an entire menstrual cycle. Women with luteal suppression generally display low estradiol levels in the early follicular phase along with a slightly decreased luteinizing hormone (LH) pulse frequency and significantly increased pulse amplitude. The rate and extent of follicular development are reduced, ovulation occurs later, and the amount and duration of progesterone secretion during the luteal phase is reduced or shortened.

Anovulation

Anovulation is the absence of ovulation and is generally caused by impairment of follicular development resulting from altered hormonal status. More specifically, estrogen and progesterone levels are reduced; however, estrogen production is sufficient to stimulate some proliferation of the uterine lining, and bleeding often occurs. As a result, women with anovulation often do not realize that they are have a menstrual irregularity. In some instances, alterations in cycle length can occur, including very short cycles (<21 days) or overly long cycles (35–150 days).

Oligomenorrhea

Literally translated, the term oligomenorrhea means "irregular menses." In practice, oligomenorrhea is used to describe a prolonged length of time between cycles (ie, >35 days).

Amenorrhea

The term amenorrhea connotes the absence of menstruation and can be subdivided into two categories: primary and secondary. Primary amenorrhea, also referred to as delayed menarche, has been redefined by the American Society of Reproductive Medicine as the absence of menstruation by age 15 years in girls with secondary sex characteristics. The age was lowered from 16 years due to the fact that age at menarche declined by 5 years in developed countries after the middle of the nineteenth century and is declining rapidly in developing countries. When amenorrhea occurs sometime after menarche, it is referred to as secondary amenorrhea. Generally, secondary amenorrhea requires the absence of at least three consecutive menstrual cycles.

Prevalence of Menstrual Dysfunction in Athletes

The prevalence of menstrual dysfunction among women in the general population who are not pregnant, lactating, or postmenopausal is estimated to be 2% to 5%, whereas the range is 6% to 79% among female athletes. This wide range of prevalence estimates seen in athletes can be largely explained by meth-odologic differences among the various studies that have attempted to measure menstrual dysfunction. Some of these methodologic issues are described.

- *Differences in the athletic population studied,* including the type of sport (ie, endurance versus esthetic versus strength/ power; individual versus team sports), the level of competition (ie, elite versus recreational versus collegiate), and the age of the athlete. Small, nonrandomized studies that sample a single sport or athletes in similar types of sports may produce biased estimates of the incidence of menstrual dysfunction. For example, it is well known that menstrual dysfunction is common among distance runners; if this population is used to represent the general female athlete population, it would likely produce an overestimation of prevalence. Conversely, if the sample is limited to female basketball or volleyball players (groups with a lower incidence of menstrual dysfunction), an underestimation of prevalence is likely to occur. To date, few studies have examined the range of menstrual disturbances in a large, heterogeneous group of female athletes.

- *Failure to control for oral contraceptive use.* Early prevalence studies in particular did not account for oral contraceptive use, or if they did, they did not indicate the rationale for use, which could confound prevalence estimates. Many female athletes take oral contraceptives to regulate their menstrual cycle; if this is not taken into account, it could confound (ie, underestimate) the true prevalence of menstrual dysfunction.
- *Assessment of menstrual dysfunction.* Most prevalence studies have used self-report menstrual history questionnaires to ascertain menstrual dysfunction. Such questionnaires rely heavily on the honesty and accuracy of the individuals completing them and are subject to response bias. Even assuming honest responses, self-report may underestimate the incidence of menstrual dysfunction because many subclinical menstrual disturbances have no overt symptoms. Even studies that have attempted to verify self-report menstrual disturbances via measures of endocrine hormones generally investigated only a single menstrual cycle. Research by De Souza and colleagues showed that data based on a single cycle grossly underestimate the actual incidence of menstrual disturbances.
- *Definitions of "menstrual dysfunction" used.* As previously indicated, researchers have used a variety of definitions for the different menstrual disturbances seen in athletes. which can have a great impact on the estimated prevalence. The more liberal the definitions used, the greater the prevalence. Johnson and associates defined amenorrhea as one or fewer menstrual periods in 6 months and found that 6% of the athletes were amenorrheic. Fo-gelholm and Hiilloskorpii reported that only 1% of athletes had amenorrhea, whereas the spectrum of menstrual dysfunction (including primary amenorrhea, secondary amenorrhea, and oligomenorrhea) among athletes not using

oral contraceptives ranged from 32% to 37% (depending on the sport type examined—esthetic, speed, endurance, weight-dependent, or ball-game). These authors did not provide a clinical definition for the menstrual disturbances they examined; it is unclear what criteria were used for the various menstrual disturbances they examined. Beals and Manore found that 31% of collegiate athletes studied reported *menstrual irregularity* (described as cycles not occurring every 28-34 days), whereas 1% had no menstrual periods, 12% had fewer than 6 menstrual periods over the past year, and 8% had more than 12 menstrual periods over the past year. Dusek found that 30% of a sample of 72 ballet dancers, runners, basketball players, and volleyball players experienced amenorrhea, defined as no menstruation for more than 3 months postmenarche. Finally, Torstveit and Sundgot-Borgen reported that 31.4% of female athletes had menstrual dysfunction, which included primary amenorrhea (defined as absence of menarche by age 16 years), secondary amenorrhea (defined as an absence of three consecutive menstrual cycles), oligomenorrhea (defined by the authors as cycles of >35 days), and shortened luteal phase (defined by the authors as cycles of <22 days). These authors did not break the prevalence estimates down by menstrual dysfunction category.

Despite differences in the definitions used for menstrual dysfunction among the above-cited studies, without exception, all found that menstrual dysfunction was most evident among athletes participating in sports that emphasize leanness.

The estimated prevalence of delayed menarche among young women in the United States is less than 1%. In contrast, Beals and Manore found that 7.4% of a sample of 425 collegiate athletes (representing 15 different sports) reported not menstruating until after age 16 (as primary amenorrhea was previously defined), and 22.2% of athletes in esthetic sports (ie, cheerleading, diving, and gymnastics) reported primary amenorrhea.

The prevalence of oligomenorrhea also seems to be significantly higher among female athletes than the general female population. Klentrou and Plyley found that 61% of elite rhythmic gymnasts from Greece and Canada ($n = 45$) regularly experienced menstrual cycles longer than 35 days. Using a slightly different definition of oligomenorrhea (ie, more than three but fewer than nine cycles in 3 months), Burrows and coworkers found the incidence among a group of English distance runners to be 21%. In a similar population (ie, English distance runners), Rosetta and colleagues found a 40% total incidence of short (<21 days) and long (>35 days) cycles.

The lack of overt symptoms makes identifying luteal suppression or anovu-lation and consequently accurately assessing their prevalence among active women difficult. Nonetheless, both menstrual disorders are hypothesized to be common among female athletes. In regularly menstruating, recreational runners, the total incidence of luteal suppression and anovulation was 78%. Similarly, Loucks and colleagues found an 80% occurrence of luteal suppression in at least 1 of 3 consecutive months among a small group (*n* = 9) of "athletic" women.

Etiology of Menstrual Dysfunction in Athletes

Although the cessation of menses coincident with physical training has long been recognized, the specific etiology has yet to determined. Endocrine and neuroendocrine experiments have shown that menstrual dysfunction in active women results from a disruption of the pulsatile secretion of LH by the pituitary gland—which is caused by a disruption of the pulsatile secretion of go-nadotropin-releasing hormone by the hypothalamus. Nonetheless, the specific factor or factors responsible for these pulsatile disruptions remain largely unknown, although many possible theories have been proposed.

In the 1970s, low body weight or body fat was thought to be the primary cause of amenorrhea seen in physically active women; however, subsequent research showed that a low body weight or body fat by itself cannot induce menstrual dysfunction. Research indicates that neither body weight nor body composition varies significantly between amenorrheic and eumenorrheic athletes.

The so-called exercise-stress hypothesis purports that the stress of exercise training, similar to other chronic stressors, activates the hypothalamic-pituitary-adrenal axis, which disrupts the gonadotropin-releasing hormone pulse generator and results in menstrual dysfunction. More recent research has shown, however, that it is not exercise per se that induces menstrual dysfunction, but rather an energy deficit. This "energy deficit or energy drain" theory holds that failure to provide sufficient calories to meet energy requirements and support the carbohydrate needs of the brain causes an alteration in brain function that disrupts the gonadotropin-releasing hormone pulse generator through an as yet undetermined mechanism.

In a series of studies, Loucks and colleagues showed that energy availability (or lack thereof) is at the root of hypothalamic menstrual dysfunction. In the first study, healthy, young, habitually sedentary, regularly menstruating women were subjected to four different experimental conditions designed to elicit energy balance and imbalance under exercise and calorie-restricted circumstances. In the exercise treatment groups, energy intake and energy expenditure (exercise) were controlled to set energy availability at an energy balance (approximately 45 kcal/kg lean body mass per day) and negative energy balance (approximately 10 kcal/kg lean body mass per day). In the nonexercising group, energy intake also was set to achieve energy balance and negative energy balance (to a similar degree as that for the exercising groups). The results indicated that exercise without a negative energy balance did not elicit significant disruptions in LH pulsatility. Low energy availability in the sedentary and exercising conditions produced marked alterations in LH pulsatility. The disruptive effects of low energy availability caused by exercise energy expenditure were smaller than those of dietary energy restriction.

In a follow-up study, it was determined that the "threshold" of energy availability (ie, the level of energy availability below which menstrual dysfunction is likely to occur) is approximately 30 kcal/kg lean body mass per day. It was shown that the restoration of normal LH pulsatility in energetically disrupted women cannot be accomplished by a single day of aggressive refeeding, which provides further evidence for a mediating mechanism between energy availability and LH pulsatility.

Effects on Health and Performance

Female athletes who experience menstrual dysfunction, particularly amenor-rhea, often show little concern for the disruption in their cycles; some even express relief at the "break." Similarly, some coaches simply dismiss menstrual dysfunction, believing it is a natural result of hard training. Nonetheless, despite these attitudes, it should be emphasized that menstrual dysfunction is not a normal response to training; rather, it is a clear indication that health is being compromised. The health consequences of menstrual dysfunction are well documented and include infertility and other reproductive problems, decreased immune function, an increase in cardiovascular risk factors, and, perhaps most importantly, decreased BMD and increased risk for premature osteoporosis.

BONE HEALTH

Spectrum of Bone Health

The third component of the triad is related to the athlete's bone health. In the initial Triad Position Stand, this component was termed osteoporosis, which is defined as a degenerative skeletal disease most common to postmenopausal women and characterized by compromised bone strength. Today, it is recognized that bone strength, as a triad component, also occurs along a spectrum that spans from low bone mass and stress fractures to osteoporosis, which is considered the most severe condition.

Bone strength not only is characterized by bone mineral content (BMC; g) and density (BMD; g/cm^2), but also by the quality of bone. The variation in bone strength is due to differences in BMC/BMD and bone quality. Bone quality includes the microarchitecture or the three-dimensional array of trabeculae. Bone quality refers to the process of bone turnover, or the dynamic nature of bone remodeling with osteoclasts breaking down bone (also known as bone resorption) and osteoblasts establishing a new matrix, or the osteoid, in the process of bone formation. Bone is a dynamic tissue those cycles over months. Osteoclasts mediate bone resorption via proteolytic digestion, followed by a delayed replacement of osteoclasts by osteoblasts, which lay down new bone or the matrix (osteoid). Until the matrix is fully mineralized, it takes several phases and hence time. Finally, bone geometry and size also are important aspects of bone quality. Differences in geometry and size are best explained by the gender difference in BMC and BMD, resulting mostly from a difference in cortical thickness between men and women who are of the same body size.

Although bone quality represents an important aspect of bone structure and strength, BMD assessed by DXA is currently the most accepted quantitative method for the diagnosis of osteoporosis and prediction of fracture risk. It is likely that in the future, measures characterizing bone quality will be combined with BMD to describe the full scope of an individual's bone strength, as has been shown by Nikander and colleagues. For the remainder of this article, however, the focus is on BMD measured by DXA, as it is currently used in the clinical setting to evaluate bone health and fracture risk in premenopausal and postmenopausal women.

Diagnosis of Low Bone Mass and Osteoporosis in Athletes

DXA has been used as a diagnostic tool for the evaluation of bone health and particularly low BMD. BMD is normally distributed and is often expressed in standard deviation (SD) units relative to its T or Z distribution. The T distribution has a mean of zero, which corresponds to the mean of young healthy women. T-scores are used for the diagnosis of osteoporosis and osteopenia and to predict fracture risk in postmenopausal women. Specifically, the World Health Organization has established cutoff scores for the diagnosis of osteoporosis and osteopenia for postmenopausal women. In postmenopausal women, fracture risk nearly doubles for every SD below the young adult mean. One more recent debate has been related to the fact that the same diagnostic strategies used for postmenopausal women (the distribution of T-scores and the comparison with the young adult mean) have been applied to premenopausal women, adolescents, and children. This seems problematic for three reasons: (1) Fracture data are lacking in premenopausal women, (2) it can be assumed that fracture risk is low in young women, and (3) peak bone mass has not yet been attained in adolescents and children. The International Society for Clinical Densitometry (ISCD) currently is proposing that BMD comparisons in premenopausal women, adolescents, and children be made relative to chronologic age, using the Z distribution.

To avoid a disease label in premenopausal women and to account for a skeleton of a young woman around or younger than age 20 years that has not yet attained peak bone mass, the ISCD recommends using Z-scores. Z-scores are expressed relative to chronologic age and allow for a better comparison of BMD values in individuals younger than age 20 years. As women become older, however, Z and T distributions are similar. According to the ISCD 2005 Official Position, a young woman is no longer considered osteoporotic or osteopenic with a low Z-score or T-score. Instead, her BMD now is considered low for chronologic age or is below the expected range for age. Although the International Olympic Committee (IOC) (IOC Position Stand, 2005) is generally in agreement with the ISCD's approach, its diagnostic criteria seem more conservative when considering athletic women. This is probably due to the fact that athletes, in general, should have higher BMD than controls, as was previously discussed. For both organizations, the diagnosis of osteoporosis is still relevant, but should not be based on densitometric criteria alone and should integrate other factors, such as hypoestrogenism or eating disorders. The aforementioned cutoff values are likely to change again, and an update of the Female Athlete Triad Position Stand through the ACSM is soon to be published as well.

In many instances and particularly in the athletic setting, DXA is not always available for the assessment and evaluation of an athlete's bone health. It is reasonable to assume, however, that an athlete's bone strength has suffered if she presents with amenorrhea for longer than 6 months or has experienced frequent phases of oligomenorrhea and possibly a stress fracture.

Prevalence of Low Bone Mass in Athletes

The prevalence of low bone mass and osteoporosis in athletes is difficult to address because of the differences in diagnostic criteria used among organizations and the fact that BMD data using DXA are not as easily and inexpensively collected. In general, using the World Health Organization classification for postmenopausal women, the prevalence of osteopenia in female athletes has been reported to be 22% to 50%, with a relatively low prevalence of osteoporosis. Considering the new ISCD and IOC criteria, women with low T-scores or Z-scores would now be considered as having low BMD for chronologic age or below the expected range (ISCD Position Statement, 2005). More recently, Torstveit and Sundgot-Borgen have applied these new criteria in a sample of 186 elite athletes and found that 10.7% had a BMD below the expected range for age.

Female athletes have higher BMD than their nonathletic counterparts. Athletes exhibit a BMD at several skeletal sites that is 5% to 15% higher than the BMD of nonathletes, even when controlled for confounding variables, such as age, body mass index, and lean body mass. Sports with loading patterns that are characterized by high impact (basketball, volleyball, gymnastics) or odd impact (squash, speed skating, and other winter sports) are strongly associated with a higher BMD, whereas repetitive low-impact (running) and non–weight bearing activities (swimming) are not.

It is not surprising that athletes, when healthy, have stronger bones than nonathletes. A study showed that low BMD is two to three times more common in controls compared with athletes. Under the condition of menstrual dysfunction and the triad, however, this positive effect of exercise on bone is diminished.

When athletes have menstrual dysfunction, their BMD is significantly below that of their eumenorrheic counterparts, and in a sense, athletes lose the skeletal advantage of their sport involvement. Athletes with amenorrhea exhibit a BMD at the lumbar spine that is 10% to 20% below the BMD of eumenorrheic athletes. Amenorrheic athletes also have significantly lower BMD at other skeletal sites compared with eumenorrheic athletes. Oligomenorrhea and amenorrhea are detrimental to bone; however, the impact of oligomenorrhea on BMD occurs likely at an intermediate stage along the spectrum of menstrual dysfunction. Finally, the cumulative exposure of low estrogen in the form of oligomenorrhea or amenorrhea during an athlete's career also needs to be considered. The longer the duration of menstrual dysfunction, in the past and at present time, the lower the BMD.

Although most athletes with menstrual dysfunction present with lower BMD compared with their eumenorrheic counterparts, there are some exceptions. It has been shown that athletes in high-impact sports, despite menstrual dysfunction, seem to be able to maintain their higher BMD compared with athletes involved in lower impact sports who also have menstrual dysfunction or eumenorrheic controls. The mechanical loading patterns of certain sports may override the deleterious effect of hypoestrogenism.

Athletes with menstrual dysfunction are at greater risk not only for low BMD, but also stress fractures. Torstveit and Sundgot-Borgen identified that 17% of elite athletes reported having a stress fracture. Although not significantly different from normally active controls, the athletes were more likely to have menstrual dysfunction than the controls. Besides stress fractures, athletes with one or more components of the triad also are more likely to report sprains, strains, and other soft tissue injuries, underlining the importance of the triad on health and the performance capabilities of young female athletes.

Etiology of Low Bone Mass in Athletes

The most important function of estrogen with respect to bone health is related to estrogen's suppressing effect on osteoclast activity. As mentioned previously, osteoclasts are bone cells that tear down bone in the process of bone re-sorption. In the hypoestrogenic state, the female athlete likely exhibits accelerated bone resorption through the impact of irregular or absent menstrual cycles. In addition, a direct effect, through low energy availability, may be possible. Some studies have shown that athletes, at risk for disordered eating, present with low BMD in the absence of menstrual dysfunction. Studies aimed at correcting the hypoestrogenic state, using estra-diol replacement (without an increase in energy intake), generally have not succeeded in the normalization of BMD after years of treatment, indicating that factors other than estrogen also are important for bone. The most convincing evidence that low energy availability may have a direct effect on bone was published in an article by Ihle and Loucks, who showed that markers of bone formation and resorption changed unfavorably within 5 days in sedentary women who were exposed to low energy availability through dietary restriction or increased exercise energy expenditure. Whether this is also the case in athletic women has yet to be determined. Nevertheless, it seems highly plausible that an energy and nutrient deficit affects metabolic substrates and hormones, including insulin, growth hormone, insulin-like growth factor-1, cortisol, and thyroid hormone, which all are considered important hormones for bone metabolism, independent of the hypoestrogenic state.

SUMMARY

The 1997 ACSM Triad Position Stand concluded with a call for additional research regarding the prevalence, causes, consequences, prevention, and treatment of disordered eating, amenorrhea, and osteoporosis in female athletes. Almost a decade later, that call has been answered, and an updated version of the ACSM Triad Position Stand is pending. In addition to renaming the triad components to reflect the full spectrum of each – ranging from health to disease – the proposed revised version of the Triad Position Stand is expected to place a greater emphasis on low energy availability as the key disorder underlying the other components of the triad, include updated information regarding the prevalence of each component of the triad and the triad as a whole, and provide greater insight into the mechanisms involved in the path-ogenesis of each disorder. Far from "setting health and social policies that ultimately discriminate against young women in the pursuit of athletic success" as more recent accusations have implied, advancing research and knowledge regarding the triad will aid in the creation of more efficacious prevention and treatment strategies so that all women can enjoy the physical, psychological, and social benefits of athletics participation to the fullest.

5

Nutrition Recommendations for Masters Athletes

More than 3000 masters athletes from 62 countries compete in Linz, Austria, in March of 2006". In 2005, 9000 "silver-haired Americans go for the gold". The National Senior Games Association announced a "major change in the NSGA rules affecting the game of basketball; a new age division of 80þ has been added for 2007".

The above-mentioned athletes are competing at the masters level. Masters athletes are defined differently by every organizational body, but for purposes of this article, masters athletes are athletes older than 50 years old. Even professional athletes are pushing the idea that sports are not only for young participants. The National Football League reported that 43 players have played until the age of 40. In the 2005 season, 9 players older than 40 were active, including a 45-year-old kicker for the Tennessee Titans.

The news that athletes are competing at older ages should not be a surprise when one considers the aging of the US population. In 2006, the oldest of the baby boomers turned 60. The Administration on Aging estimates that 7918 people will turn 60 every day, or about 330 every hour.

Although exact numbers are unavailable, it is accurate to say that today's generation of older adults is more active than their parents or grandparents. Twenty-three percent of health club memberships in the United States belong to adults older than age 55. Consider the increase in participation in the Huntsman World Senior Games held annually in Utah. This competition is open to all athletes age 50 or older. In 1987, 500 participants competed in a variety of sports; in 2005, 9000 athletes from around the world competed in basketball, tennis, cycling, mountain biking, racquetball, road racing, swimming, triathlon, track and field, volleyball, and softball.

HEALTH BENEFITS OF ATHLETIC PARTICIPATION

The literature on the health benefits of participating in masters athletics indicates that these athletes have favorable lipid profiles, normal insulin and glucose levels with no age-related deterioration of glucose tolerance, good bone health, and improved mood states compared with age-matched sedentary controls. More extensive reviews on the physiologic and psychological benefits of participating in vigorous activity at the masters level of competition have been published, but one thing is clear: The benefits to health continue as long as the older athlete is active. When activity ceases because of injury or disinterest, the health benefits recede.

RESTING METABOLIC RATE AND CHANGES IN BODY COMPOSITION

Aging brings on alterations in resting metabolic rate (RMR) and changes in body composition. Aging is associated with declines in all components of energy expenditure: RMR, thermic effect of food, and energy expenditure. Early research suggested an inverse relationship between RMR and aging (the older one got, the more decline in RMR was seen), but more recent studies suggest that the age-related decline in RMR can be attenuated by regular exercise. Van Pelt and colleagues studied RMR in men and women. Sixty-five healthy women (21–35 years old and 50–72 years old) were recruited to study age-related decline in RMR. Subjects were divided into groups of controls, endurance-trained runners, or swimmers. The primary finding from the study is that the decline expected in RMR with aging is attenuated in older women who remain physically active. The research group conducted a similar study with men (n ¼ 137; 19–36 years old and 52–75 years old). They reported that adjusted RMR declines with age even in physically active men, but the decrease in RMR is related to reductions in training volume and energy intake, which contribute to altered body composition. In the group of older men who maintained a high level of training and adequate energy intake, there was no significant difference in RMR compared with the younger age groups. These data are applicable to masters athletes and may provide motivation for continued participation in sports.

Women in particular are concerned with weight gain after menopause. Postmenopausal women have higher body fat levels and more central obesity than premenopausal women, but several investigations reveal that lifestyle, especially physical activity, is more responsible for alterations in body composition than hormone status.

Data from the Third National Health and Nutrition Examination Survey also indicated that women age 25 to 55 who met or exceeded the exercise guidelines to be moderately active 5 days a week or vigorously active for 3 days a week had lower body mass index, percent body fat, and waist-to-hip ratios than less active women.

NUTRITION RECOMMENDATIONS

Energy Intake

There are few published data on the energy needs of masters athletes; the key factor for predicting energy needs in masters athletes is training volume. The Dietary Reference Intakes (DRIs) for energy and macronutrient intakes can be used as a guide in establishing energy requirements. The DRIs set estimated energy requirements for four different levels of exercise. Using the "active" physical activity level, Table 1 shows estimated energy requirements for older adults. These levels should be used only as a guide; competitive masters athletes with heavy training loads could require more calories to fuel training and activity.

Carbohydrate

The DRIs suggest dietary carbohydrate should be in the range of 45% to 65% of total calories. For athletes, calculating carbohydrate needs based on grams per kilogram of body weight is more likely to meet the athlete's need for fuel. Consider an older female athlete who weighs 120 lb and has an estimated energy need of 2116 calories. Forty-five percent of energy from carbohydrate would yield 238 g of carbohydrate for daily needs. Using the recommendations of 5 to 7 g/kg/d for general training needs, this woman would need 272 to 380 g of carbohydrate. The typical US diet provides 4 to 5 g/kg/d, and athletes who train daily and compete at high intensity need more carbohydrate. Endurance athletes require 7 to 10 g/kg/d, and athletes participating in ultraendurance events need more than 10 g/kg/d.

Carbohydrate feedings during exercise that lasts more than 1 hour can improve performance and help athletes have a "kick" at the end of a sprint. It is recommended that 30 to 60 g of carbohydrate (in food or beverage) be consumed every hour. This is not a large volume of food, and athletes should be encouraged to experiment during training with foods that are portable, easy to eat, and do not cause gastrointestinal upset. Energy bars are often eaten because of their convenience, and perhaps because of their persuasive marketing to athletes, but there is nothing magical about energy bars. Recovery from hard exercise (>90 minutes) is enhanced with a carbohydrate feeding in the immediate postexercise period. Athletes should aim to get 1.5 g/kg immediately after exercise if they are training daily. An additional carbohydrate feeding 2 hours later enhances muscle glycogen synthesis. These recommendations are for athletes who train hard and train daily; a 5-km road racer who competes once a month does not need to worry about recovery carbohydrate.

Protein

Usual aging is associated with declines in lean muscle mass. The term sarcopenia has been coined to describe the decline in skeletal muscle mass and concomitant loss of muscle strength with aging. The prevalence of sarcopenia may be 30% for adults older than age 60 years, and it can lead to reduced function and disability for older men and women. Physical activity, especially progressive resistance training, may be the best antidote to sarcopenia. Nutritional strategies also are being studied to assess the appropriate level of protein and amino acids in the diet.

Protein recommendations for masters athletes have not been established, but it is suggested that the same guidelines for younger athletes are appropriate. Protein in the range of 1.2 to 1.7 g/kg/d should provide adequate supplies of amino acids for muscle synthesis and repair. There is debate over the adequacy of the current Recommended Dietary Allowance (RDA) for protein for older adults. Several studies suggest that the current RDA of 0.8 g/kg/d is insufficient for maintaining positive nitrogen balance or providing sufficient anabolic stimulus for muscle repair.

Two considerations for protein intake for masters athletes are warranted. The first is adequate energy intake; the body's primary need is for energy, and protein can be converted to glucose if the body needs fuel. Assessing energy and protein needs in masters athletes is important to ensure that protein is used for anabolic functions and not for energy needs. Second, the timing of protein intake may influence the anabolic stimulus for muscle repair and growth. Ingestion of small amounts of protein (0.1–0.2 g/kg/h) can enhance muscle anabolism during recovery from endurance and resistance exercise. To date, research studies showing this effect have used essential amino acids. Recommending that masters athletes consume small snacks of foods that provide essential amino acids may enhance muscle building and recovery. Foods and fluids that meet these criteria include milk, eggs, cheese, yogurt, lean meat, fish, and poultry.

Fat

The DRIs recommend a range of fat intake of 20% to 35% of total calories. Heart healthy fats (monounsaturated and long-chain polyunsaturated fats) are recommended to provide essential fatty acids and improve blood lipids levels. No recommendation for dietary fat is available for masters athletes, and the American Dietetic Association recommends that athletes not restrict their fat intake because no benefit to performance with a low-fat diet has been identified.

Micronutrients

There has been little research to date on the micronutrient needs of masters athletes. Although there is evidence of benefit to altering the micronutrient needs of older adults in the general population, there are few guidelines for older adults who are physically active, much less engage in regular, strenuous exercise. For adults older than 50 years, the DRIs have established increased needs for vitamin D, calcium, and vitamin B_6. Other nutrients of interest for older adults are folate and vitamin B_{12}. For women older than 50 years, the iron requirement is decreased to the same level needed for men. Limited research exists for thiamine, riboflavin, choline, and zinc.

Vitamin D

In a study of 18 French male masters athletes with a mean age of 63 years, it was found that despite an increased energy intake compared with the French recommended dietary allowance, the men were deficient in vitamin D intake. The average intake was

2.1 lg/d, which is far below the recommended levels. Older adults have higher requirements of vitamin D because the skin is less able to synthesize vitamin D from the sun. In addition, there is less 25-hydroxyvitamin D circulating in the blood with advancing age. To prevent bone loss, the adequate intake of vitamin D is doubled to 10 lg/d in men and women older than 50 years and tripled to 15 lg/d for adults older than 70 years compared with younger adults.

Calcium

Just as the need for vitamin D is increased for protection of bone health in older adults, so are calcium needs. The adequate intake has been established at 1200 mg/d for men and women older than 50 years. This recommendation is based on evidence that calcium absorption decreases with age. In addition, clinical trials in women older than 50 years have found that intakes greater than 1000 mg/d reduce bone loss. Although there have been studies of varying intensities of physical activity on calcium needs, there is inconclusive evidence at this time that calcium needs should be adjusted for level of physical activity.

Vitamin B_6

Vitamin B_6 is involved in many metabolic pathways that produce energy during exercise. In the muscle, vitamin B_6 is necessary for the breakdown of glycogen in muscle, and it assists in converting lactic acid to glucose in the liver. Research suggests that the requirements for vitamin B_6 are greater in adults older than 50 years. In addition, there is a gender difference in the vitamin requirement that does not exist in younger adults. Men older than 50 years should consume 1.7 mg/d, and women older than 50 years should consume 1.5 mg/d. Research on the need for vitamin B_6 in exercise is equivocal, and results are inconclusive to warrant changing the dietary requirement in exercising individuals.

Folate

Although aging does not seem to have an effect on folate absorption or use, it is a crucial nutrient for older adults. Research has found that low folate status is a risk factor for cognitive decline. The mechanism by which this decline occurs seems to be through the methylation pathway of homocysteine metabolism.

As a result of folate deficiency, the pathway is disturbed, and S-adenosylhomo-cysteine accumulates. The accumulation of S-adenosylhomocysteine inhibits methylation reactions, possibly resulting in cognitive dysfunction. The RDA for folate for all adults is 400 lg/d of Dietary Folate Equivalents.

Vitamin B_{12}

It has been proposed that there is a decline in vitamin B_{12} status in older adults as plasma vitamin B_{12} levels decrease with age, and serum methylmalonic acid increases with age. There are several possible explanations for this decline with increasing age, including decreased gastric acidity, atrophic gastritis, bacterial overgrowth, malabsorption of food-bound vitamin B_{12}, lack of liver stores of vitamin B_{12}, and impaired binding proteins. Despite this evidence, the RDA for vitamin B_{12} for older adults is the same as for younger adults at 2.4 lg/d. For adults older than age 50, however, it is recommended that most vitamin B_{12} be obtained by consuming foods fortified with synthetic vitamin B_{12} or by taking a supplement containing vitamin B_{12} because the food-bound form is more difficult to absorb with aging.

Iron

Iron is the one micronutrient that is needed in lesser amounts for women after menopause. The RDA is reduced to 8 mg/d for women older than 50 years, which is the same level for men. For men and women who engage in regular, endurance exercise there is a greater loss of iron. In addition, decreased iron stores have been documented in athletes because iron has a shorter half-life in these individuals. A conservative estimate is that athletes need 30% more iron than individuals who do not exercise. No distinction has been made, however, with respect to the age of the athlete. It is possible that masters athletes may require 10.4 mg of iron a day.

Other Vitamins and Minerals

Regular and strenuous exercise may have an effect on thiamine, riboflavin, and choline, although more research is needed before specific recommendations can be made. There is limited evidence that thiamine requirements may be increased for individuals consistently engaged in active sports. Normal physical activity does not have a substantial effect, however, on thiamine needs.

In addition, older adults may need more thiamine, although this may be compensated for by decreased energy expenditure. The current RDA of 1.2 mg/d for men and 1.1 mg/d for women is sufficient for masters athletes. Similarly, riboflavin requirements may be increased for individuals who are very physically active, but there are no data to suggest how much is needed. The needs of older adults are no different from those of younger adults, so the RDA of 1.3 mg/d for men and 1.1 mg/d for women is adequate. Plasma choline concentrations may be depleted as a result of strenuous exercise, although more research is needed to confirm this effect. There also may be reduced transport of choline across the blood-brain barrier in elderly individuals, which would suggest greater needs. At this time, however, the DRI is the same for older adults as younger at 550 mg/d for men and 425 mg/d for women.

Zinc has not been studied in relation to physical activity; however, it has been studied in elderly patients. It is possible that zinc metabolism is altered in older adults, but more research is needed before conclusions can be drawn. Aging does not have any negative effects on zinc absorption. The RDA for masters athletes is the same as for all adults at 11 mg/d for men and 8 mg/d for women. Low zinc status has been linked to lower plasma total protein thiol groups in the exercising elderly. Oxidative stress immediately lowers plasma total protein thiol groups, and this could be even more pronounced in the exercising elderly if the DRI for zinc is not met.

Although studies have looked at the effect of exercise on magnesium levels, there is no clear evidence to suggest that exercise depletes magnesium stores in the body. In addition, research does not indicate a need for greater magnesium requirements in adults older than age 50. The recommended RDA of 420 mg/d for men and 320 mg/d for women is sufficient for masters athletes.

Antioxidants

Research has shown that exercise leads to oxidative stress in skeletal muscle through the production of lipid peroxides and free radicals. It has been postulated that antioxidants, which protect the body from cellular damage, may aid in recovery by reducing the damage of oxidative stress in skeletal muscle. Research shows that antioxidants may assist in recovery, although they do not have an effect on performance. It also has been proposed that exercise enhances the body's response to oxidative stress by increasing the production of antioxidant enzymes. It is unknown if the same response occurs in the exercising elderly as in young adults because few studies have focused on masters athletes. It is known, however, that regardless of exercise, oxidative stress increases with age.

Rousseau and associates conducted a study of the exercising elderly compared with sedentary counterparts and exercising and sedentary young adults. It was found that even high intakes of antioxidants coupled with exercise did not counteract the oxidative stress induced by advancing age, whereas anti-oxidant intake and exercise training were protective against oxidative damage in young athletes. Rousseau and associates concluded that masters athletes have specific antioxidant requirements as they age, particularly for the carotenoids. Further research is warranted to explore these issues in depth.

Vitamin C

Several studies have looked at the vitamin C status of athletes. There is no evidence at this time that athletes require additional vitamin C greater than the RDA. In addition, advancing age has no effect on the absorption or metabolism of vitamin C. The RDA for men and women older than age 50 is 90 mg/d and 75 mg/d. Vitamin C supplementation is popular, and the Tolerable Upper Intake Level (UL) established in the DRIs at 2000 mg/d should be used as a guide for masters athletes.

Vitamin E

Vitamin E is another antioxidant that has been widely studied. Vitamin E may be beneficial in protecting the body from the oxidative stress resulting from exercise. There is not enough research at this time, however, to warrant a change in the requirements for athletes. There is limited evidence that regular exercise in adults older than 60 years alters vitamin E status, but it is unknown whether requirements should be adjusted as a result of regular or strenuous exercise. There are currently no data to suggest that aging impairs the absorption or use of vitamin E. The RDA of 15 mg/d for adults older than age 50 is sufficient, regardless of activity level. The UL is set at 1000 mg/d and should be followed by masters athletes choosing to take supplements.

Carotenoids

There is not enough evidence at present to establish a DRI for beta-carotene and the other carotenoids; however, this does not diminish their importance in the diet. The current recommendation for older adults is to consume more carotenoid-rich fruits and vegetables. Beta-carotene supplements other than as a source of provitamin A to prevent vitamin A deficiency are not advised, however, because their potential to cause harm is great. Research has found that plasma concentrations of lycopene, beta-carotene, and alpha-carotene were low in exercising elderly participants despite a high intake of these carotenoids. Further research should be conducted to elucidate the carotenoid requirements of masters athletes.

Whole foods are the preferred source for the daily consumption of micronutrients. Although there is little research to suggest altering the DRI requirements for masters athletes, masters athletes should be striving to meet the DRI for all micronutrients through their diet. Research has shown that this is not the case, however. Nieman and coworker showed that female marathon runners are deficient in vitamin D and zinc. Chatard and colleagues found that healthy Frenchmen between the ages of 57 and 72 who engaged in regular cycling, running, swimming, tennis, and walking did not meet the RDA for magnesium or vitamin D.

The use of supplements is popular, particularly among athletes. Supplement use can be the difference between masters athletes who meet the RDA and those that do not. In a study comparing the dietary intake of 25 female master cyclists and runners who took supplements versus those who did not, it was found that athletes who took supplements consumed significantly more vitamin C, vitamin E, calcium, and magnesium. On further analysis of dietary intake without accounting for the supplements, these same individuals consumed average levels below the RDA for vitamin D, vitamin E, folate, calcium, magnesium, and zinc. For athletes taking supplements, the UL should be adhered to for all vitamins and minerals.

FLUID NEEDS

Hydration is crucial for all athletes, but masters athletes have to pay special attention to fluid intake. Aging brings physiologic changes to thirst sensation, sweating rates, renal adaptation to altered fluid and electrolyte status, and blood flow responses that can impair thermoregulation in older athletes. Although no data are published to recommend a specific fluid plan or preferred beverages, guidelines for younger athletes can be used to establish a fluid plan for masters athletes. Assessing the athlete's daily fluid intake and monitoring intake during training and competition can establish a baseline for developing a hydration strategy.

SUMMARY

Very little is known about the nutrient intakes, nutritional status, or nutritional needs of masters athletes. As the population ages and more people remain physically active and engaged in competitive sports in later life, more research is needed to identify nutritional strategies to fuel these athletes.

6

Nutritional Considerations in Joint Health

Osteoarthritis, a debilitating joint disorder, is the most common form of arthritis in the United States, where it affects an estimated 21 million people. In 2004, the direct and indirect health care costs associated with all forms of arthritis were approximately $86 billion. Joint discomfort from osteoarthritis and other joint disorders may reduce physical activity in individuals experiencing this condition, resulting in energy imbalance and weight gain. Increased weight can exacerbate existing problems, as additional stress on joints stimulates risk of additional joint disorders. Dietitians play a role in preventing or reversing the problem of joint disorders by promoting nutrient-rich diets that support joint health through improvement in cartilage metabolism. In addition, counseling individuals on weight management and active lifestyles are key strategies for the management of joint health.

JOINT

Joints are structures in the body that provide movement and mechanical support. Although there are several types of joints in the human body, this article focuses on synovial joints, such as those in the knees, arms, and shoulders. These joints, found at the ends of bones, have a space that allows for a wide range of motion. Formed by endochondral ossification, joints are strengthened by a dense fibrous capsule that is reinforced by ligaments and muscles. The capsule is filled with synovial fluid, a clear liquid that contains hyaluronic acid, a lubricant that also provides nutrients to the joint tissues. The surfaces where two bones meet are covered with articular cartilage. Articular cartilage consists of four layers of tissue (Fig. 1). First, a thin superficial layer provides a smooth surface for two bones to slide against each other. The second layer is very resistant to shear stresses. An intermediate layer is mechanically designed to absorb shock and distribute load or weight efficiently. The fourth or deepest layer is highly calcified and anchors the articular cartilage to the bone.

A unique aspect of articular cartilage is the isolation of its component cells from each other and from other cell types. It is one of the few tissues in the human body that does not have its own blood supply. It obtains its nutrition principally from diffusion of synovial fluid in the synovial cavity.

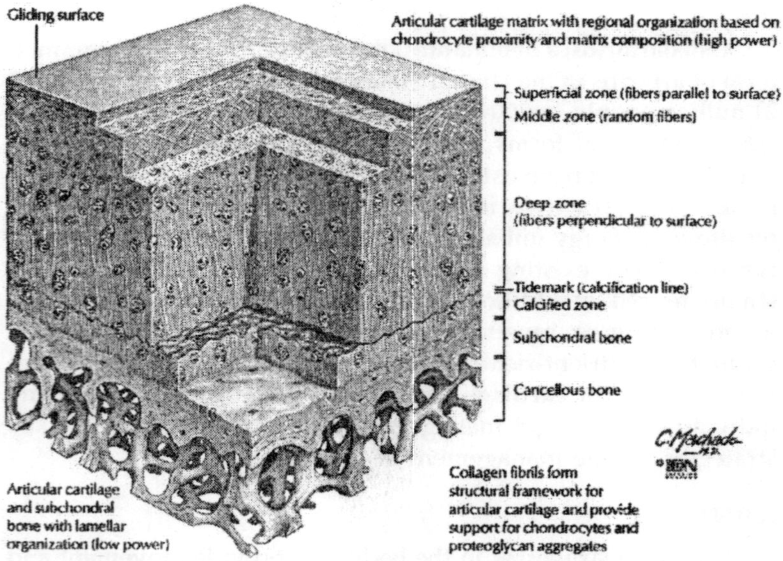

Fig. 1. Layers of cartilage in a joint. (Courtesy of Netter Images. Available at: www. NetterImages.com.)

Articular cartilage is able to provide support and flexibility because of the structure of its extracellular matrix. This matrix contains proteoglycans, which are responsible for the compressive stiffness of the tissue and its ability to withstand load, and type 2 collagen, which provides tensile strength and resistance to shear, water, chondrocytes, and other molecules. The collagen fibers are arranged in arches, a horizontal orientation near the surface of the cartilage. This orientation allows the cartilage to resist stress and to transmit weight.

The water and proteoglycans provide cartilage with elasticity and play a crucial role in reducing friction. Most proteoglycans in articular cartilage are in the form of aggrecan, aggregates of proteoglycan monomers bound to a hyaluronic acid backbone by a noncovalent association with a link glycoprotein. The highly charged, polysulfated glycosaminoglycan components of the aggrecan molecules attract cations and water, resulting in osmotic pressure in the tissue owing to the constraint of the molecular configuration caused by containment within the collagen meshwork.

The chondrocytes maintain a balance between production and degradation of cartilage extracellular matrix. Matrix turnover is modulated by chondrocytes that secrete degradative enzymes and enzyme inhibitors. The number and activity of chondrocytes affect the anatomic and tribologic features of cartilage. The chondrocyte itself is regulated by various cytokines and growth factors that can alter the homeostatic balance toward an anabolic or catabolic direction.

Most load on articular cartilage is produced by contraction of the muscles that stabilize and move the joints. Although cartilage is an excellent shock absorber, it is usually 1 to 2 mm thick in most parts of the joint, which is too thin to serve as the only shock-absorbing tissue in the joint. Subchondral bone and periarticular muscles provide additional protective effects.

BASIC NUTRITIONAL REQUIREMENTS OF HEALTHY JOINTS

A balanced, nutritionally adequate diet is required to maintain healthy joints (Box 1). Key nutrients include the following:

Calcium. The adult body contains about 1200 g of calcium, approximately 99% of which is present in the skeleton. Bone mineral consists of two chemically and physically distinct calcium phosphate pools – an amorphous phase and a loosely crystallized phase. The skeleton contains two major forms of bone: trabecular (spongy) bone and cortical (dense) bone, both of which constantly turn over in a continuous process of resorption (loss) and reformation (gain). In later life, resorption predominates over formation. Growth of bone requires a positive calcium balance. Peak bone mass seems to be related to intake of calcium during the years of bone mineralization. The age at which peak bone mass is attained is uncertain, but probably is not less than 25 years. The recommendation for optimal bone formation is consumption of 1200 mg/d of calcium for males and females between the ages of 11 and 24 years. For optimal maintenance of bone mineral density with aging, 1500 mg has been suggested. Dairy products or foods fortified with calcium offer the best sources of calcium along with additional nutrients, such as lactose, vitamin D, and phosphorus, which seem to support calcium absorption.

Phosphorus. This nutrient is an essential component of bone mineral. Approximately 85% of all phosphorus in the body is found in the skeleton. Major contributors of phosphorus in the food supply are protein-rich foods such as milk, meat, fish, and poultry.

Cereal grains provide about 12% of dietary phosphorus, whereas diets based heavily on processed foods receive an additional 20% to 30% of phosphorus from food additives. Recommended intakes for phosphorus are 800 mg/d for children between the ages of 1 and 10 years, 1200 mg/d for individuals 11 to 24 years, and 800 mg/d for individuals older than 24 years old. Dietary phosphorus is more abundant than calcium in most US diets.

Protein. Overall, protein's role in healthy joint formation is its contribution of amino acids and nitrogen for growth. Without adequate protein, optimal bone and joint formation is compromised. Especially important are sulfur-containing amino acids, such as the nonessential amino acid cysteine, which contributes sulfur. In animal studies, there have been reports of reduced levels of sulfur in joints associated with osteoarthritis.

Vitamin C. Ascorbic acid stimulates collagen synthesis and modestly stimulates synthesis of aggrecan.

Vitamin D. Normal bone and cartilage metabolism depends on the presence of vitamin D. Suboptimal levels of vitamin Dare reported to cause adverse effects on articular cartilage turnover. In tissue culture, vitamin D has been shown to have a direct effect on the synthesis of proteoglycan bychondrocytes.

In addition, researchers have shown that dietary intake of vitamin D in patients with osteoarthritis is less than 80% of the recommended daily allowance. In the Framingham study comprising 556 participants, the risk of osteoarthritis progression increased threefold in participants in the middle and lower tertiles for vitamin D intake and serum levels of vitamin D.

Vitamin E. Research suggests that vitamin E may enhance chondrocyte growth, provide protection against reactive oxygen species, and modulate the development of osteoarthritis. It has been shown that many osteoarthritis patients have dietary intakes of vitamin E that are below the recommended daily allowance of 400 IU/d.

Zinc. Low zinc levels have been reported in patients with osteoarthritis. The recommended daily allowance for zinc in males is 11 mg, whereas for females it is 8 mg. Vegetarians may need 50% more zinc than nonvegetarians, owing to decreased absorption of zinc from plant sources.

In addition to these nutrients, healthy joints require that individuals get adequate levels of collagenous materials in their diet. Collagen naturally occurs in the gristle of meats. Recommendations to reduce meat consumption, which aim to reduce saturated fat and decrease risk for cardiovascular disease, have increased speculation that the amount of collagen in the average Western diet may be declining.

Many consumers prefer lean, boneless meats without connective tissue. The adoption of lactovegetarianism also may reduce the amount of collagen in the diet. Concerns about bovine spongiform encephalopathy, commonly known as mad cow disease, also have contributed to a decline in the consumption of meat, which may have resulted in decreased collagen consumption. While essential nutrients for joint health may be decreasing, there is a concomitant increase in obesity and overweight, putting additional stress or overload on joints.

JOINT DISORDERS

Causes of Joint Problems

Athletic activities can influence joint problems from a variety of different causes. Joint problems can arise from normal use in individuals with existing joint diseases or from overuse or excessive stress specific to a sport (eg, joint pain from running or cycling or constant repetitive stress on a specific knee). These causes including the following:

Stress (microfractures, osteochondrophytes). Many activities, including sports-related activities, cause excess stress on joints, which leads to microfractures in the surrounding bone. This damage can lead to the formation of osteochondrophytes and calluses that cause thickening of the joint area.

Dietary habits. Two aspects of dietary habits can affect joint health: an early-in-life deficiency of nutrients necessary for optimal bone and joint formation and overconsumption of total calories (resulting in overweight or obesity). In Western societies, excess caloric intake is more likely to be a problem than early deficiency of nutrients.

Injury and trauma. Power and contact sports with a high risk of injury increase the risk of severe degenerative disease of the joints involved.

Disease. The most common type of joint disease is osteoarthritis. Although the term *osteoarthritis* suggests an inflammatory disease, osteoarthritis is a disease of the synovial joint, in which all of the tissues are affected, including the subchondral bone, synovium, meniscus, ligaments, supporting neuro-muscular apparatus, and cartilage, in which biochemical and metabolic alterations result in the breakdown of this tissue. Some inflammatory cells may be present in osteoarthritis, but inflammation is not the primary disease state.

It is believed that degeneration of cartilage in osteoarthritis is characterized by two phases: a biosynthetic phase, during which the chondrocytes in cartilage attempt to repair damage to the extracellular matrix, and a degradative phase, in which the activity of enzymes produced by the chondrocytes digest the matrix, matrix synthesis is inhibited, and the consequent erosion of cartilage is accelerated.

Obesity. Although there are conflicting data on the linear, causal correlation between overweight and the frequency and severity of joint disease, it is generally accepted that degenerative joint disease occurs more frequently in obese individuals. Coggon and associates reported that the risk of osteoarthritis of the knee increased from 0.1 with a body mass index (BMI) of less than 20 kg/m^2 to 13.6 for a BMI of 36 kg/m^2 or greater. In addition, it has been reported that if overweight and obese individuals reduced their weight by 5 kg or until their BMI was within the recommended normal range, 24% of surgical cases of knee osteoarthritis would be avoided. Some researchers have suggested that the increased risk of joint problems is not only the added mechanical stress brought about by overweight, but also the metabolic disturbance associated with obesity that has an additional effect on cartilage metabolism. This view is supported by evidence that osteoarthritis of the fingers, which is not associated with mechanical stress, seems to occur more frequently in obese individuals.

Aging. By age 70, most adults have some form of osteoarthritic joint disease. Although not specifically a result of aging, it may be due to the fact that many elderly individuals have a generalized vitamin deficiency.

Congenital deformity. Another cause of joint disorders is skeletal deformity and joint malposition. In such cases, uneven stress from the deformed or misaligned joint causes the cartilage tissue to be worn down or injured over time.

PREVENTING AND ADDRESSING JOINT DISORDERS

Currently, there is no cure for joint disorders such as osteoarthritis, so treatment focuses on reducing pain and inflammation with the goal of maintaining mobility and avoiding unnecessary stress to the painful joint area. Management strategies include exercise, reduction in weight, and nonpharmacologic and pharmacologic interventions.

Lifestyle Treatments: Exercise, Stretching, Aerobic Activity, and Weight Management

Targeted and well-dosed physical stress helps keep avascular cartilage supplied with nutrients and free to metabolize waste products. Because of this and other factors, a physically active lifestyle is an important aspect of the complex treatment of joint disorders. Various kinds of therapy are recommended for treating joint disorders, including functional training; isometric, isotonic, and isokinetic exercises; postural training; and general strengthening exercises.

Stretching exercises are important to help muscles, tendons, and ligaments retain strength and ensure that no further restrictions in mobility develop. Exercises should be moderate in nature to prevent stress to the joints. In addition, relaxation is important (at least 4-6 hours each day).

Dietary Treatments: Optimal Nutrition

Maintaining healthy joints starts with adequate nutrition. Athletes should get adequate levels of protein to maintain and repair muscles, tendons, ligaments, and joints. Fruits and vegetables provide antioxidants that can help reduce inflammation and improve recovery from and adaptation to exercise. Essential fats, especially omega-3 fatty acids, are beneficial for promoting prostaglandins that control inflammation and pain pathways. Some essential fatty acids, such as omega-6 fatty acids, are easy to obtain from dietary sources because they are readily available in plant oils. A 1:1 or 2:1 ratio of omega-6 to omega-3 fats in the daily diet has been suggested. The amount of omega-3 fatty acids can be achieved by eating fish two to three times per week and using flax oil regularly.

In animal studies, high levels of vitamin C (150 mg/d) in the diet resulted in less severe joint damage in guinea pigs with surgically induced osteoarthritis compar ed with guinea pigs receiving low levels (2.4 mg/d). In the Framingham Osteoarthritis Cohort Study, a moderate intake of vitamin C (120-200 mg/d) resulted in a threefold lower risk of osteoarthritis progression, but did not have an impact on the incidence of the disease. A multicenter, double-blind, randomized, placebo-controlled, crossover trial was conducted on 133 patients with radiographically verified symptomatic osteoarthritis of the hip or knee joints. The patients received 1 g of calcium ascorbate (containing 898 mg of vitamin C) or placebo daily for 14 ± 3 days, separated by 7 ± 3 days washout. Calcium ascorbate was reported to reduce pain significantly compared with placebo, although the demonstrated effect was less than half that commonly reported with nonsteroidal anti-inflammatory drugs (NSAIDs).

Clinical studies have reported benefits from vitamin E administered for the treatment of symptomatic osteoarthritis over a short-term period. Two large studies, performed over a longer period, found no evidence of benefits in terms of reduced pain or stiffness or improved physical function.

Nonpharmacologic and Pharmacologic Treatments

No medications have been shown to reverse the damage to joints caused by injury or disease, so pain relief is the main goal for individuals with osteoarthri-tis and other joint disorders. Many patients with joint pain use NSAIDs. On average, 30% pain relief and 15% functional improvement have been reported. Although NSAIDs may suppress inflammation, they do not improve the natural history of the disease. Another problem with NSAIDs is that they are associated with an increased risk of side effects, including the following :

- Epigastric discomfort
- Gastric or duodenal ulcers
- Gastrointestinal bleeding
- Exacerbation of the degenerative process of osteoarthritis by decreasing production of glycosaminoglycan synthesis

Another class of medications for the treatment of joint pain is the cyclooxy-genase-2 (COX-2) inhibitors, which target COX-2, an enzyme responsible for inflammation and pain. COX-2 inhibitors were associated with fewer gastrointestinal side effects than the NSAIDs in several large studies. Concerns about cardiovascular effects led to the COX-2 inhibitor rofecoxib being withdrawn from the market on September 30, 2004, however.

The systemic administration of glucocorticoids is another approach to joint pain used by some clinicians. This approach is not considered effective for osteoarthritis. Depot glucocorticoids may have a pain-reducing effect over many weeks if given by intra-articular or periarticular injection. Although this approach is recommended in several guidelines for the management of patients with peripheral joint osteoarthritis, the long-term effect of treatment on cartilage metabolism and the progression of osteoarthritis is unclear. A specialist should administer intra-articular injections, and they should be given at most two or three times per year to the same joint.

SUPPLEMENTS AND HERBS FOR OPTIMIZING JOINT HEALTH

Herbal Products

Various herbal products have been studied for the treatment of joint disorders, including green tea extracts, Asian herbal remedies (eg, *Tripterygium wilfordi* Hook F, SKI 306X [a mixture of extracts from *Clematis mandshurica, Tricosanthes kirihwii,* and *Prunella vulgaris*]), and devil's claw (*Harpagophytum procumbens*).

- Green tea contains polyphenolic compounds called catechins. The cate-chins in green tea include (−)-epigallocatechin 3-gallate (EGCG), (−)-epigal-locatechin, (−)-epicatechin 3-gallate (ECG), and (−)-epicatechin. A polyphenolic fraction from green tea has been reported to prevent collagen- induced arthritis in mice. In a study that used a bovine in vitro model of cartilage degradation, EGCG and ECG were shown to inhibit interleukin (IL)-1–induced proteoglycan release and type II collagen degradation in cartilage explants. In a human in vitro model, EGCG was shown to suppress IL-1 (5-induced inducible nitric oxide synthase mRNA and protein expression and the production of nitric oxide. Further studies are required, however, to determine whether oral consumption of green tea can result in sufficiently high concentrations of catechins in joints to provide the same effects seen in the in vitro studies.
- Tao and colleagues reported the effects of a Chinese herbal medicine called *Tripterygium wilfordii* Hook F in a clinical trial using patients with rheumatoid arthritis. They found that an extract of the plant suppressed symptoms of rheumatoid arthritis compared with a placebo control.
- The compound SKI 306X (an herbal product extracted from the herbs *Clematis mandshurica, Trichosanthes kirilowii,* and *Prunella vulgaris)* has been reported to inhibit IL-1-induced proteoglycan degradation in rabbit articular cartilage explants and to decrease lesions in a collagen-induced osteoarthritis model in rabbits. The complex nature of these extracts and their variability has prevented elucidation of the active ingredients in this compound, however, and their specific mechanisms of action.
- Extracts of the root of devil's claw *(Harpagophytum procumbens),* a plant originally found in the savannas of South West Africa, is believed to have anti-inflammatory and analgesic effects, which may be associated with its component harpagoside. A review of the literature concluded that there is some evidence that *Harpagophytum* powder containing 60 mg of harpagoside provides some relief to patients with osteoarthritis of the spine, knee, and hip.

Glucosamine Sulfate and Chondroitin Sulfate

Glucosamine sulfate and chondroitin sulfate supplements are the most widely used dietary supplements for the treatment of osteoarthritis, with an annual sales of nearly $730 million in 2004. Glucosamine is an amino monosac-charide that is the most fundamental building block required for the biosynthesis of several classes of compounds that require amino sugars, such as glycosaminoglycans and proteoglycans. The raw material for glucosamine is derived from chitin, a biopolymer present in the exoskeleton of marine invertebrate animals. Chondroitin sulfates are a class of glycosaminoglycans required for the formation of proteoglycans found in joint cartilage.

The rationale for the use of glucosamine and chondroitin is based on the assertion that osteoarthritis is associated with a local deficiency in some key nutritional substances, and that providing these substances addresses this deficiency and supports cartilage repair. Glucosamine sulfate has been shown to be capable of stimulating proteoglycan synthesis and regeneration of cartilage in animals after experimentally induced damage and inhibiting the degradation of proteoglycans. It also has been suggested that chondroitin sulfate may increase proteoglycan synthesis and inhibit the activity of degradative enzymes.

Clinical research with glucosamine sulfate and chondroitin sulfate

Numerous clinical trials have tested the efficacy of glucosamine sulfate and chondroitin sulfate to reduce pain and provide functional improvement in patients with joint disorders, such as osteoarthritis. These studies were evaluated in a meta-analysis by McAlindon and colleagues, who reviewed 15 placebo-controlled glucosamine or chondroitin trials. The authors of the meta-analysis reported that trials of glucosamine and chondroitin preparations for the management of osteoarthritis symptoms showed moderate-to-large effects, but that quality issues and likely publication bias suggest that these effects are exaggerated.

GAIT trial

Many of the design flaws of glucosamine sulfate and chondroitin sulfate studies, including the failure to adhere to the intention-to-treat principle, the enrollment of small numbers of patients, potential bias because of sponsorship by a manufacturer of dietary supplements, and inadequate masking of the study agent, were addressed in the GAIT (Glucosamine/chondroitin Arthritis Intervention Trial), a study sponsored by the National Institutes of Health.

In GAIT, Clegg and coworkers investigated glucosamine sulfate, chondroitin sulfate, and the two supplements in combination in a multicenter, double-blind, placebo-controlled and celecoxib-controlled study with 1583 patients with symptomatic knee osteoarthritis who were randomly assigned to receive 1500 mg of glucosamine sulfate daily, 1200 mg of chondroitin sulfate daily, both glucosamine sulfate and chondroitin sulfate, 200 mg of celecoxib daily, or placebo for 24 weeks. Up to 4000 mg of acetaminophen daily was allowed as rescue analgesia. The mean age of the patients was 59 years, and 64% were women. The primary outcome measure was a 20% decrease in knee pain from baseline to week 24.

The investigators reported that glucosamine sulfate and chondroitin sulfate were not statistically significantly better than placebo in reducing knee pain by 20% (the primary outcome they had defined). Compared with the rate of response to placebo, the rate of response to glucosamine sulfate was 3.9% higher (P ¼.30), the rate of response to chondroitin sulfate was 5.3% higher (P ¼.17), and the rate of response to combined treatment was 6.5% higher (P ¼.09), whereas the response in the celecoxib control group was 10% higher (P ¼.008). The investigators concluded that glucosamine sulfate and chondroitin sulfate alone or in combination did not reduce pain effectively in the overall group of patients with osteoarthritis of the knee.

Methylsulfonylmethane

Methylsulfonylmethane (MSM) is another dietary supplement that is taken for the treatment of joint pain from arthritis. Its benefits for patients with osteoarthritis were investigated in a randomized, double-blind, placebo-controlled trial with 50 men and women (40–76 years old) with pain from osteoarthritis of the knee who were enrolled in an outpatient medical center. The patients received MSM 3 g or placebo twice each day (6 g/d) for 12 weeks. The outcomes included the Western Ontario and McMaster University Osteoarthritis Index visual analog scale

(WOMAC), patient and physician global assessments, and SF-36 (an overall health-related quality-of-life measurement).

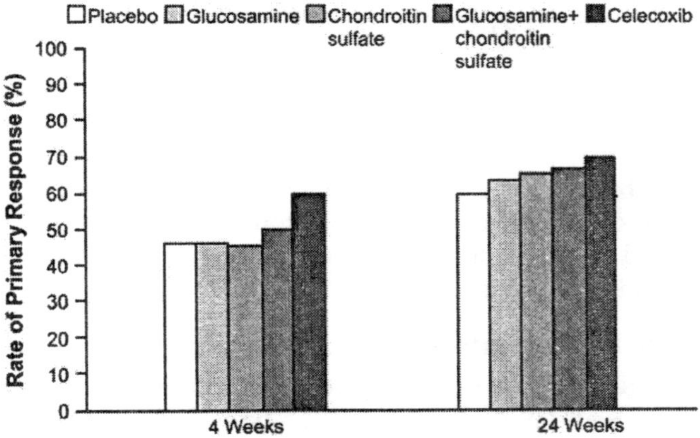

Fig. 2. Rates of primary response in the five groups in GAIT at 4 and 24 weeks. A primary response was defined as a 20% decrease in the summed score for the pain subscale of the WOMAC index. (From Clegg DO, Reda DJ, Harris CL, et al. Glucosamine, chondroitin sulfate, and the two in combination for painful knee osteoarthritis. N Engl J Med 2006;354:795–808; with permission.)

The investigators reported that MSM resulted in significantly decreased WOMAC pain and physical function impairment (P <.05) compared with placebo, but no notable changes were found in WOMAC stiffness and aggregated total symptom scores. MSM also produced improvement in performing activities of daily living compared with placebo on the SF-36 evaluation (P <.05). They concluded that MSM (3 g twice a day) improved symptoms of pain and physical function during a short intervention without major adverse events, although the long-term benefits and safety in managing osteoarthritis could not be confirmed by this pilot trial.

S-Adenosyl-L-methionine

The dietary supplement S-adenosyl-L-methionine (SAMe) has been reported to be effective for the management of a variety of problems, including depression, liver disease, and arthritis. It has been suggested that SAMe can reduce pain in osteoarthritis because it reduces inflammation, increases proteoglycan synthesis, or has an analgesic effect. It is unknown whether SAMe is an inhibitor of COX-2. Studies using human articular chondrocytes have shown SAMe-induced increases in proteoglycan synthesis. A double-blind crossover study compared SAMe (1200 mg) with celecoxib (Celebrex; 200 mg) for 16 weeks to reduce pain associated with osteoarthritis of the knee. Sixty-one adults diagnosed with osteoarthritis of the knee were enrolled, and 56 completed the study. The investigators reported that SAMe had a slower onset of action, but was as effective as celecoxib in the management of symptoms of knee osteoarthritis. They concluded that longer studies are needed to determine the long-term efficacy of SAMe and the optimal dose to be used.

Collagen Hydrolysate

Collagen is a vital component of structural matrix throughout most tissues and organs in the human body. It is concentrated in cartilage, where it plays a significant role in the integrity of joint-related connective tissues. The important role played by collagen in joints is vividly shown by the severe generalized arthritis associated with collagen gene mutations.

The amount of collagen in the diet can be increased by consuming specific foods, such as meats with gristle or connective tissue still intact. Collagen also can be found in foods containing gelatin. Dietary supplements also can be used to increase the amount of collagen contributed by the diet. An example of such a supplement is collagen hydrolysate, which is prepared by enzymatic hydrolysis of collagenous tissue, such as bone, hide, and hide split from pigs and cows. Collagen hydrolysate is soluble in cold water and is composed of proteins with a molecular weight of 3 to 6 kD.

Collagen hydrolysate provides high levels of amino acids. Among these are glycine and proline, two amino acids that are essential for the stability and regeneration of cartilage. To synthesize a single picogram of collagen type II, more than 1 billion glycine molecules and 620 million proline molecules are required. In the absence of these amino acids, the anabolic phase of cartilage metabolism can be impaired.

In studies of rats and humans, concentrations of the amino acids proline, hy-droxyproline, and glycine after administration of collagen hydrolysate (10 g in humans) increased significantly compared with placebo. In a single-blind, randomized, and placebo-controlled study of 60 male sports students, the amino acid concentrations in peripheral blood after a daily intake of 10 g of collagen hydrolysate for 4.5 months were measured. It was found that levels of the amino acids glycine, proline, and hydroxyproline were significantly higher in the treated group than in the control group. The concentrations of alanine, asparagine, glutamic acid, and tryptophan also were higher.

Mechanism of action

It has been shown that about 90% of orally administered collagen hydrolysate is resorbed within 6 hours from the gastrointestinal tract. It also has been found thatcollagen hydrolysate hasa special affinity for cartilage, and that this affinity to cartilage has a stimulating effect on the synthesis of chondrocytes.

Clinical research on collagen hydrolysate

Collagen hydrolysate has been studied for the management of joint pain in four open-label and three double-blind studies. The earliest of these, by Krug, studied the clinical effect of collagen hydrolysate on degenerative joint disease in patients with knee osteoarthritis with tibial, femoral, or retropatellar involvement or with degenerative disc disease of specific parts of the spine. Patients received 5 to 7 g of collagen hydrolysate by mouth for 1 to 6 months. The author reported results on 56 patients: 10 (24%) had very good success, 18 (44%) had noticeable improvement, and 13 (32%) reported no improvement. The author did not report the statistical significance of the findings.

In 1982, Go¨tz reported the results of a study in which 60 juvenile patients diagnosed with retropatellar osteoarthritis received collagen hydrolysate treatment (one 7-g sachet per day by mouth) for 3 months. The sachet also included 24,000 U of vitamin A and 120 mg of the sulfur-containing amino acid L-cysteine. Go¨tz reported that after treatment, 75% of patients showed improvement: 45% of patients were symptom-free, and 30% had clearly improved symptoms; the remainder of the patients did not improve. No P values were provided in this report.

An open-label study of 154 patients with osteoarthritis provided additional evidence of the clinical efficacy of collagen hydrolysate. Patients with diagnosed osteoarthritis of the knee, hip, or lower spine were randomized among three treatment groups: therapeutic exercises; therapeutic exercises plus collagen hydrolysate with vitamin A and L-cysteine; or collagen hydrolysate, vitamin A, and L-cysteine without therapeutic exercise. The collagen hydroly-sate, vitamin A, and L-cysteine were given as one sachet per day by mouth. After 3 months of treatment, the percentage of patients with a very good response was 26% for the supplement-only group, 20% for the supplement plus exercise group, and 6% for the exercise-only group. Similar results were found for good response (supplement only, 43%; supplement plus exercise, 36%; and exercise only, 14%), whereas the opposite results were found for patients who were considered unchanged (supplement only, 6%; supplement plus exercise, 14%; and exercise only, 43%).

Collagen hydrolysate has been studied in populations other than patients diagnosed with osteoarthritis. An observational study investigated the effects of collagen hydrolysate in athletes who had joint pain, but who did not have osteoarthritis.

In this study, 100 participants with hip, knee, or shoulder pain resulting from intense physical activity were treated with orally administered collagen hydrolysate (10 g/d) for 12 weeks. Of the 88 patients who could be evaluated in the study, 78% of patients achieved pain reduction after taking collagen hydrolysate for 12 weeks (68 patients improved, 19 patients were unchanged or worsened, and 1 patient was incompletely documented for pain on movement).

In addition to these open-label trials, collagen hydrolysate has been studied in a prospective, randomized, double-blind, placebo-controlled clinical trial conducted by Adam. Researchers recruited 81 patients with osteoarthritis of the knee or hip and used a complex crossover design to compare four different nutritional supplements that included collagen hydrolysate (10 g in the form of 20 capsules, each 500 mg, by mouth).

They found that 81% of patients taking collagen hydrolysate achieved meaningful pain reduction compared with 23% of patients taking a control substance (egg albumin). In addition, 69% of patients taking collagen hydrolysate had a 50% or greater decrease in the consumption of analgesics compared with 35% of the patients taking egg albumin. The author noted that the results from treatment with all nutritional supplements, including collagen hydrolysate, were significantly different from egg albumin, but he did not define statistical significance.

Another study of collagen hydrolysate by Moskowitz was a prospective, randomized, double-blind, placebo-controlled clinical trial. The study included sites in Germany, the United Kingdom, and the United States and recruited 389 patients with knee osteoarthritis. Patients were randomly assigned to receive 10 g of collagen hydrolysate per day or placebo, by mouth, for 24 weeks. The primary outcome measures were the WOMAC pain score, function score, and patient global assessment. After 24 weeks of treatment, there were no statistically significant differences for the total study group for differences of mean score for pain. Moskowitz reported, however, that one group of patients (the German patients, n ¼ 112) experienced a statistically significant benefit from collagen hydrolysate in terms of pain reduction (P ¼.016) and functional improvement (P ¼.007), but not patient global evaluation (P ¼.074).

The benefits of collagen hydrolysate for patients with mild symptoms of osteoarthritis were examined in a randomized, placebo-controlled, double-blind study with 250 adults diagnosed with mild symptoms of osteoarthritis of the knee. A total of 190 patients completed the study (88 treatment and 102 placebo patients). Treatment consisted of oral administration of collagen hydroly-sate (10 g/d) or placebo for 14 weeks. Isokinetic and isometric leg strength was assessed using a Biodex Multi-Joint System B2000. A 6-minute walk test and a 50-foot walk test were used to assess functional mobility, and joint pain, stiffness, and perceived functional mobility were assessed using the WOMAC Index, the Lequesne Index, and the Knee Pain Scale.

After 14 weeks of treatment, there were no statistically significant differences between the treatment groups for measures of pain, stiffness, mobility, or flexibility measurements. The collagen hydrolysate-treated group showed statistically significant improvement, however, in three out of six isokinetic leg strength measures (peak torque/body weight for extension at 60°/sec~, peak torque/body weight for flexion at 60°/sec~, and total work/body weight for extension at 60°/sec~; P<.05 compared with placebo for all three tests). The investigators stated the findings suggest that collagen hydrolysate may contribute to early changes in knee cartilage (M. Carpenter, personal communication, 2006), which is consistent with animal data.

SUMMARY

Osteoarthritis is a widespread condition that causes pain, disability, and decreased quality of life. Dietitians can play an important role in managing patients with osteoarthritis by supporting healthy eating habits, which should include the nutrients that support healthy joints. They also can encourage patients who are obese to reduce weight and increase activity levels.

Joints require many nutrients to stay healthy and to regenerate new tissue, including calcium, phosphorus, protein, vitamin C, vitamin D, vitamin E, and zinc. It also is important to include collagenous materials in the diet to maintain joint health, although many individuals may be cutting back on the amount of collagen in their diet. Joints are threatened further by overweight.

Joint disorders can result from many different causes, including stress to joints, poor dietary habits, injury or trauma, disease, obesity, aging, and congenital deformity. Regardless of the cause, there is no cure for joint disease. Treatment for joint disorders such as osteoarthritis focuses on reducing the pain and inflammation of affected joints, with the goal of maintaining mobility and maximizing quality of life.

Treatments for patients with osteoarthritis range from lifestyle changes, such as exercise, stretching, aerobic activities, and weight management, to dietary and nutritional interventions, including increasing levels of such nutrients as omega-3 fatty acids, vitamin C, and vitamin E. In addition, pharmacologic treatments, herbs, and nutritional supplements have been investigated for patients with osteoarthritis.

Drugs that have been used to manage symptoms of patients with osteoarthritis include NSAIDs, COX-2 inhibitors, and glucocorticoids. Herbal products include green tea extracts, SKI306X, and devil's claw. Nutritional supplements that have been studied in osteoarthritis patients include glucosamine and chon-droitin sulfate, MSM, SAMe, and collagen hydrolysate. Research with these drugs and supplements has provided varying results about their efficacy in patients with osteoarthritis; additional research is needed to determine the optimal treatments for patients with this disorder.

7

Micronutrient Requirements for Athletes

Vitamins and minerals are necessary for many metabolic processes in the body and are important in supporting growth and development. Vitamins and minerals also are required in numerous reactions involved with exercise and physical activity, including energy, carbohydrate, fat and protein metabolism, oxygen transfer and delivery, and tissue repair. The vitamin and mineral needs of athletes have always been a topic of discussion. Some researchers state that athletes require more vitamins and minerals than their sedentary counterparts, whereas other researchers do not report greater micro-nutrient requirements. The intensity, duration, and frequency of the sport/ workout and the overall energy and nutrient intakes of the individual all have an impact on whether or not micronutrients are required in greater amounts. This article evaluates the vitamin and mineral needs of athletes.

DIETARY REFERENCE INTAKES

The Dietary Reference Intakes (DRI) for all known vitamins and essential minerals for healthy individuals living in the United States were updated between 1997 and 2005. Adequate Intake (AI), Recommended Dietary Allowance (RDA), Estimated Average Requirement (EAR), and Tolerable Upper Intake Level (UL) all are under the DRI heading. The RDA is the dietary intake level that is sufficient for approximately 98% of healthy individuals living in the United States. The AI is a projected value that is used when the RDA cannot be established. The EAR is a value used to estimate the nutrient requirements of half of the healthy individuals in a group. The UL is the maximum quantity of a nutrient most individuals can consume without resulting in adverse side effects. In most cases, if energy intakes are sufficient, the micronutrient requirements of athletes are similar to healthy, fairly active individuals; using the DRI for evaluating nutrient needs would be suitable. Some athletes may have greater requirements, however, as a result of disproportionate losses of nutrients in weat and urine. For these athletes, supplementation may need to be considered on an individual basis. Many athletes supplement with vitamins, minerals, and ergogenic aids on their own. The UL provides guidelines to athletes who supplement, which should prevent negative effects from occurring owing to oversupplementation.

IMPORTANCE OF ACCURATE DIETARY INTAKE ASSESSMENT

Although this article focuses on micronutrients, a total evaluation of an athlete's energy intake is necessary because even if an athlete is consuming the correct amount of micronutrients (especially if he or she is supplementing with a vitamin-mineral supplement), if energy requirements are not being met, athletic performance still would be suboptimal. Clark and colleagues examined the preseason and postseason intakes of macronutrients and micronutrients in division I female soccer players. They reported that despite meeting total energy requirements (carbohydrate needs were not met), vitamin E, folate, copper, and magnesium intakes were suboptimal (<75% of the DRI). The evaluation of an athlete's diet must be conducted properly to ensure accuracy. It is common for athletes (and nonathletes) to underreport their dietary intake. Consequently, it is imperative that athletes are taught how to estimate accurately portion sizes and fluid intake, the amount and frequency of snacking, any weight management practices they may perform, and changes in their food patterns during seasons and off-seasons.

MICRONUTRIENT INTAKE AND NUTRITION STATUS AMONG ATHLETES

Dietary Intake Assessment and Nutritional Status in Male Athletes

Assessing dietary intake among any individual is difficult and is often criticized because of the inherent lack of accuracy.

Nonetheless, dietary records are still the best method presently available to estimate dietary intake. Although dietary records often provide information about intake at a particular point in time, longer term studies can help to provide a more accurate assessment of dietary intake, even if one point in time is assessed per year. Leblanc and coworkers analyzed the diets of French male athletes training at the National Training Centre in Clairefontaine. There were 180 athletes, 13 to 16 years old, who participated in this 3-year dietary survey. Despite the long-term nature of this study, calcium and iron were the only micronutrients evaluated. Each year, a 5-day food record was collected from these athletes. Leblanc and coworkers reported insufficient energy intake for all athletes. They also reported that calcium intake was below recommendations during the first year, whereas iron intake was sufficient; however, calcium and iron intakes significantly improved ($P < .05$) over the 3-year period. The researchers stated that the increase in calcium and iron intake may have been a result of a physiologic adjustment to growth or to the positive effects of the nutrition courses provided during their stay at the Centre. Rico-Sanz and colleagues also reported lower than recommended intakes of calcium in eight male soccer players (average age 17 years) who were part of the Puerto Rican Olympic soccer team, despite an adequate energy intake.

Iglesias-Gutierrez and associates evaluated the dietary intake and nutritional status of adolescent Spanish soccer players of similar age to those studied by Leblanc and coworkers (14–16 years old; n ¼ 33). The soccer players consumed an adequate amount of iron; however, 48% of these athletes were iron deficient (without anemia). These results suggest that even with adequate intakes of micronutrients, the impact of training may require greater amounts of certain mi-cronutrients. A nutrition intervention, including education and monitoring transient and long-term micronutrient changes (intake and blood values), is required to make definitive recommendations, however. It has been suggested that nutrition educationbeprovided to athletes atanearly age and continued throughout adolescence, not only to optimize athletic performance, but also to promote healthy dietary practices throughout the life span.

In a more recent study, Paschoal and Amancio examined the dietary intake and nutritional status of eight Brazilian elite male swimmers, 18 to 21 years old. Four-day dietary records indicated adequate energy and micronu-trient intake, with the exception of calcium, for which only four of the athletes consumed the recommended amount. The biochemical indices of nutritional status all were within normal limits for the micronutrients. These researchers also reported that 62.5% and 25% of the swimmers consumed amino acid and antioxidant supplements. Similar to other researchers, Paschoal and Aman-cio strongly recommended nutrition education for balanced dietary intake and education about supplementation.

Rankinen and associates also evaluated the dietary intake and nutritional status of athletes (Finnish elite male ski jumpers) (n ¼ 21), but compared them with age-matched controls (n ¼ 20). Dietary intake was assessed via 4-day dietary records. There were no differences between groups in age and height, although the ski jumpers had a lower mean body weight and percent body fat (assessed via dual-energy x-ray absorptiometry). Energy intake was significantly lower (P ¼.001) in the ski jumpers compared with the control participants. Despite this difference in energy intake, thiamine, riboflavin, folate, vitamin C, calcium, and iron intakes were similar between groups; however, vitamins D and E, zinc, and magnesium were significantly lower in the ski jumpers compared with the controls. Although the ski jumpers had significantly lower intakes of these micronutrients, their biochemical markers of nutritional status were within normal limits. Although nutritional status was within normal limits, the cross-sectional nature of this and many other studies to determine nutritional status among athletes may not accurately capture deficiencies that could be occurring over time. Blood (plasma or serum) concentrations of micronutrients are not always the best measure of status.

Dietary Intake Assessment and Nutritional Status in Female Athletes

There seems to be more research on the dietary intake of female athletes than male athletes, probably because of a higher prevalence of disordered eating among women, especially in sports that require a specific body weight to compete or in sports that also highly value esthetics. Ziegler and colleagues evaluated 18 female competitive figure skaters, 14 to 16 years old, during preseason, the competitive season, and off-season using 3-day dietary records. Energy intake was below energy needs, although energy intake did not differ significantly over the three seasons. Nonetheless, throughout the competitive season, 78%, 50%, and 44% of the skaters had intakes less than 67% of the RDA for folate, iron, and calcium. The biochemical indicators of nutritional status were within normal limits, although long-term assessments are required to evaluate the impact of the less-than-adequate intake of the aforementioned nutrients. Ziegler and colleagues emphasized the need for nutrition education among these athletes, especially throughout their competitive season.

Hassapidou and Manstrantoni compared the dietary intake of elite Greek female athletes in four different sports (volleyball, middle distance running, ballet dancing, and swimming) with a nonathletic control group. They evaluated dietary intake using 7-day weighed dietary records over two seasons, the training season and the competitive season. The investigators reported a lower than recommended intake of iron in the athletic and nonathletic groups, but a higher than recommended intake of vitamin C in all participants, which they stated was "characteristic of the population of the Mediterranean countries". Although micronutrient intakes did not differ between athletes and nonathletes, biochemical indices to assess status were not conducted. An additional study on dietary intake conducted in female Greek athletes (volleyball players) found that these adolescent athletes did not consume recommended intakes for calcium, iron, folate, magnesium, zinc, vitamin A, and the B vitamins. Neither of these groups of researchers evaluated nutritional status; nevertheless, the lower than recommended intake could lead to less than optimal performance and growth (in the adolescent athletes).

Beals conducted a more complete study on 23 nationally ranked female adolescent volleyball players. Nutrient intake was assessed using 3-day weighed food records. Iron, vitamins C and B_{12}, and folate status were determined through blood samples. Beals found that these athletes consumed fewer calories than they expended (energy intake = 2248 ± 414 kcal/d, energy expenditure = 2815 kcal/d). They also consumed less than the recommended intakes for folate, B-complex vitamins, vitamin C, iron, calcium, magnesium, and zinc. With respect to their nutritional status, three of the athletes had iron deficiency anemia, one athlete had a marginal vitamin B_{12} status, and four athletes had marginal vitamin C status. Beals also reported a high percentage of athletes who had past or present menstrual disorders (amenorrhea, oligomenorrhea, or irregular menstrual cycles). The combination of low energy and micronutrient intake and menstrual irregularities shows the need for long-term studies evaluating dietary intake and nutritional status among athletes of all levels and ages.

In another comprehensive study, Kim and coworkers compared the nutritional intake, iron status, and immunologic patterns of Korean female Judo athletes to control participants. Three-day dietary records were used to evaluate intake. In general, vitamin and mineral intakes were within recommendations; however, calcium and iron intakes were less than 100% of the recommendations, whereas intakes of phosphorus, thiamine, and riboflavin were greater in athletes compared with controls. None of the participants were iron deficient; however, iron, thiamine, and niacin intakes were positively associated with the immunologic variables measured. Although more research is required on the dietary intake and nutritional status of all athletes, further investigation is needed in the area of specific vitamins and minerals with immunologic function in athletes, especially endurance athletes.

Athletes of all levels of competition can be negatively affected by poor dietary intake. Heptathletes are so varied in their training and competition, by the mere nature of their sport, that they may be at greater risk for nutritional deficiencies. Mullins and coworkers assessed the dietary intake (using 4-day dietary records) and nutritional status of 19 female heptathletes, 26 ± 3 years of age, during their training season. These athletes consumed more than 67% of the recommended intakes for all nutrients, with the exception of vitamin E, despite the fact that more than 50% of this group took vitamin supplements. Biochemical markers indicated normal iron status. The cross-sectional nature of this study, similar to some of the previously discussed studies, may not accurately reflect dietary intake and nutritional status.

In two separate studies, Gropper and colleagues evaluated the copper and iron intake and status of 70 female collegiate athletes (18-25 years old) from across different sports. Depending on the sport, copper intake ranged from 41% to 118% of the recommended intakes. Of the athletes, 41% did not consume two thirds of the RDA for copper. Serum copper and ceruloplasmin concentrations were within normal limits for all athletes. With respect to iron intake and status, 25% of the athletes did not consume two thirds of the RDA for iron, and these athletes displayed suboptimal serum ferritin, iron, or transferring saturation concentrations. Athletes whose serum ferritin concentration was 15 (ig/L or less also displayed serum iron concentrations of less than 60 Hg/dL and transferrin saturation of less than 16% (both below normal). Despite the fact that these were athletes from different sports, and iron deficiency was not apparent, iron depletion was present in many of these athletes across different sports and different ages. Certain studies have suggested that iron-depleted women have decreased maximal oxygen consumption (VO_2max) as a result of decreased iron storage. Some studies have observed alterations in metabolic rate, thyroid hormone status, and thermoregulation with iron depletion and iron deficiency anemia, although some researchers have not observed these alterations. Mild iron deficiency anemia also has been shown to affect psychomotor development, intellectual performance, and immune function negatively. The fact the iron deficiency anemia is one of the most common nutritional deficiencies throughout the world, especially in women, further emphasizes the need for proper nutrition education and intake among female athletes.

The previously discussed studies all have been cross-sectional in nature, which provides a snapshot of the athletes' intake and status, but do not allow for further interpretation. Petersen and associates evaluated 18 female collegiate swimmers and 6 female collegiate divers preseason and after 16 weeks of training. There were no changes in energy intake over time; however, the athletes significantly improved their dietary quality as evidenced by increases in iron, vitamin C, and vitamin B_6 intake. The investigators also reported improved iron status in these athletes, with increases in hemoglobin and hemat-ocrit, with a subsequent decrease in serum transferrin receptors. Clark and coworkers assessed dietary intake in female collegiate soccer players preseason to postseason and reported marginal intakes (<75% of the DRI) for vitamin E, folate, copper, and magnesium, with no improvements over the season as Petersen and associates reported. Although these studies evaluated preseason to postseason dietary intake or nutritional status, research examining intake over a longer period is needed to assess fully any impact of poor dietary intake on nutritional status and performance.

Dietary Intake Assessment and Nutritional Status in Special Populations of Female Athletes

Female athletes may be more restrictive in their dietary intake than male athletes, placing them at greater risk for nutritional deficiencies and impaired performance and health. Beals and Manore evaluated the diet and nutritional status of female athletes with subclinical eating disorders (n ¼ 24), compared with those of controls (n ¼ 24). The group with subclinical eating disorders had significantly lower energy intake than the control group (1989 kcal/d versus 2300 kcal/d; P ¼.004); however, energy expenditure did not differ between groups. Average micronutrient intake and iron, zinc, magnesium, vitamin B_{12}, and folate status did not differ between groups (and were within normal limits). Athletes in both groups used vitamin-mineral supplements, which likely improved nutritional status.

Aside from disordered eating, many female athletes are vegetarians for various reasons, which also could affect nutritional intake and status. Janelle and Barr compared the nutrient intakes of vegetarian (n ¼ 23) and nonvegetar-ian (n ¼ 22) athletes, 20 to 40 years old, using 3-day dietary records. The vegetarian athletes had lower intakes of riboflavin, niacin, vitamin B_{12}, zinc, and sodium intakes, while consuming higher intakes of folate, vitamin C, and copper compared with the nonvegetarians. Within the subgroup of the vegetarians, vegans consumed lower calcium and vitamin B_{12} compared with lactovegetarians. Despite the health-conscious nature of many vegetarians, dietary intake still may be inadequate and is definitely not the same among subgroups of vegetarians. Vegetarian athletes may need more information on proper nutritional intake to ensure adequate energy and micronutrient intake for optimal performance and health.

Dietary Intake Assessment and Nutritional Status in Female and Male Athletes

Numerous researchers evaluated the dietary intake of female and male athletes from similar sports. These studies can help shed some light on gender differences within the same sports. Although the total nutrient intake of athletes is important, evaluating the diversity of athletes' meals and snacks in providing nutrients is also important. Ziegler and colleagues evaluated the contribution of breakfast, lunch, dinner, and snacks on the macronutrient and micronu-trient intake of 46 male and 48 female elite figure skaters who participated in the 1999 US National Figure Skating Championships. Three-day dietary records were used to assess dietary intake. With respect to micronutrient intake, they reported that breakfast was the main source of dietary folate (36%), whereas breakfast and dinner were the main sources of iron (29% and 27%) and calcium (32% and 29%). Ziegler and colleagues concluded that these figure skaters needed to be educated about the benefits of consuming breakfast and about consuming a variety of foods throughout the day to maintain proper energy and micronutrient intake.

A larger study of the National Figure Skating Championship competitors was conducted in which 4-day diet records and fasting blood samples and anthropo-metric variables were assessed 2 months after the National Championships. Forty-one figure skaters 11 to 18 years old participated in this study. The researchers compared their intakes with the Third National Health and Nutrition Examination Survey (NHANES III) and recommended intakes. Ziegler and colleagues reported that the mean intakes for vitamins were greater than required intakes except for vitamins D and E. In addition, compared with NHANES III, the figure skaters consumed lower amounts of vitamins B_{12} and E, but greater amounts of vitamin C and thiamine (female skaters only). Male and female figure skaters consumed lower amounts of magnesium and zinc compared with recommended intakes. Male figure skaters also consumed lower amounts of iodine, whereas female figure skaters consumed lower amounts of magnesium, zinc, calcium, iron, and phosphorus compared with recommended intakes. Although biochemical indices of nutritional status were within the normal range, electrolyte concentrations indicated dehydration. Ziegler and colleagues emphasized the need for dietary interventions and nutrition education for these athletes to lead to optimal performance and health.

In a more recent study from the same group of researchers, Jonnalagadda and colleagues assessed the food preferences and nutrient intakes of elite male (n ¼ 23) and female (n ¼ 26) figure skaters using 3-day dietary records. They reported that male figure skaters had a higher preference for grains, meat, dairy, fats, fruit, and sweets, whereas female figure skaters had a higher preference for fruits and grains. Total energy intake and vitamins E and D, magnesium, and potassium intake were less than two thirds of the recommended intake for males and females. Female skaters also consumed less than two thirds of the recommended intakes for folate, pantothenic acid, calcium, and phosphorus. The researchers did not assess biochemical indices of these athletes; nutritional status could not be determined. Regardless, decreased intakes, combined with intense training, can lead to impaired performance and health.

Constantini and associates assessed the iron status of Israeli male and female gymnasts 12 to 18 years old compared with summers, tennis players, and table tennis players. They all trained for about 25 hours per week, lived in the same national center for gifted athletes, and ate in the same dining room. Hemoglobin concentrations were less than 14 g/dL in 45% of the male gymnasts compared with only 25% of the nongymnasts and less than 13 g/dL in 25% of premenarcheal female gymnasts compared with 15% of nongymnasts. Iron depletion (serum ferritin levels <20 ng/mL) was observed in 36% of the male gymnasts and 30% of the female gymnasts.

The prevalence of iron deficiency and depletion in the gymnasts compared with the other athletes was much greater and may be due to the pressures of maintaining a low body weight, even in males. Dubnov and Constantini reported similar high rates of iron depletion and iron deficiency, however, in 103 male and female national basketball players. They reported that 15% of males and 25% of females were iron depleted, whereas 18% of males and 38% of females were iron deficient. These researchers recommend iron screening and nutritional counseling for athletes.

SUPPLEMENTATION AND ATHLETIC PERFORMANCE

Based on the aforementioned review, it seems that some athletes may need to supplement as a result of inadequate dietary intake or impaired nutritional status. Does supplementation improve performance, however? Tsalis and colleagues evaluated whether the iron status of healthy adolescent swimmers was altered during a 6-month training season, and if increased daily iron intake (via supplement or food) would affect iron status or performance. Twenty-one male and 21 female Greek swimmers 12 to 17 years old were separated into three groups: (1) Group A received an iron supplement of 47 mg/d, (2) group B followed a diet high in iron (providing about 26 mg/d), and (3) group C served as the control group. Data were collected at baseline and at the end of three training phases.

The investigators found significant variations in iron status during the training season; however, they did not find significant differences in iron status or performance among the three groups, which could have been due to the fact that these athletes were neither iron depleted nor iron deficient.

Vasankari and associates found no improvement in exercise-induced oxidative stress in Finnish runners who were supplemented with vitamin C. Although Bryant and colleagues reported diminished membrane damage with 400 IU/d of vitamin E in trained cyclists (22.3 ± 2 years old, who participated in four separate supplementation trials—placebo, 1 g/d of vitamin C, 400 IU/d of vitamin E, or 1 g/d of vitamin C plus 200 IU/d of vitamin E), 1 g/d of vitamin C promoted cellular damage. Neither vitamin E nor vitamin C (alone or taken together) improved exercise performance.

Although these particular researchers did not find a positive effect on nutritional status or performance with supplementation, the nutritional status of the athletes is probably the key factor in why these trials were not as effective. It would seem that athletes who were deficient in particular micronutrients would benefit the most from supplementation, in terms of nutritional status and athletic performance. Conversely, with respect to vitamin C, Peake stated, "... it remains unclear if regular exercise increases the metabolism of vitamin C. However, the similar dietary intakes and responses to supplementation between athletes and non-athletes suggest that regular exercise does not increase the requirement for vitamin C in athletes."

LIMITATIONS IN RESEARCH

Although a great deal of research has been conducted on vitamins and minerals and athletes, more research is required. In addition, the research that has been published has limitations, including, but not limited to, the following: (1) small sample sizes; (2) mostly conducted in female athletes; (3) variations in type of sport studied; (4) variations in levels of training and fitness of athletes studied; (5) deficient in solid longitudinal data; (6) variations in methodology or study design (many have been cross-sectional); (7) differences in the types and amounts of supplementation used; and (8) some studies use a combination of vitamin and mineral supplements, making it difficult to ascertain the effects of one particular vitamin or mineral.

GENERAL RECOMMENDATIONS

Based on this review, athletes seem to consume inadequate amounts of many mi-cronutrients (and energy); however, not all athletes have impaired nutritional status, which could be a result of study design and not their true status. Maughan stateditwell inhis review, "When talented,motivatedandhighly trained athletes meet for competition the margin between victory and defeat is usually small. When everything else is equal, nutrition can make the difference between winning and losing."

Economos and associates published a review article in which they reviewed 22 research studies on the nutritional intake of athletes. Based on their review, they recommend an energy intake of greater than 50 kcal/kg/d for male athletes who train for more than 90 min/d and 45 to 50 kcal/kg/d for female athletes who train for more than 90 min/d.

They also recommend that athletes who consume low-energy diets focus on adequate intakes of iron, calcium, magnesium, zinc, and vitamin B_{12}. "There is no special food that will help elite athletes perform better; the most important aspect of the diet of elite athletes is that it follows the basic guidelines for healthy eating". Athletes should work with a registered dietitian with expertise in sports nutrition to establish his or her nutritional and performance goals—goals that will lead to consistent eating and training, leading to improved performance. With respect to micro-nutrients, it seems that if energy intake is sufficient, balanced, and varied, and nutritional status is within normal limits, vitamin-mineral supplementation is not warranted. Supplementation may be warranted for athletes who restrict energy intake, participate in sports with weight restrictions, or limit certain foods and food groups.

SUMMARY

The micronutrient intake and status of athletes has been assessed in numerous researcher studies; however, limitations exist in many of these studies, owing to the cross-sectional nature of the study design. From the published data, however, it seems that athletes who consume adequate energy and micronutrients would not benefit from supplementation. Longitudinal research is required (including supplementation studies) to follow athletes over time and evaluate dietary intake, nutritional status, and effects of performance properly.

8

Determination of Energy Needs

Many of the world's nutrition problems relate to a failure to match energy intake to energy requirements. In many countries, chronic undernutrition is a leading cause of mortality, especially in infants and children. In most industrialized countries, however, excess dietary energy is the major problem, with obesity and its sequelae being a major cause of morbidity and mortality. Most adults succeed in maintaining their body weight within fairly narrow limits, indicating that the match between energy intake and energy expenditure is quite close. These control mechanisms are not perfect, however, and it has been estimated that the body fat content of the average male doubles between the ages of 20 and 50 years, and that of women typically increases by 50%.

Training and competing in sport involve a range of activities of varying energy demands. Athletes face a spectrum of challenges in meeting their individual energy demandsaranging from difficulties in achieving sufficiently high energy intakes to meet very high energy needs, to the need to restrict energy intake to achieve and maintain a low weight (body mass) and body fat level. This chapter will overview the factors that determine the energy needs of athletes and recreationally active people, and will comment on the energy intakes reported by athletes in a variety of sports.

The food that we eat provides the fuels and building materials for life, supplying both the structural elements of the body and the means of sustaining the body's energy-requiring processes. Energy is needed for all biosynthetic pathways and for maintaining the internal environment of the body. After the body's basal needs have been met, additional energy is needed to fuel muscular activity, whether this is carried out for occupational, recreational, or sporting purposes. The individual components considered to make up total energy requirements of an individual include:

- Basal or resting metabolic rate (the energy required to maintain body systems). This should be measured in a thermoneutral environment.
- Thermic effect of food (the increase in energy expenditure following the intake of food that is associated with the digestion, absorption, and metabolism of food and nutrients).
- The thermic effect of activity, including the energy cost of spontaneous movements as well as planned muscular activities such as exercise.
- The cost of growth.

The primary factors that determine the energy requirement of athletes in training are body size and the training load. The importance of body mass is often underestimated, but the active tissue mass influences the basal metabolic cost of living as well as the energy cost of exercise. Total energy expenditure can be expected to vary between athletes who range in size from the female gymnast or marathon runner at less than 40 kg to the heavyweight weightlifter at 120 kg and the sumo wrestler in excess of 200 kg. The total training load will increase energy requirements above those of normal daily living and in some individuals may be as high as 50% of total daily energy expenditure. The three important components of any training program*a*intensity, duration, and frequency*a*will all influence total energy expenditure.

Energy costs of exercise

In the simple locomotor sports that involve walking, running, or cycling, the energy cost of activity is readily determined and can be shown to be a function of speed. Whether body mass is supported by the muscles as in running, or the athlete is seated as in rowing or cycling, or where it must be moved against gravity as in cycling uphill, then this too is an important factor in determining the energy cost. For walking, running, and cycling at low speeds, there is a linear relationship between velocity and energy cost, if the energy cost is expressed relative to body weight. At higher speeds, the relationship becomes curvilinear and the energy cost increases disproportionately. In cycling a large part of this is due to the need to overcome air resistance, which increases as the square of velocity. The effect of air resistance becomes significant at the speeds involved in cycling, and explains the attention paid by elite cyclists to methods of reducing it. Bicycle design, cycling position, and clothing all affect the aerodynamics and hence the energy cost.

At the speeds involved in walking and running through still air, air resistance is not a significant factor, but the relationship is nonetheless curvilinear. The reason for this seems to be a reduced mechanical efficiency as velocity increases. At very low speeds, the energy cost of walking is less than that of jogging, because of the smaller vertical displacements of the centre of mass; as velocity increases, however, the cost of walking increases faster than that of running, and at speeds in excess of about 6-7 km $\cdot h^{-1}$, running is less energetically demanding than jogging. As a rough approximation, the energy cost of walking or jogging is about 1 kilocalorie per kilogram of body mass per kilometer of distance covered. There are, however, large differences between individuals in the energy cost of even simple activities such as running, and these differences in the efficiency of movement may translate into substantial differences in energy demand.

It is often recommended that 20-30 min of moderate intensity exercise three times per week is sufficient exercise to confer some protection against cardiovascular disease: if this exercise is in the form of jogging, the energy expenditure will be about 4 MJ (1000 kcal) per week for the average 70-kg individual. The energy cost of running a marathon is equivalent to only about 12 MJ (3000 kcal). However, even a small daily contribution from exercise to total daily energy expenditure will have a cumulative effect on a long-term basis. For obese individuals, whose exercise capacity is low, the role of physical activity in raising energy expenditure is necessarily limited, but this effect is offset to some degree by the increased energy cost of weight-bearing activity.

There have been several attempts to identify the factors that might account for the differences in running economy which exist among runners. When elite and non-elite runners are compared, there is generally a slightly shorter stride length and correspondingly higher stride frequency in the elite runners when running at the same speed. Some studies have shown that the extent of vertical oscillation of the centre of gravity does not vary between runners of different levels of ability, but other studies have found differences. It seems unlikely that any single variable can account for differences in running economy, but rather that many different factors each make a small contribution to the observed differences that exist between individuals.

In most sports, the pattern of energy is variable, and is therefore even more difficult to quantify: in field games such as soccer, play consists of sprints, periods of jogging at submaximal speed, walking, and resting. The overall energy cost depends on many factors, including the total distance covered. It must also always be remembered that the fitter the individual, the higher the overall rate of energy expenditure. Estimates made from match analysis suggest that most top-class soccer players cover a total of about 8-12 km during a game.

The distance may vary between the two halves, and also depends on the level of play and the position of the individual in the team. The daily energy expenditure during typical training of English professional players has been estimated to be approximately 6.1 MJ (1500 kcal). The only technique that might be expected to give a reliable estimate of energy expenditure in a situation such as this is the doubly labeled water method, but this has not yet been applied to the wide range of team sports.

Tables of the energy cost of a wide range of different sports activities are available, but these have to be considered as crude approximations at best. The body mass and fitness level of the performer will have major influences on the energy cost of training, and even when these factors are similar, there may be differences in the mechanical efficiency, as well as in the energy expenditure during other daily activities. Because of this, applying mean values may not be helpful when providing advice for an individual.

Evidence suggests that the metabolic rate may remain elevated for at least 12 and possibly up to 24 h after very prolonged intense exercise. The athlete training at near to the maximum sustainable level, who already has a very high energy demand, will find this increased further by the elevation of postexercise metabolic rate, and this will increase the difficulties that many of these athletes have in meeting their energy demand. It seems unlikely, however, that metabolic rate remains elevated for long periods after more moderate exercise. The recreational exerciser, for whom the primary stimulus to exercise is often control of body weight or reduction of body fat content, will not therefore benefit to any measurable extent from this effect.

Energy costs of growth or changing body mass

The requirement for growth is an important factor in the energy needs of young athletes who have not reached full maturity. In these cases, energy intake must exceed expenditure if growth is to take place. Some athletes, mostly in events where a high power output is an important part of successful performance, will also benefit from an increased body mass, and an increase in muscle mass rather than in fat mass is usually desired. In some events, such as the heaviest weight categories in weightlifting and in the combat sports, and in the throwing events in track and field, a high absolute mass may be important, and a high body fat content is often seen in the most successful competitors. If the body mass is to increase, there must be an excess of energy intake over expenditure, The reverse situation, a need to reduce body mass and especially to reduce the body fat content, is also frequently encountered. There are particular problems in reducing the energy take to a level that will result in a loss of body mass without compromising the ability to sustain the training load. In seasonal sports such as soccer or rugby, a substantial gain in body fat is not unusual in the off season, and the preseason training for these athletes often involves a combination of sudden increases in the training load in combination with a restriction of energy intake.

Determining individual requirements for energy

As with the general population, there is likely to be a large variability in energy requirements between athletes, even when body mass and training loads are similar. The reasons for this remain obscure.

Each athlete must identify their own energy requirement and their own ideal body mass and body fat content. An adequate energy intake is achieved when body weight and body fat content are maintained at a level that is appropriate for the sport and healthy for the athlete. In a small number of sports situations, there appears to be a conflict between the demands of performance at elite level and a body composition level that is optimal for health. Examples of such sports are primarily those where performance is based on subjective aesthetic assessment, including women's gymnastics and ice dancing, but also include long-distance running. Additional needs for growth and development must be added to the cost of daily activity where young athletes are involved, and an increase in body mass, and in body fat content, is a normal part of the maturation process.

The energy requirements of an individual can be determined by a number of methods, each of which has some advantages and disadvantages. The most common laboratory-based method is indirect calor-imetry, in which energy expenditure is calculated from the rates of oxygen consumption and production of carbon dioxide. Of course this requires equipment such as a Douglas bag, ventilation hood, or metabolic chamber in which expired air samples can be accurately collected and analysed. Disadvantages of this technique include expense and the need for specialized equipment and trained personnel. Most importantly, the technique usually interferes with the performance of normal daily living and exercise activities, meaning that it measures an artificial situation of daily energy expenditure. On the other hand, it can be used to measure the individual components of energy expenditure *a*for example resting metabolic rate, the thermic response to a meal, and the energy cost of various exercise activities.

More recently, the doubly labeled water (DLW) technique has been developed and validated to estimate energy expenditure. In this technique, the subject ingests a sample of water that has been labeled with stable (non-radioactive) isotopes of both hydrogen and oxygen ($^2H_2{}^{18}O$). Energy expenditure can be calculated via the periodic monitoring of the concentration of these isotopes in body fluids to compare the different rates of disappearance of these isotopes (see Expert Comment 1).

This technique has no effect on the daily activities of the subject and measures the total energy expenditure, so it is particularly useful for monitoring energy expenditure in the field over a period of days or weeks. Nevertheless, the cost and availability of the DLW sample and analyses restrict the use of this method to the realms of research. Indirect calorimetry and DLW estimates are rarely used in the management of individual athletes, except perhaps where they are used to investigate the case of an athlete who has an apparent disturbance of energy balance.

The most accessible and practical way to assess the energy requirements of the athlete is to use prediction equations based on assessments of resting metabolic rate and the energy cost of daily activities. Several equations are available to predict resting metabolic rate from factors such as age, height, weight, or lean body mass. Once resting metabolic rate is estimated, it must then be multiplied by various activity factors to determine the total daily energy expenditure. At the simplest level, an overall activity factor is applied to the whole day to represent the athlete's typical exercise level. At the most complex level, an athlete might complete an intricate activity diary, with the energy cost of each activity undertaken over the day being separately added to calculate the final prediction of total energy expenditure. In most cases the factorial information used to predict the cost of activities is generically derived. However in some research projects or cases of individual therapy, measurements may be made of the exact energy cost of an individual's exercise activities for example, the cost of their typical training and competition activities. While this protocol can provide a general estimation of an athlete's energy requirements, the possibility for substantial error should be taken into account.

Even if athletes do not have access to facilities for estimation of their energy requirements, they should be able to identify when they are in energy balance by monitoring long-term changes in body mass as part of their training diary. The athlete should be weighed at the same time of day, and under the same conditions many athletes use their early morning weight, taken just after waking and going to the toilet but before breakfast, as their true body weight. Small fluctuations from day to day should be ignored, and hydration status should also be taken into account as a cause of variations in body weight. However, trends in weight change over a week or more, whether upwards or downwards, indicate an imbalance between energy intake and expenditure. Assessment of body composition, and more specifically of body fat content, requires more sophisticated procedures.

Energy intake of athletes

If body weight and performance levels are to be maintained during periods of intense training, the high rate of energy expenditure must be matched by an equally high energy intake.

Available data for most athletes suggest that they are in energy balance within the limits of the techniques used for measuring intake and expenditure. This is to be expected, as a chronic deficit in energy intake would lead to a progressive loss of body mass. Because they often fall at or beyond the extremes of the normal range, the dietary habits of athletes in different sports have been extensively studied.

Extreme endurance activities that involve very high levels of energy expenditure on a daily basis are now rarely encountered in occupational tasks. The average daily metabolic rate of lumberjacks was estimated in the 1930s to be about 4 times the basal metabolic rate, and similar values have been reported elsewhere, suggesting that this may be close to the upper limit of physical exercise that can be sustained on a long-term basis. In the short term, sporting activities can involve much higher levels of energy output: the world record for distance run in 24 h is 286 km, which requires an energy expenditure of about 80 MJ (20 000 kcal). Such an effort, however, results in considerable depletion of the body's energy reserves, and must be followed by a period of recovery.

Very high levels of daily energy expenditure are more often a feature of training than of competition, but there are some competitive events that require high levels of activity to be sustained for many consecutive days. One of the most obvious examples is the multistage cycle tour, of which the most famous is the Tour de France. Measurements on some of the competitors have shown that the successful riders manage to maintain body weight in spite of a mean daily energy expenditure of 32 MJ (8000 kcal) sustained over a 3-week period. Those cyclists who are unable to meet the daily energy requirement are unable to complete the race. In multiday running events, it appears that intake and expenditure may be less well balanced, although individual case histories of successful runners undertaking non-stop races have reported intakes of 25-50 MJ (6000-12 500 kcal) per 24-h period over periods of 5-9 days. There is a tendency in these races for performance to deteriorate over time, and this may be in part due to the growing energy deficit.

Of course, most athletes spend more time in the training phase then they do in competition, and in many cases, the energy requirements of the one or more sessions of daily training are greater than the energy cost of the event. These are divided into sports involving a strong endurance base and lengthy training sessions (e.g. distance running, cycling, triathlon, rowing, and swimming) as well as sports with a greater emphasis on skill, speed, and power (e.g. team sports, gymnastics, track and field athletics, lifting sports). It is difficult to make direct comparisons of the results of different studies since they are usually conducted on athletes of different levels of ability from different countries, as well as being influenced by the technique used to collect the dietary survey results. Nonetheless, it is interesting to see how the components of daily energy expenditure predict the typical energy intakes reported in different types of sport. For example, higher energy intakes are typically reported by endurance athletes than non-endurance athletes due to the substantial energy demands of prolonged sessions of moderate-to high-intensity training. On the other hand, athletes with large body mass, particularly due to high levels of lean body mass or muscle mass (e.g. body builders and throwers) reported higher energy intakes than athletes of small stature (e.g. gymnasts).

It should be remembered that dietary surveys cannot present the *actual* and *usual* energy intakes of athletes. Rather they present the results of what athletes *report* eating during a *particular* period of time. Experts in dietary survey methodology are keenly aware that such studies rely on the athlete accurately reporting what they consumed, and on the study period being a true representation of their usual eating patterns. Errors occur because athletes eat differently during the period of the dietary survey, or because they fail to be accurate and truthful about everything they eat and drink. In general, dietary surveys underestimate the true intakes of most people, because subjects undereat or under-report their usual intake while they are being studied.

The female athlete

There has been much interest recently in the eating patterns of female athletes. Across the board, female athletes tend to report a lower energy intake than male athletes involved in the same sporting activities, even when differences in body mass and lean body mass are taken into account. For example, when the reported energy intakes of the groups of athletes presented in Figs 1.2-1.5 are presented per kilogram of body mass, the typical female athlete reported a daily energy intake of 172 kJ $\cdot$kg^{-1} for endurance sports and 125 kJ $\cdot$kg^{-1} for non-endurance sports. By contrast, male athletes typically reported daily energy intakes of 227 kJ $\cdot$kg^{-1} (endurance) and 183 kJ $\cdot$kg^{-1} (non-endurance). Even allowing for differences in the range of athletes studied. The modern female athlete trains at a similar volume and intensity to that of her male counterpart. None the less, some studies have found that female athletes report energy intakes that seem barely able to cover the energy cost of their training, let alone basal metabolic needs, or intakes that are similar to the reported energy consumption of sedentary controls. These reports are more understandable in the case of "aesthetic sports" where a low body fat level must be achieved primarily by energy restriction rather than energy expenditure. However, it is also prevalent in the case of female endurance athletes such as distance runners where low energy intakes are an anomaly in view of the considerable training requirement.

There is no obvious physiological explanation for this finding. There are, of course, many possible sources of methodological errors in the calculation of energy intake and expenditure, but it seems odd that these should apply specifically to female athletes in sports where low body mass is important. It is tempting to try to explain low energy intakes in terms of metabolic adaptations leading to a lower resting metabolic rate or a reduced energy cost of activity in these athletes. This is a common excuse or frustration claimed by the many female athletes who feel that they can't lose weight/body fat despite "hardly eating anything". In fact, if metabolic "efficiency" does occur, it is found in individuals and isolated situations rather than the widespread situations in which it is claimed. Several studies have convincingly shown that there are no aberrations in the energy requirements of groups of female athletes. The use of the doubly labeled water method for the assessment of energy expenditure has been particularly useful in addressing this issue. Studies using this technique to investigate energy balance in female athletes have shown that energy expenditure is generally greater than reported energy intake, even though body weight is maintained, suggesting an under-reporting of energy intake.

If under-reporting is the major contributor to energy discrepancies, the true energy intakes of female athletes will be higher than estimated from the present overview of dietary surveys.

However, it is also likely that some level of energy restriction occurs either chronically or periodically in these athletes compared to true energy requirements, due to activities related to body fat loss. This pattern will vary between individual female athletes or over time in the same athletes. There is considerable evidence that restrained eating practices or low energy availability may be involved in the development of the menstrual dysfunction that is common among female distance runners, gymnasts, and other athletes who are preoccupied by weight and body fat issues.

Practical considerations for achieving energy intake

Most people manage to balance energy intake and energy needs over the long term, but situations of extreme energy requirement are harder to manage. Athletes in endurance sports often find it difficult to achieve the very high energy intakes necessary to sustain hard training on a daily basis, and may need advice on dietary strategies to achieve this. This becomes particularly important for the athlete who has to work or study in addition to training, and whose opportunities for eating are therefore limited. The athlete who trains two or even three times per day also has particular problems. Most athletes do not like to eat for some hours before training, and the appetite is likely to be suppressed for some hours after a hard session. By contrast, other athletes need to restrict energy intake to reduce or maintain body weight and body fat levels. This can be difficult to achieve in the face of hunger, customary eating patterns, or the eating habits of peers. These athletes may also need to address their requirements for other nutrients within a reduced energy allowance.

Practical considerations for manipulating energy intake to achieve high or low energy goals are demonstrated in the case histories provided in this chapter.

9

Fuels Used in Exercise: Carbohydrate and Fat

INTRODUCTION

All exercise imposes an increased energy demand on the muscles. If the muscles are unable to meet that demand, the exercise task cannot be performed. When the exercise intensity is high or the duration is prolonged, there may be difficulty in supplying energy at the required rate, and fatigue ensues. For simple activities such as running or swimming, the rate at which energy is required is a function of speed, and the time for which a given speed can be maintained before the fatigue process intervenes is inversely related to speed. In most sports situations, however, the exercise intensity, and hence the energy demand, is not constant. For example, games such as soccer or tennis involve brief periods of high-intensity effort interspersed with variable periods of rest or low-intensity exercise. Even in sports such as running or cycling, the energy demand will vary with changes in pace or in other factors such as wind resistance or the topography of the course. Muscles have adapted, and can be trained, to meet the varying demands as far as possible. Given the wide range of the requirements placed on muscle it is not surprising that several different strategies are employed to meet these demands.

Energy is required by muscle cells to perform work and can only be used in the form of adenosine triphosphate (ATP). All the energy-requiring processes in muscle are powered by the energy released when ATP is converted to adenosine diphosphate (ADP) with the release of an inorganic phosphate group (PO_4^{2-}, Pi); this applies as much to the pumping processes that maintain the ionic gradients across muscle membranes as to the contractile mechanisms that make the muscle "move".

Only a small amount of ATP is present within the muscle cells, amounting to about 5 mmol $\cdot kg^{-1}$. This is about 3.4 g, so with about 20 kg of skeletal muscle in the average healthy young man, this is about 70 g of ATP in total. Most activities, however, use only a fraction of the total muscle mass, so much less than this is available. The ATP content of the muscle is never allowed to fall by more than about a third, but even if it fell to zero the amount of energy available is very small and would only sustain about one second of exercise at maximum intensity. Because the content is so small and must be maintained, the ATP present in the muscle cannot be considered to be an energy store. Storage of ATP sufficient to support exercise of more than a few seconds' duration would impose an impossible weight burden. The muscle does have a second source of readily available energy in the form of creatine phosphate (CP), which is present within the muscle cell at a concentration about 3-4 times that of ATP. Although the muscle content of ATP is closely regulated, that of CP can fall to almost zero after a few seconds of maximum exercise. The resynthesis of ATP from ADP by transfer of a phosphate group from CP is catalysed by the enzyme creatine kinase in a reaction that is extremely rapid. These mechanisms can supply energy at a very high rate and can thus support a high power output, but their capacity is limited and they cannot sustain this level for long. For more prolonged exercise, an alternative fuel must be used.

Glycogen, consisting of very large branched polymers of glucose, is stored within the muscle cells, and glycogenolysis can supply relatively large amounts of energy to the muscles. Unlike the CP content of muscle which is small and, at least in the resting state, rather constant, the amount of energy available from the glycogen store is large and highly variable. Human skeletal muscle normally contains about 14-18 g $\cdot kg^{-1}$ of glycogen (80-100 mmol glu-cosyl units per kg wet weight of muscle), but the range can be much wider than this. If glycogenolysis proceeds only as far as lactate, the muscles can produce 4 mol of ATP for each mol of glucosyl units consumed. This series of reactions, which constitutes anerobic glycogenolysis, is rapid although the maximum rate of ATP production that can be achieved is less than can be supplied from CP. As the name indicates, it proceeds without the involvement of molecular oxygen. When rates of glycogenolysis are high, much of the lactate formed will leave the muscle and appear in the blood. If glycogenolysis is allowed to go to completion with the oxidation of the pyruvate through the tricar-boxlic acid cycle (TCA cycle) to carbon dioxide and water rather than to lactate, the amount of ATP formed is much greater, being 39 mol per mol glucosyl units. Although the amount of energy that can be liberated from the glycogen stores is thus increased, the rate at which it is available is much less.

Table: Maximum rates of ATP resynthesis (nmol min⁻¹ gram muscle⁻¹).

Creatine phosphate hydrolysis	440
Lactate formation	180
Carbohydrate oxidation	40
Fat oxidation	20

An alternative source of carbohydrate fuel available to the muscles is blood glucose, which is derived from the liver. The total amount of glycogen stored in the liver varies greatly: in the postabsorptive state, a range from 14 to 80 $g \cdot kg^{-1}$ has been reported. Assuming a liver weight of 1.8 kg, the mean value from these studies for the total liver glycogen content is about 80 g, which is much less than the amount of glycogen stored in the muscles (about 300-400 g). Although short-term fasting has little effect on the muscle glycogen content if no exercise is performed, a 12-h fast can cause the liver glycogen to fall by more than half. This reflects the important role of the liver in maintaining the blood glucose concentration and thus ensuring a constant supply of glucose to vital tissues, especially the brain. To do this, liver relies on the enzyme glucose 6-phosphate dehydrogenase, which releases free glucose that is then able to leave the cells. This enzyme is not present in muscle, so the sugar phosphates that are formed when glycogen is broken down are trapped within the cells. If glucose rather than glycogen is the starting point, one ATP molecule is needed to convert the glucose to glucose 6-phosphate, so the net gain in energy to the cell is three molecules of ATP for each molecule of glucose broken down rather than the four when glycogen is the starting point. This, together with the limitation on the rate at which glucose can enter the muscle cells, makes glycogen a more suitable fuel when the energy demands are high. Manipulation of diet and exercise patterns can cause the glycogen content of both liver and muscle to vary widely. In addition to its store of glycogen, the liver can release glucose produced by the process of gluconeogenesis in which glucose is synthesized from other substrates, including lactate and amino acids as well as glycerol derived from triglycerides. Although the process is relatively expensive in energy terms 12 molecules of ATP are required for each molecule of glucose produced gluconeogenesis can account for more than half of the glucose released by the liver in some situations, and may be particularly important in prolonged exercise when the liver glycogen store is depleted. The supply of gluconeogenic precursors is generally increased during exercise and in starvation, both situations where there may be a need for extra carbohydrate to be made available.

Not all of the lactate produced by active muscle fibers will be used by the liver for gluconeogenesis. Although muscle is often a net producer of lactate, it also has a high capacity for the oxidation of lactate. Heart muscle cells are exceptionally good at using lactate as a fuel for energy supply, but skeletal muscle, especially the Type I muscle fibers, can also do this. In many exercise situations, lactate produced by one muscle, which is working at a high percentage of its capacity, will be taken up and oxidized by another muscle. This may also happen within the same muscle: lactate released by one muscle fiber may be taken up and used as a fuel for oxidation by another fiber within the same muscle without ever reaching the bloodstream. This depends on the biochemical characteristics of the muscle fibers, which determine the relative capacities for lactate production and oxidation, and on the fiber recruitment patterns.

Muscle also has the capacity to obtain energy from the oxidation of fat in the form of free fatty acids derived from triglyceride: each triglyceride molecule can be broken down to release three molecules of fatty acids and one of glycerol. The body stores large amounts of triglycerides within the adipose tissue and, to a much smaller extent, within the muscle cells themselves. Again, the extent of these stores varies greatly between individuals, although, unlike the body's carbohydrate stores, they are not susceptible to large changes in the short term. Free fatty acids released from the adipose tissue are transported to the muscle in the plasma where they are bound to albumin. Within the muscle cells, the fatty acids are oxidized to carbon dioxide and water.

The rate at which energy can be produced by fat oxidation is, however, much less than can be achieved by oxidation of carbohydrate, and the amount of energy released per unit of oxygen consumed is less for fat (19.7 kJ·l O_2^{-1}) than for carbohydrate (21.4 kJ·l O_2^{-1}). Translated into marathon running terms, this difference may be highly significant. The 70-kg runner who completes the race in about 2[1]/2 h requires a power output of about 80 kJ·min^{-1} throughout the race. If carbohydrate (CHO) oxidation met the entire energy requirement, the oxygen consumption would be about 3.74 l·min^{-1} whereas an oxygen consumption of about 4.06 l·min^{-1} would be necessary if fat oxidation provided all the energy.

Assuming a maximum oxygen uptake of 5l·min^{-1}, CHO oxidation requires that the runner uses 75% of his maximum, compared with 81% if fat was the sole fuel. The main advantage of fat as a fuel is that it is an extremely efficient storage form, releasing approximately 37 kJ·g^{-1} compared with 16 kJ·g^{-1} for carbohydrate. Each gram of CHO stored also retains some additional water because of the osmotic effect it exerts, further decreasing the efficiency or "compactness" of CHO as an energy store. The energy cost of running a marathon is about 12 000 kJ; if this could be achieved by the oxidation of fat alone, the total amount of fat required would be about 320 g, whereas 750 g of CHO and additional associated water (perhaps as much as 2 kg) would be required if CHO oxidation were the sole source of energy. Apart from considerations of the weight to be carried, this amount of CHO exceeds the total amount normally stored in the liver and muscles. The total storage capacity for fat is extremely large, and for most practical purposes the amount of energy stored in the form of fat is far in excess of that required for any exercise task.

All of these fuels are used by muscle to produce energy during exercise, but the proportions in which they contribute to the total energy requirement will depend on a number of different factors including the intensity and duration of the exercise, nutritional status, and the physiological and biochemical characteristics of the individual.

PHYSIOLOGICAL FACTORS AFFECTING EXERCISE METABOLISM

The capacity to perform exercise and the metabolic response to exercise both vary greatly between individuals. Many factors contribute to these differences, which are particularly apparent in highly trained elite athletes. The key to successful sprinting is the ability to generate a high power output, and elite sprinters are characterized by a large muscle mass and a highly developed capacity for anaerobic energy production. The muscles of endurance athletes are not large, but have a high capacity for aerobic metabolism. These athletes also have a cardiovascular system that is extremely effective at delivering oxygen to the muscles. Measurement of the maximum oxygen uptake (^O$_{2max}$) shows that sprinters commonly achieve values that are little greater than those of untrained individuals, whereas the ^O$_{2max}$ of endurance athletes may be twice as great.

The physiological and biochemical response to an exercise task is largely determined by the fraction of the individual's ^O$_{2max}$ that the task represents. Running at a speed that requires 100% of V^{r}O$_{2max}$ for the sedentary individual may require less than 50% of ^O$_{2max}$ for the distance runner. Where technique is important, as for example in swimming or cross-country skiing, the differences between the elite competitor and the novice are even more marked. Whereas fatigue will occur within a few minutes of the onset of exercise at 100% of ^O$_{2max}$, exercise at 50% of ^O$_{2max}$ represents a fairly comfortable level of effort that can be continued for many hours.

The metabolic response to exercise is also influenced by the biochemical characteristics of the muscles performing the work. Although muscle is often considered to be a homogeneous tissue, skeletal muscle fibers may have very different biochemical and contractile properties. Type I muscle fibers are often referred to as slow-twitch or oxidative fibers, whereas Type II fibers are also classified as fast-twitch or glycolytic fibers (see Expert Comment 1). Although the classifications based on the speed of muscle shortening (twitch times) or on the enzyme activities may appear more useful, they may be misleading. Type II fibers all have a relatively high glycolytic capacity, but some, the Type IIa fibers, also have a high oxidative capacity, which may be even greater than that of the Type I fibers. The Type II fibers, which were formerly referred to as Type IIb fibers have a low oxidative capacity and a high glycolytic capacity. Type I fibers are well supplied with blood due to the large number of capillaries around each fiber, and have a high capacity to oxidize a range of substrates, including glycogen, blood glucose, lactate, and fat.

The individual muscle fibers are organized into motor units. All the fibers in a motor unit belong to the same fiber type, and the same nerve serves all fibers in the unit so that all are activated simultaneously. The recruitment pattern of the muscle fibers is determined by the effort required, and is organized such that the motor units consisting of Type I fibers are the first to be recruited. Only sufficient motor units to accomplish the required task are activated. In low-intensity exercise, this can be achieved by the activation of some of the Type I fibers with no involvement of Type II fibers, but if high forces are required, then the Type II fibers are recruited to help.

Thus the patterns of substrate metabolism that are observed during exercise can be largely explained in terms of the biochemical characteristics of the muscle fibers and their recruitment patterns. The biochemical characteristics of the muscle fibers can be modified by the patterns of use or disuse imposed upon them, but the speeds of contraction are relatively fixed. Endurance training has the effect of increasing the capacity of all of the muscle fiber types for oxidative metabolism, and may lead to the Type II fibers of the well-trained individual having a higher oxidative capacity than that of the Type I fibers of the sedentary individual.

Substrate utilization in high-intensity exercise

In the transition from rest to maximum exercise, the rate of energy turnover in the exercising muscles can increase by as much as 1000-fold. The supply of oxygen to the working muscles increases only rather slowly at the onset of exercise, and takes at least 1-2 min to reach its peak value. The maximum rate at which the aerobic system can supply energy exercise is also rather low relative to the rates of energy demand in high-intensity exercise. The duration of maximal-intensity activity is severely limited, however, as fatigue occurs rapidly. Studies on animal muscle in which the resynthesis of ATP is prevented have shown that the amount of work that can be performed is very small only about three normal twitch contractions are possible under these conditions.

However, the maximum activity of the enzyme creatine kinase, which transfers a phosphate group from creatine phosphate (CP) to ADP resulting in the resynthesis of ATP, is higher than that of ATPase which catalyses the breakdown of ATP to ADP. This ensures that the ATP content of the muscle is kept high as long as there is adequate CP available. Only when the CP content has fallen to less than half the resting value will a fall in the ATP level be apparent. When only a few muscle contractions are involved and the duration of the exercise is no more than 1-2 s, all of the energy required will be provided from these sources. In the postexercise period, the muscle CP and ATP content will return to normal within a few minutes, with the energy for their resynthesis being derived from oxidative metabolism.

When the duration of the exercise is increased to a few (5-10) seconds, significant falls in the muscle ATP and CP content are observed. Although it was thought at one time that no lactate would be produced in exercise lasting less than 10 s, sprinting over a distance of 40 m (in about 5 s) has been shown to cause a large increase in the lactate content of the quadriceps muscles. There was no change in the muscle ATP content in that study, even when the distance run at full speed was extended to 100 m.

Muscle CP content fell significantly after 40 m of sprinting, but did not fall further when the distance was extended, indicating that CP breakdown did not contribute to energy provision at this stage. In a maximal cycling task of 30 s duration, CP breakdown and lactate formation by glycolysis contribute about equally to the total energy requirement during the first 6 s of exercise. Only about 35% of the muscle CP content is used in the first 6 s of exercise, and a further substantial contribution is made over the next 24 s during which time the power output falls progressively. The muscle ATP content remains essentially unchanged after 6 s, but falls by almost half at the end of the 30-s period. Large amounts of muscle glycogen are used, with reductions of about 16% of the resting value after 6 s and 30% after 30 s. These findings suggest that major demands on the muscle glycogen store will be made in training sessions consisting of multiple short sprints.

The rate of energy provision by glycogenolysis is not normally limited by the availability of glycogen within the muscle. Even in maximum exercise, large amounts of glycogen remain within the muscle at the point of fatigue. If repeated sprints are performed, however, the glycogen content of the muscles will be reduced. In particular, the Type IIx muscle fibers, which have a high capacity for glycogenolysis, may lose most of their glycogen. If this happens, sprinting ability will be seriously impaired. It is important therefore to ensure that the muscle has an adequate glycogen store before exercise begins. Where high-intensity training or competitions occur on successive days, replacement of these stores by consumption of a diet rich in carbohydrate is essential to ensure optimum performance.

The need for a high CHO intake is well recognized among endurance athletes, but sprinters and games players often do not appreciate that the muscle glycogen stores may be substantially depleted in training as well as in competition and must be replaced.

It has long been known that the maximum speed which can be achieved by elite sprinters begins to decline towards the end of a 100-m race, and in maximal cycle ergometer tests the peak power output is observed within 1-3 s of the onset of exercise. The reasons for this now become apparent. In the initial acceleration phase, most of the energy is derived from CP breakdown, and after only a few seconds the CP content of the muscle has fallen to the point where the rate of resynthesis of ATP by this mechanism cannot be sustained. Almost immediately during the exercise, the rate of glycolysis is dramatically increased but the maximum rate of energy production is still less than can be achieved by transfer of phosphate groups from CP.

In most field games such as soccer, the pattern of activity consists of sprints lasting no more than a few seconds (typically 1-2 s) followed by recovery. During these high-intensity bursts, most of the energy will be supplied by CP, with glycolysis contributing more as the distance increases or if there has not been complete recovery from the previous sprint. The resynthesis of CP after exercise has been reported to be complete within a few minutes after work, but more recently it was shown that the CP content of muscle did not return to the pre-exercise level even 60 min after high-intensity exercise where exhaustion was reached after about 3 min. If a second sprint is performed before CP levels have been restored, the speed and duration may be reduced. Restoration of CP levels during recovery will not be delayed if low-intensity exercise is performed, even though this increases the total energy demand on the muscles.

As the exercise becomes more prolonged, the contribution of glycolysis to energy production is increased, leading to the accumulation of the end-product lactate in the muscle and blood. In exercise lasting from about 10 s to about 2-3 min anaerobic glycolysis will be the main source of energy. In longer events, oxidative metabolism gradually becomes more important. When the exercise duration exceeds about 2-3 min, aerobic processes supply more than half the total energy requirement. In the shorter events, most of the fuel used will be in the form of muscle glycogen, but glucose derived from the blood becomes more important as the duration increases.

At the pH that exists within muscle, the lactic acid that is formed by glycolysis is almost totally dissociated to form the negatively charged lactate anion and a proton (a positively charged hydrogen ion, H^+). Some of these protons are buffered within the muscle, and some leave the muscle, but if the exercise is sufficiently intense and prolonged the accumulation of protons will cause the intramuscular pH to fall. This may reduce the rate of energy production by glycolysis as a result of inhibition of phosphofructokinase (PFK), one of the key enzymes, although other changes in the muscle have the effect of stimulating PFK activity. It may also interfere more directly with the contractile process within the muscle. Whatever the mechanism involved, the end result is a subjective sensation of fatigue and an inability to continue exercising.

One of the most striking effects of endurance training is to increase the rate at which work can be performed before significant accumulation of lactate and protons occurs within the muscle and blood. A running speed which, in the untrained state, results in a high rate of anaerobic glycolysis with its associated lactate production, fall in muscle pH, and fatigue, can be accomplished with little or no anaerobic glycolysis in the trained state.

SUBSTRATE UTILIZATION IN PROLONGED EXERCISE

During prolonged exercise at constant intensity, the muscle relies almost entirely on oxidative metabolism for energy production. The exception to this is the first few minutes of exercise when anaerobic metabolism will make a contribution to energy production until a more or less steady state of oxygen consumption is attained. In the competitive situation, of course, the exercise intensity is rarely constant, and anaerobic metabolism may be required during prolonged races where there are tactical bursts during the event, where uphill stretches are encountered, and during a sprint finish. In many games, the total exercise duration is about 90 min; the oxygen uptake will normally be elevated throughout this period, but the immediate energy requirements of the many short bursts of activity will be met by anaerobic metabolism. Oxidative metabolism will provide energy for the resynthesis of ATP and CP and the removal of lactate during recovery periods.

The major fuels contributing to oxidative metabolism during prolonged exercise are fat and carbohydrate. It is often assumed that protein breakdown does not contribute to energy production during exercise, but, although there is disagreement as to the extent to which this occurs, some protein is oxidized during prolonged exercise. The use of protein as a fuel will be increased when other substrates, especially carbohydrate, are not available, but under normal conditions, protein oxidation probably accounts for not more than about 5% of the total energy requirement in exercise lasting up to 2-3 h. Although the body's protein content can be used as a source of substrate for oxidation, there is no significant store of protein. The loss of structural and functional proteins can only be tolerated to a limited extent without some impairment of health and performance.

The relative contributions of fat and CHO are determined largely by the intensity and duration of the exercise. The greater the exercise intensity, the greater is the reliance on CHO as a fuel. In low-intensity exercise, at less than 50% of ^O_{2max}, fat is the predominant fuel, accounting for more than half of the total energy production, with oxidation of blood glucose and muscle glycogen contributing about equally to the remainder. At about 60-65% of ^O_{2max}, the contributions of fat and CHO are roughly equal, and above this level of exercise CHO is the major fuel.

In moderate-intensity exercise corresponding to about 70-75% of ^O_{2max}, which can usually be sustained for 2-4 h and is approximately the intensity at which the faster marathon runners are working, muscle glycogen will be the major fuel. At higher exercise intensities, the rate of CHO utilization increases still further, and once the muscle begins to rely on anaerobic glycolysis to supplement the energy produced by oxidative metabolism, the rate of glycogen utilization increases sharply. Although the total amount of glycogen stored in all the body's muscrles is about 300-400 g, only a part of this will be available during exercise. Unlike the glycogen stored in liver, muscle glycogen cannot contribute directly to the blood glucose pool, as discussed above. As glucose units are split off from glycogen, a phosphate group is added to each glucose molecule and these phosphorylated sugars cannot cross the cell membranes. In liver, but not in muscle, a phosphatase enzyme releases free glucose, which can then leave the cell. The CHO stored in inactive muscle can be made available if it is released in the form of pyruvate, lactate, or alanine which can freely cross cell membranes and which can then be used by active muscle as a fuel or taken up by the liver for gluconeogenesis. This does not, however, happen to any great extent in resting muscle.

Even when the exercise intensity remains constant, the pattern of substrate utilization changes with time. As exercise progresses, the glycogen stores in the working muscle become depleted, and the muscle is forced to rely on other fuels to an increasing extent. Since the 1960s the muscle biopsy technique has been used to follow the changes in muscle glycogen occurring during exercise. The glycogen content of the quadriceps muscles falls progressively during exercise at 70% of ^O$_{2max}$, and the point of exhaustion coincides with the time when the muscle glycogen is almost completely depleted. This is certainly true of exercise carried out in cool or temperate conditions, but may not apply in warm weather when there seems to be plenty of glycogen left in the muscles at the point of fatigue. The decline in the muscle glycogen content is paralleled by its decreased contribution to energy provision.

The rate of energy production is maintained by a corresponding increase in the oxidation of free fatty acids, which are taken up from the plasma. As exercise progresses, the plasma free fatty acid concentration rises due to an increased rate of breakdown of triglyceride in the adipose tissue. This is a result of an increase in the circulating level of catecholamines (adrenaline and noradrenaline), which stimulate the process of lipolysis, and a decrease in the circulating level of insulin, which inhibits lipolysis. The rate at which muscle uses fatty acids is determined largely by their availability, so the increased plasma concentration has the effect of causing the muscle to use more fat. This increased rate of fat oxidation has the effect of reducing CHO oxidation by the muscle, so it seems to be the increased supply of fatty acids rather than the falling glycogen concentration which shifts the muscle's choice of fuel towards fat.

In prolonged cycling exercise at about 70% of $V^{r}O_{2max}$, fatigue is generally associated with the depletion of glycogen in the quadriceps muscles. Once this point is reached, the individual is unable to continue working at the same exercise intensity, although it is possible to continue if the work intensity is reduced. Fat oxidation, even though supplemented by the oxidation of glucose derived from the blood, is unable to support the desired rate of energy production. A good example is the marathon runner who "hits the wall": fat oxidation can supply enough energy for a walking pace, but running pace is not possible without a supply of carbohydrate.

In some situations, the output of glucose by the liver fails to keep pace with the rate of utilization by muscle, and the blood glucose concentration begins to fall. Although a low blood glucose level (hypo-glycemia, usually defined as a blood glucose concentration of less than 2.5 mmol $\cdot l^{-1}$) is not in itself usually the factor limiting exercise performance, it is essential that the supply of glucose to the brain is maintained.

The metabolic response to exercise is influenced by many factors, some of which have important implications for performance. The need for glyco-gen to be available as a fuel when exercise of moderately high intensity is performed means that the athlete engaged in endurance training must ensure an adequate dietary intake of CHO. The body does not have the metabolic capacity to convert its fat stores to CHO. If the muscle glycogen is not replaced between training sessions, the muscle will be forced to rely on fat as a fuel; although the muscle will adapt by increasing its capacity to oxidize fat, it will not be possible to sustain the training intensity and performance will deteriorate. In competition, where the role of CHO is even more crucial, increasing the muscle glycogen content by consumption of a high-CHO diet will increase endurance capacity. The need to ensure an adequate muscle glycogen store prior to competition is well recognized in some sports, such as marathon running, but many sportsmen pay little attention to this aspect of their preparation for competition.

SUMMARY

Muscle metabolism is fueled by a variety of substrates, according to the intensity and duration of exercise, and the characteristics of the athlete's preparation and environment. Limitations to exercise metabolism include inadequate supplies of substrates that can provide the muscle fiber with a sufficiently rapid supply of energy. In future chapters in this book, dietary strategies aimed at enhancing the availability of muscle substrates will be discussed. Although the major focus is on practices to enhance the availability of muscle CHO availability, other strategies include enhancement of the muscle creatine phosphate content or the muscle's ability to utilize the considerable stores of body fat. These strategies will form the key planks of an athlete's sports nutrition plan, and must be adapted to suit the specific physiological needs and practical opportunities of the athlete's training and competition schedule.

10

Protein and Amino Acid Requirements of Athletes

INTRODUCTION

Foods with a high protein content have long been seen as a natural part of the diet of athletes, and the idea that a high-protein diet will help the athlete prepare for competition is an attractive one. Our understanding of the role of protein in exercise has changed dramatically over the last few centuries, ranging from the belief that it was the major fuel for muscle contraction (encouraging the intake of large amounts of protein by athletes) to the belief that exercise does not change the body's need for protein (distracting scientists from being interested in protein). This chapter will consider the recent evidence for special requirements of protein and amino acids arising from high-level exercise as well as the ability of athletes to meet these demands from their typical eating patterns.

General overview of protein metabolism

Amino acids are a family of chemicals with a common structure that includes an amine ($-NH_2$) group and a carboxyl ($-COOH$) group. A total of 20 different amino acids are present in the body. A 70-kg athlete typically has a body pool of ~ 12 kg of amino acids, with the vast majority of this existing in the form of protein (amino acid polymers) and a small amount (about 200 g) existing as free amino acids. Over the day, there is a constant process of protein turnover, with protein breakdown and protein synthesis occurring simultaneously, and amino acids continuously exchanging between the various amino acid pools. Skeletal muscle accounts for the largest reservoir of body protein as well as a significant proportion of the free amino acid pool. All body proteins have structural roles (e.g. skin) or functional and regulatory roles (e.g. enzymes and hormones), and most serve both roles.

New amino acids can enter the free amino acid pool from three sources*a*from dietary intake, from the breakdown of body protein, and from new synthesis within the body. Some amino acids cannot be manufactured within the body and must be recycled from body protein or consumed as dietary sources. These are known as the essential amino acids.

On the other hand, amino acids leave the free amino acid pool via secretion into the gut, incorporation into new proteins, oxidation as a fuel source, or incorporation into body fat or carbohydrate stores. There is a huge amount of cycling between body pools and net changes can reflect a change in breakdown rates as well as a change in synthesis rates.

In general, however, there is a limited capacity to store new proteins, and protein intake in excess of requirements is deaminated, with the nitrogen being incorporated into urea and excreted primarily in the urine, and the carbon skeleton being oxidized or stored as fat or carbohydrate.

Table: Essential and non-essential amino acids: these essential amino acids cannot be synthesized and must be supplied in adequate amounts in the diet.

Essential	Non-essential
Isoleucine	Alanine
Leucine	Arginine
Lysine	Asparagine
Methionine	Aspartate
Phenylalanine	Cysteine
Threonine	Glutamate
Tryptophan	Glutamine
Valine	Glycine
	Histidine
	Proline
	Serine
	Tyrosine

Although the overall structure of the body is fairly stable, many of the component tissue proteins have a relatively short life span in the body. Most structural proteins and enzymes are synthesized and degraded at high rates, and as much as 20% of the basal rate of energy expenditure is the result of protein turnover. This process is obviously important in the repair of damaged tissue and in wound healing, but is also an ongoing process in healthy tissue.

The half-life of some proteins is extremely short less than 1 h for some enzymes in the liver. Changes in the amount of these enzymes is an important factor in the control of their activity, and a high rate of turnover is therefore essential if the tissue is to be responsive to changes in metabolic requirements. In the liver, a high rate of turnover of the enzymes that regulate fuel homeostasis allows regulation to occur rapidly in response to feeding and to short-term fasting. Some proteins are much more stable, with half-lives measured in days and weeks rather than hours. Skeletal muscle adapts to training and detraining with a time course that can be measured in days, giving some indication of the rate of turnover of the enzymes involved in the process of adaptation.

MEASURING PROTEIN TURNOVER

The classical way to measure net protein turnover is to monitor the balance between the nitrogen consumed (from dietary protein) and the nitrogen excreted (mostly in urine). A positive nitrogen status (intake is greater than excretion) signals that there is a net gain of body protein, while negative nitrogen status signals a net loss of body protein. A long-term negative status should be avoided since it means that the body is losing protein that would otherwise have a structural or functional role. Unlike the case for fat and carbohydrate, the body has little capacity to store protein simply as an energy reserve. Positive nitrogen status, representing a gain in body protein, occurs during growth and pregnancy, but is also desired by athletes who wish to increase their muscle mass to enhance their size and strength. Unfortunately, reliable measurements of nitrogen balance are difficult and expensive to achieve. There is generally an overestimation of nitrogen status because there is a trend to overestimate nitrogen intake (the true amount absorbed from food) and to fail to collect total nitrogen losses (in sloughed skin, sweat, feces, etc.). There are also some discrepancies in the calculation and assumptions of nitrogen balance, which are affected by energy balance, and appear to take time to equilibrate when there is a change to a very high or very low protein intake. Data from existing nitrogen balance studies therefore need to be examined with care.

Metabolic tracer techniques offer a newer way to monitor protein turnover. Here, individual amino acids are "labeled" and their uptake, oxidation, or incorporation into various amino acid/ protein pools can be tracked. The benefits of this new knowledge must also be balanced against problems such as expense, and some doubts as to the validity of various assumptions. For example, it may not be suitable to assume that the behavior of a single amino acid reflects the fate of all amino acids or total body protein pools. Nevertheless this technique has greatly added to our understanding of protein metabolism during and after exercise.

The effect of exercise on protein metabolism

Muscles consist largely of protein (although water is the largest component, accounting for about 75% of the total mass), and the functional properties of the muscles depend on their protein composition. It is also readily apparent that regular exercise has a number of highly specific effects on the body's protein metabolism. Strength training results in increases in muscle mass, indicating an increased formation of actin and myosin, and it is tempting to assume that this process is dependent on protein availability. Endurance training has little effect on muscle mass, but does increase the muscle content of mitochondrial proteins, especially those involved in oxidative metabolism. Hard exercise also results in an increased level of muscle damage, usually at the microscopic level, and there is clearly a role for protein in the repair and recovery processes.

The changes that comprise the adaptive response to exercise are selective, and are specific to the training stimulus. They are also dependent on the availability of an adequate intake of protein in the diet, but apparently cannot be accelerated by increasing protein intake above normal levels. Exercise also has a number of acute effects on protein metabolism, and the response to a hard bout of exercise represents a challenge to the muscle that is similar in many ways to the responses that follow infection or injury.

Effects of an acute bout of exercise on protein metabolism

Skeletal muscle has the capacity to metabolize a number of amino acids, particularly the branched-chain amino acids leucine, isoleucine, and valine. This includes the degradation of the branched-chain acids to form the chemical intermediates that take part in the tricarboxylic acid (TCA) cycle of oxidative metabolism. Although the majority of substrate used to fuel submaximal exercise comes from fat and carbohydrate stores, there is a small contribution from protein sources (3-6%) to the total energy cost of the exercise bout. This can be tracked directly by measuring the oxidation of a specific amino acid, typically leucine, or indirectly by measuring plasma urea concentrations. Such measurements typically show that the rate of leucine oxidation increases with the intensity and duration of exercise, and is greater in situations of glycogen depletion or low carbohydrate availability. Thus protein metabolism during bouts of prolonged endurance exercise is affected by the type of exercise and the dietary strategies used by the athlete. There are concerns, however, that the use of leucine as a tracer may not represent the overall rate of amino acid oxidation. The effects of protein ingestion following a bout of endurance exercise on protein synthesis has not been well studied, largely because of the limitations of the methodology. It appears that the response varies according to the intensity of the exercise, but may also vary according to the protein subfraction for example, the responses of the mitochondrial proteins may be different from those of muscle fiber proteins.

By contrast, resistance training does not appear to increase leucine oxidation, perhaps reflecting the fact that such high-intensity exercise is fueled by non-oxidative pathways using high-energy phosphate and glycogen sources. Studies using new techniques have been able to monitor fractional rates of muscle protein breakdown and synthesis in response to resistance training. During the hours following the bout of exercise, there is an increase in protein breakdown but also an increase in protein synthesis. If subjects exercise but remain fasted, the net effect is catabolic (breakdown is greater than synthesis), but less negative than with fasting alone. In other words, resistance training helps to enhance protein status or reduce the catabolic state achieved by fasting and rest. However, when subjects consume a source of protein containing essential amino acids (~ 7 g essential amino acids or

~ 20 g high-quality protein) and a substantial source of carbohydrate (~ 50-100 g), there is a net anabolic effect (synthesis exceeds breakdown). This interaction occurs when the protein-carbohydrate feeding occurs after exercise, but according to very recent research, it may be even more pronounced when the feeding occurs immediately before the resistance training bout. These new data show potentially exciting ideas for sports nutrition strategies, but it must be remembered that these studies deal with the microresponse to an acute bout of exercise. We have yet to find evidence that the immediate muscle protein response to exercise is extended beyond the first few hours or will lead to a significant improvement in muscle size and strength in the long term.

Chronic effects of exercise on protein metabolism – the effect of training

The outcome of a training program is the result of the cumulative effects of a series of workouts. The net effect of a resistance training program is an increase in muscle size and strength, resulting from the series of transient increases in muscle protein balance following each exercise session. After the first few months or years of such a program, however, there is usually little further change in muscle mass. Endurance exercise appears to stimulate increases in mitochondrial proteins, but again, there is little change in muscle mass, and there may even be a decrease in the total muscle protein content.

There is some evidence that repeated bouts of exercise cause an adaptation to the protein response to exercise. For example, studies show that experienced strength training athletes achieve nitrogen balance at lower protein intakes than novice trainers. Further studies are needed to confirm these findings and translate them into protein requirements for athletes. It is likely that protein requirements are elevated at the onset of a training program or after a sudden increase in training volume and intensity, but that this increase in requirement is transient.

RECOMMENDATIONS FOR PROTEIN INTAKES BY ATHLETES

The requirement for dietary protein is influenced in part by the type of protein that is consumed. The body has an absolute requirement for nitrogen in the form of the amino groups that make up part of the structure of amino acids, and these can be used in the manufacture of the non-essential amino acids. The essential amino acids, which cannot be synthesized by humans, must be obtained from the diet. Different proteins contain different proportions of the various amino acids, and each of the essential amino acids must be supplied in an amount that meets the needs. In general, foods from animal sources contain substantial amounts of all the essential amino acids, but foods from other sources do not generally contain these amino acids in the same proportions as are found in animal tissues. However, various foods from plant sources can combine with each other to "complement" the amino acid profile of the total meal. Vegetarian eaters need to plan menus to achieve such mixing and matching of foods, although it is now recognized that this can occur over a day rather than at the same meal.

The protein requirements of the general population have been the subject of extensive investigation, and it is now generally accepted that a daily requirement of about 0.6 g of protein per kilogram body mass per day will meet the needs of most of the adult population, provided that a variety of different protein sources make up the diet and that the energy intake of the diet is adequate to meet the energy expenditure. Protein requirements are increased during times of growth such as adolescence and pregnancy. Nutrition experts in various countries have interpreted these results into a range of recommended daily allowances or intakes, with some differences between countries due to differences in the way that the safety margin has added to the daily requirement.

It is now recognized that protein requirements are increased by exercise, but few countries have included special recommendations for the protein requirements of athletes in their dietary recommendations. The exception appears to be the Dutch Nutrition Board which has set a specific guideline that physically active individuals should achieve a protein intake of 1.5 $g \cdot kg^{-1} \cdot day^{-1}$*a*well above the intake recommended for the sedentary population. Despite the lack of official recommendations, experts in sports nutrition have interpreted the result of various nitrogen balance studies to produce some guidelines for protein intakes by various athletic groups. These are also included in Table 3.3. These guidelines represent a departure from the early views of sports scientists, but they fail to meet the enthusiasm of many resistance training athletes who feel that optimal gains in muscle mass and strength are achieved only with very large intakes of protein.

Is there a need for high-protein diets and protein supplements?

If athletes have increased requirements for protein compared to their sedentary counterparts, it is tempting to consider that high-protein diets and special protein supplements are needed. However, an athlete's energy intake provides the factor that underpins their success in meeting many of their nutrition goals. With a moderate to high energy budget, high protein intakes can be achieved even within the boundaries of the typical ratios of protein in Western eating patterns. The following examples illustrate this point.

From a diet containing 12-15% of energy from protein:

70-kg athlete (typical male) 12 MJ (3000 cal) = 90-112 g protein = 1.3-1.6 g $\cdot kg^{-1}$ 20 MJ (5000 cal) = 150-188 g protein = 2.1-2.7 g $\cdot kg^{-1}$ 60-kg athlete (typical female) 8 MJ (2000 cal) = 60-75 g protein = 1-1.3 g $\cdot kg^{-1}$ 12 MJ (3000 cal) = 90-112 g protein = 1.5-1.9 g $\cdot kg^{-1}$. Thus, even without focusing on protein-rich foods or expensive protein products, most athletes have the potential to meet their protein requirement. Special dietary advice and menu planning may be needed to help some athletes meet these needs within their overall sports nutrition goals. This will be especially important for athletes with restricted energy budgets, limited finances, or practical constraints on eating.

Recommendations about timing of protein intake

Recent attention has focused on the timing of protein intake in relation to training rather than on the amount required. In the recovery period, muscle glycogen synthesis is a priority, but synthesis of new proteins should perhaps be seen as being of equal or even greater importance. Because little attention has been paid to this area until recently, we do not yet know how dietary or other factors may be manipulated to influence these processes. The supply of essential amino acids and the hormonal environment are the two obvious factors that may be important. Nutritional status can influence the circulating concentration of a number of hormones that have anabolic properties, the most obvious and important example being insulin. The diet can also supply amino acids for incorporation into proteins. A fall in the intracellular amino acid concentration will restrict the rate of protein synthesis, and there is some evidence that the muscle amino acid concentration does fall after exercise. Ingestion of protein or amino acids immediately after exercise, and even before exercise, can promote muscle protein synthesis, but no long-term studies have yet been conducted to establish whether these effects result in an improved adaptation of the muscle to the training stimulus.

Protein intakes of athletes

There have been a large number of studies of protein intake in different athletic groups, using a variety of different methods of assessment. These studies have found a wide range of values for the habitual protein intakes reported by athletes within groups and between groups. The general finding is, as predicted from the examples above, that athletes typically ingest sufficient protein to meet their needs, provided that adequate energy and a variety of different foods is consumed.

Notwithstanding the differences between and within groups, there are some interesting trends in the protein intakes reported by athletes. Mean protein intakes of groups of male endurance and team athletes are generally ~ 90-150 g per day, providing 12-16% of energy intake and an intake of 1.2-2.0 $g \cdot kg^{-1} \cdot day^{-1}$. Groups of female endurance and team athletes generally report a lower mean intake of protein: ~ 60-90 g per day, representing 1.1-1.7 $g \cdot kg^{-1} \cdot day^{-1}$. Lower intakes of protein are generally due to lower energy intakes rather than a lower contribution of protein to total energy intake.

Protein intakes reported by strength training athletes are generally higher in absolute amounts, and in terms of the percentage contribution to energy intake*a*daily intakes of 150-250 g of protein, representing 14-20% of energy, are common. Sometimes, however, because of the large body size of these athletes, protein intakes expressed per kg body mass are similar to or even lower than those reported by endurance athletes. Very high values for protein intake are sometimes encountered, especially in body builders. Individual values as high as 4.0 $g \cdot kg^{-1} \cdot day^{-1}$ have been reported in the precom-petition period, providing 30-60% of total energy intake.

Concerns as to the adequacy of protein intake are generally found in athletes with low energy intakes. However, athletes who follow extreme dietary practices or restricted eating may also have a low protein intake. This is particularly the case with athletes who consume a diet extremely high in carbohydrate. Because of the common association between protein and fat in the diet, attempts to eliminate fat from the diet will often result in severe reductions in protein intake. Some distance runners habitually eat diets containing 85% carbohydrate: inadequacies of both essential fatty acids and the essential amino acids must be a real possibility in this situation. This is also the case for athletes with disordered eating practices who consume so-called vegetarian diets, which are really badly constructed diets in which animal protein is avoided but not replaced with suitable plant protein sources. Athletes whose diets are restricted in terms of energy, variety, or budget may need counseling in food choices to ensure that their protein requirements are met, but the use of high-protein supplements is seldom or never justified. Being a vegetarian or a vegan is in no way incompatible with success in sport, and many elite athletes, especially in endurance sports, eat a diet from which animal products are largely or even completely absent.

The recognition that the protein requirements of youngsters are higher, on a body mass basis, than those of adults, raises some special concerns as to the adequacy of dietary protein intake in the adolescent athlete. Published studies suggest that most young athletes achieve a dietary protein intake of about 1.6 $g \cdot kg^{-1} \cdot day^{-1}$, and that even in those sports where energy intake is commonly restricted there is no good evidence of an inadequate intake. It is equally clear, however, that there is a limited amount of information available on the protein requirements of the growing athlete who is engaged in intensive training: it is possible that there are substantial increases in the requirement during periods of rapid growth, as during the adolescent growth spurt. Special attention must be paid to the dietary intake of athletes who are training hard at this time, especially in sports where restriction of energy intake is commonly practiced to reduce or restrict body fat mass (e.g. gymnastics). Where energy, and especially carbohydrate, intake is inadequate, protein oxidation by the exercising muscles is increased, so the adequacy of protein intake cannot be considered independently of the overall diet.

Are very high protein intakes harmful?

Excess protein in the diet is not beneficial, but neither is it normally harmful as the excess amino acids will be used as an energy source and the nitrogen and sulphur content excreted. Although many people are concerned about possible harmful effects of the excess nitrogen on the kidneys, there is no evidence of any harmful effects in normal individuals even when extremely high intakes are sustained over prolonged periods. Anyone with a history of liver problems or impaired renal function, however, should be advised to take care to ensure that the handling capacity of these tissues is not exceeded. Possibly the most common problem associated with high protein intakes is the unnecessary expense. Since protein-rich foods, particularly from animal sources, are often among the most costly items in a shopping basket, athletes may be spending their sometimes limited resources on unnecessary food choices. Of particular concern is the expense of protein supplements including products supplying individual amino acids. While some sports foods or supplements may be useful to meet sports nutrition goals when everyday foods are impractical to consume, there is rarely a need to supply protein sources alone.

11

Micronutrients: Vitamins and Minerals

INTRODUCTION

For normal health to be maintained, a wide range of vitamins, minerals, and trace elements must be present in adequate amounts in the body tissues, and the dietary intake must be sufficient to meet the requirement for these micronutrients. Many vitamins and minerals play key roles in energy metabolism or the production of body tissues, and the adverse effect of deficiencies of these components is well recognized and easily demonstrated. Marginal deficiency states may have little effect on the sedentary individual for whom performance is not critical, but small impairments of exercise capacity may have profound consequences for the serious athlete. Regular intense exercise training may also increase micronutrient requirements, either by increasing rates of utilization or by increasing losses from the body. Consequently, athletes are greatly interested in answers to the following questions.

1 To what extent are requirements for micronutrients increased by regular exercise? Should there be special guidelines for intakes of micronutrients by athletes?

2 How should optimal status with regard to micronutrients be measured in athletes? Do athletes have poorer micronutrient status than non-athletes?

3 Do micronutrient intakes above the recommended daily intakes further enhance exercise performance?

This chapter will explore the roles of micronutrients in the health and performance of the athlete, with the focus on situations in which there is a risk of inadequate intake, and the evidence for benefits arising from intakes above recommended daily intakes.

VITAMINS

Biological functions of vitamins

Vitamins are organic compounds that are needed by the body in small amounts to enable key reactions of daily living to occur. Since these compounds cannot be manufactured by the body, they must be provided by dietary sources. Many vitamins, particularly from the B group, act as cofactors for reactions involved in energy metabolism for example, glycolysis, the tricarboxylic acid cycle, the beta-oxidation of fatty acids, and oxidative phosphorylation. Vitamin C activates an enzyme regulating the synthesis of carnitine, which transports fatty acids into the mitochondria for oxidation. Other B vitamins act as cofactors for the synthesis of heme, which is involved in oxygen transport in blood and muscles.

A severe deficiency of these vitamins will interfere with the activity of these enzymes, and therefore reduce body function and health. Indeed, most of the vitamins were first recognized because of the deficiency syndromes that result when they are not present in the diet in adequate amounts. Marginal deficiency states may have a small impact on function, which is barely noticed by sedentary individuals, but of critical importance for high-performance athletes for whom success is decided by fractions of seconds and meters. Various depletion studies have shown that inadequate vitamin status is associated with impaired capacity for exercise, especially when there is a compromised status of more than one micronutrient. With this knowledge, it is intuitively attractive to believe that supplying additional amounts of these vitamins may be beneficial in "supercharging" energy turnover or other key functions in exercise metabolism.

Dietary intakes and vitamin status of athletes

Although an increased rate of flux through the various pathways involved in exercise metabolism may increase the utilization of some vitamins, studies have not been conducted to define with any degree of accuracy the vitamin requirements of highly active people. Indeed, the setting of recommended dietary intakes and allowances involves the addition of a "safety" margin for individuals with higher requirements, which could be expected to cover the needs of athletes. Of course, these deliberations could be rendered moot by the potential of the dietary patterns of athletes to provide generous amounts of vitamins and other micro-nutrients. With regular strenuous training, there must be an increased total food intake to balance the increased energy expenditure: without this, hard training cannot be sustained for long. Provided that a reasonably varied diet is consumed, a high-energy diet can be expected to provide vitamins in amounts well in excess of these recommended intakes. Even taking into the account the inaccuracies of dietary survey techniques, studies of athletes from a variety of sports typically report intakes of vitamins from food sources alone that easily meet the recommended daily intakes or allowances.

It is difficult to precisely determine the vitamin status of an individual. A diagnosis of vitamin deficiency is best made from a variety of sources of information, including an assessment of dietary intake, some biochemical or hematological measurements, and clinical signs and symptoms. Individually, each of these parameters must be judged cautiously in making a judgement of vitamin status. However, together they help to build a reasonable picture of an adequate or inadequate status. Most studies using biochemical measures of vitamin status do not reveal differences between the results of athletes and sedentary controls. This suggests that athletic training, *per se*, does not increase the risk of micronutrient deficiency, or at least does not increase the requirement disproportionately in relation to the effect on energy intake. However, these data need to be interpreted with care because of the insensit-ivity of most indices to states of marginal inadequacy. In other words, these results do not entirely exclude minor but functionally important differences between athletes and controls, or the possibility that an inadequate status may be present in some individuals in the group. Nevertheless, the available information suggests that frank vitamin deficiencies are rare among athletes, just as they are among the general population.

Athletes may put themselves at risk of inadequate vitamin intake by either restricting intake of energy, or failing to include a variety of nutrient-rich foods in their eating patterns. Energy restriction is common among athletes who are concerned about body weight and body fat levels. Many athletes follow weight-loss programs, fad diets and disordered eating practices for prolonged periods in an attempt to reach a perceived ideal body size and physique. Poor practical nutrition skills, inadequate finances, and an overcommitted lifestyle that limits access to food and causes erratic meal schedules may also restrict dietary variety. The best management is to educate the athlete with regard to the quality and quantity of their food intake. However, a low-dose, broad-range multivitamin/ mineral supplement may be useful when the athlete is unwilling or unable to make dietary changes, or when the athlete is traveling to places with an uncertain food supply and eating schedule.

EVIDENCE THAT VITAMIN SUPPLEMENTATION ENHANCES PERFORMANCE

Athletes often see dietary supplements as a form of "insurance policy". Even when there is no evidence that a deficiency may exist or that intakes above the normal level may be beneficial, they feel they should take vitamin supplements "just in case". This practice is generally harmless, except perhaps in the financial sense, but there are some concerns over the possible harmful effects of excessive intakes of the fat-soluble vitamins (A, D, E, and K) over long periods. The water-soluble vitamins are simply excreted if consumed in amounts in excess of the requirement, but the fat-soluble vitamins can accumulate in the body tissues and may reach toxic levels.

Whether supplementation with vitamins enhances athletic performance and recovery has been the subject of a number of studies. However, these studies have failed to find any sound evidence that vitamin supplementation provides a benefit to the performance of sport or exercise activities, except in cases where it was used to correct a pre-existing deficiency. Early studies that showed beneficial effects of supplementation on performance were usually poorly designed, often with no proper control group against which to compare the effects of supplementation. These studies should be regarded as a testament to the power of the placebo effect rather than evidence of the beneficial effects of supplementation.

Vitamins of special interest to athletes: antioxidant vitamins

Athletes engaged in very hard physical training and sedentary individuals participating in unaccustomed exercise show signs of muscle damage in the postexercise period, and there is evidence of free radical-induced damage to muscle membranes and subcellular structures. There is some evidence for an adaptive increase in antioxidant status in response to regular exercise, and this may help protect against further damage. Supplementation of the diet with antioxidant nutrients (particularly vitamins C and E) has been proposed as a possible way of further reducing the harmful effects of exercise. Some studies suggest that the severity of muscle damage as assessed by circulating levels of muscle-specific proteins that have leaked out into the blood can be reduced by supplementation with large doses of anti-oxidant vitamins but the evidence is not entirely convincing, and further information is required before any specific recommendations can be made.

There is little evidence that any favorable changes to antioxidant status transfer into a performance benefit, although it is possible that true changes occurring over the relatively short periods of most studies are too small to be detected. Another dimension to the antioxidant story is also emerging which suggests that small levels of oxidants in cells play an important role in body function for example to act as signals for pathways promoting adaptive change, or as part of the immune system function. Therefore, any antioxidant supplementation needs to be carefully applied in case it interferes with positive oxidant-mediated function. In the absence of clear recommendations regarding antioxidant needs, athletes are advised to consume a diet that is rich in food sources of anti-oxidants. Supplementation may be most justified in situations where there is a sudden increase in training stress for example, a sudden increase in training load, or exposure to altitude or a hot environment.

MINERALS

Biological functions of minerals and evidence for benefits of supplementation

At least 20 different minerals are required in adequate amounts to sustain normal function of tissues and cells. Many of these are required in only trace amounts, but others must be supplied in greater quantities. Deficiencies of all of these elements are theoretically possible, but in practice, deficiencies are generally uncommon, with the possible exceptions of iron, calcium and, in some parts of the world, iodine. Since iron and calcium play an important role in the health and performance of athletes, and high-level training may have an effect on iron and calcium status, these minerals will be considered separately. Otherwise, dietary surveys and mineral status studies generally show that athletes consume adequate intakes of minerals and trace elements, and show similar biochemical and hematological status to their sedentary counterparts.

The major electrolytes sodium, potassium, and chloride all play important roles in water homeo-stasis and in the distribution of water between the intracellular and extracellular spaces. Sodium is important for regulation of blood pressure, but this is more of an issue for the recreational athlete and indeed for those in the population who take no exercise than for the elite performer.

Magnesium plays a number of vital roles in the regulation of energy metabolism, acting as a co-factor and activator for a number of enzymes. Magnesium is also involved in calcium metabolism and in the maintenance of electrical gradients across nerve and muscle cell membranes. Magnesium homeostasis in athletes has received recent attention due to the potential for increased magnesium losses and requirements in those undertaking regular exercise. For example, magnesium is lost in sweat in concentrations that may be higher than those in the blood, leading to concern about magnesium deficiency in athletes training and competing in hot climates, where large amounts of sweat are lost from the body. Magnesium deficiency is often proposed as a cause of exercise-induced muscle cramps, even though there is no experimental evidence to support this hypothesis. In some countries, including Germany, this idea is so fixed that sports drinks intended for athletes invariably have added magnesium, even though the same products are sold in other countries without the addition of magnesium salts. Experimental magnesium deficiency results in a variety of symptoms, but these do not include muscle cramp.

Zinc is also involved as a cofactor in many enzyme reactions, and has many other roles, including an important function in the promotion of tissue repair processes. More recently, zinc supplementation has been promoted on the basis of a potential role in enhancing immune function and increasing resistance to minor illness and infection. Most of the body zinc content of about 2 g is present in muscle (60%) and bone (30%), and measurements of zinc levels in blood may not be very meaningful. Low concentrations are present in sweat, and exercise may stimulate urinary loss. This increased loss associated with exercise may account for the concern of many athletes, but there is no evidence that these losses are sufficient to cause concern. Small amounts of zinc are present in many foods, including both animal and vegetable products, and no benefit of regular supplementation for health or for performance has been established. Copper is another divalent cation with important biological functions including modulation of enzyme activity and also a role in the synthesis of hemoglobin, catecholamines, and some peptide hormones. Once again, deficiencies are rare as copper is found in a wide range of foods, including shellfish, liver, wholegrain cereals, legumes and nuts.

Selenium has an antioxidant function, since it forms an integral part of the glutathione peroxidase enzyme, which helps to protect cells against the damage that can result from free radicals. There is some evidence that selenium plays a role in protecting against some cancers. In regions of the world where the soil is low in selenium, vegetables will have a low selenium content and deficiencies are possible. However, these regions are generally well recognized, with appropriate measures for fortification in place. Most people now eat foods produced in diverse geographical locations, so the risk of specific deficiencies is much less than in former times when most fresh produce was grown locally.

An adequate dietary iodine intake is essential for synthesis of the thyroid hormones thyroxine (T4) and triiodothyronine (T3), and thyroid deficiency was once common in parts of the world where the availability of iodine is low. Recognition of the role of iodine led to iodization of salt in these regions. In most countries, intakes are well in excess of requirements, and there is no evidence to suggest a greater requirement in physically active individuals.

A variety of other elements, including cobalt, molybdenum, manganese, chromium, and phosphorus, play important metabolic roles and are required in the diet in small amounts. Deficiencies of all of these elements are sufficiently rare that the possibility of their being encountered in athletes is negligible. However, many of these elements, including cobalt, chromium, and phosphate, are used as supplements by athletes, despite a lack of evidence either for an increased requirement or for a beneficial effect of specific supplementation on performance.

Minerals of special interest to athletes: iron

Iron deficiency anemia is regarded as the most commonly occurring nutritional deficiency in the world. In developing countries or among high-risk groups, iron deficiency can affect 30-40% of the population, whereas the prevalence of iron deficiency anemia in the general community is typically 1-3%. Since the 1970s, athletes have come under scrutiny as one such high-risk group. In early studies of long-distance runners, exercise scientists commented on some confusing hematological findings. These athletes were found to have reduced hemoglobin concentrations in their blood (a sign of anemia); this characteristic seemed unfavorable for the performance of events that rely on the delivery of oxygen to working muscles.

Later, this phenomenon was found to be a false or dilutional anemia, resulting from the acute increase in plasma volume that accompanies heavy aerobic training. Termed "sports anemia", it is not considered a pathology or disadvantage to performance, and does not respond to iron supplementation therapy. Of course, a low blood hemoglobin concentration may result from deficiency of other micronutrients such as vitamins B_{12} or folate, and should be investigated.

The body's iron is found in three main pools: storage iron (ferritin and hemosiderin found predominantly in the spleen, liver, and bone marrow); transport iron (transported by the protein carrier, transferrin); and oxygen transport iron (hemoglobin in the blood and myoglobin in the muscle). The majority of iron in the body is carefully recycled, with iron from destroyed red blood cells (erythro-cytes) being salvaged for storage or reincorporation into new blood cells. Iron status is a result of the balance between the small amounts of dietary iron that are absorbed each day and the sum of the small iron losses from skin, sweat, and the gastrointestinal and urinary tracts. Important functions of iron and iron-related compounds in the body are:

- transport of oxygen in the blood (hemoglobin) and muscle (myoglobin);
- as a component of enzyme systems such as the electron transport chain, and enzymes involved in DNA synthesis; and
- as a catalyst in the production of free oxygen radical species.

Iron drain is thought to progress through a number of stages with different functional and diagnostic criteria. The end stage of iron deficiency anemia is detected by blood iron status measures that are below population reference standards and also below the "normal or usual" concentrations for an individual. At this stage, there is inadequate iron available in the bone marrow for the normal manufacture of hemoglobin and erythrocytes, leading to the production of red blood cells that are small and pale. Anemia causes a reduction in exercise performance. In cases of severely reduced hemoglobin levels, individuals may report breathlessness on even the mildest exertion, and may be unable to carry out everyday activities and work tasks. Impaired functioning of iron-related enzymes may result in reductions in brain function, temperature control, and immunity, which exacerbate the symptoms of impaired exercise tolerance.

Although the effects of gradually reduced hemoglobin on performance have not been systematically studied, it is believed that even a small decline in hemoglobin levels (e.g. 1-2 g·$100ml^{-1}$) will reduce the competition performance of athletes. Since the range of "normal" hemoglobin levels is reasonably wide, it is possible that an athlete may show a level that is within reference standards, but is below the level that is "usual" for them and is required for their optimal performance. Although a low hemoglobin level may be relatively easy to detect, it is difficult to confirm optimal iron status from a single blood test. Fluctuations in iron status measures may occur without any change in true iron status. For example, concentrations of all parameters are increased by hemoconcentration (for example, in the severely dehydrated athlete) just as parameters are diluted when there is an increase in blood volume. Ferritin levels are increased in response to acute stress*a*such as a strenuous training session, infection or illness, further confusing the picture in athletes in training.

Therefore, it is valuable to standardize the time and conditions of iron status monitoring, and to establish a history of iron status results from the individual athlete to establish a feel for what is normal and "optimal" for them. Athletes often believe that the "more is better" principle applies to hemoglobin levels *per se* and may undertake specialized training, such as altitude training, to stimulate the production of erythrocytes. However, in the absence of hemoconcentration due to dehydration, very high hemoglobin levels are usually explained by genetic individuality or drug use (e.g. erythro-poietin (EPO)).

The most contentious issue about the iron status of athletes is whether iron depletion, in the absence of anemia, reduces exercise performance. Low serum ferritin levels have become synonymous with reduced iron status, and the effect on performance has been investigated mostly by studying the effects of iron supplementation on the performance of individuals with low ferritin levels. In general, there is little evidence that low ferritin levels, in the absence of anemia, are associated with reduced performance of a single exercise task, or that iron supplementation enhances the performance of athletes with moderately low serum ferritin but normal hemoglobin levels. Studies in which a performance improvement was seen after iron supplementation in subjects with low ferritin levels also show an increase in hemoglobin levels in response to the therapy, suggesting that the subjects had sub-optimal hemoglobin levels prior to the supplementation. However, studies have failed to address the complaint commonly made by athletes with reduced iron stores that they fail to recover between a series of competitions or training sessions.

Therefore, at the present time there is no evidence to suggest that a moderately reduced ferritin level *per se* is detrimental to performance, or that endurance athletes should receive routine iron supplementation. However, low ferritin levels may become progressively lower and eventually lead to problematic iron deficiency. For this reason, it makes sense to routinely assess the iron status of athletes with high risk of iron deficiency and implement a treatment plan where iron status is declining.

Causes of iron deficiency

Athletes are often considered a high-risk group for iron deficiency, but the causes of iron deficiency in athletes are the same as those in sedentary populations: iron requirements and/ or losses exceed iron intake over a sufficiently lengthy period of time. Iron requirements are increased during periods of growth, reflected by the higher recommended dietary allowances for iron during adolescence and while pregnant. Iron needs are higher in females of reproductive age than in males because of the need to replace the monthly menstrual blood losses. Given the individual characteristics of athletes it is not possible to make general recommendations as to iron requirements of people who exercise, but there is a general appreciation that there is an increase in iron requirements and iron turnover in those who undertake prolonged and heavy training. Even though the small losses from mechanical trauma and gastrointestinal blood loss might seem inconsequential, they may lead to iron drain over a prolonged period unless there is a compensatory increase in iron intake or absorption. Of course, iron losses may also occur due to medical problems that cause substantial or prolonged blood loss such as tumors, gastrointestinal ulcers, surgery, or severe bruising.

Prevention and treatment of iron deficiency and anemia

Evaluation and management of iron status should be undertaken on an individual basis by a sports medicine expert, and preferably by a team including the physician and dietitian. Cases of frank iron deficiency anemia warrant immediate iron therapy supported by a long-term management plan. Low iron status, indicated by serum ferritin levels lower than 20 ng ml^{-1}, should be considered for further assessment and treatment, and the prevention and treatment of iron deficiency may also include iron supplementation. The long-term management plan should be based on dietary counseling to increase the intake of bioavailable iron, and appropriate strategies to reduce any unwarranted iron loss should also be implemented.

Iron is found in a range of plant and animal food sources in two forms: as heme iron, found only in flesh- or blood-containing animal foods, and organic iron which is found in both animal foods and plant foods. Whereas heme iron is relatively well absorbed from single foods and mixed meals (15-35% bioavailability), the absorption of non-heme iron from single plant sources is low and variable (2-8%). The bioavailability of non-heme iron is affected by the presence of enhancing or inhibiting factors in foods eaten at the same meal. Inhibiting factors include phytates (found in wholegrain cereal foods and soy protein), polyphenols (found in tea and red wine), calcium (found in milk and cheese), and peptides from plant sources such as soy protein. Enhancing factors include vitamin C (found in citrus, tropical, and berry fruits, and some vegetables), peptides from meat/fish/chicken, alcohol, and some foods with a low pH due to fermentation or the presence of citric or tartaric acids. Until recently, the absorption of heme iron was considered to be relatively unaffected by other dietary compounds, but updated study techniques have shown that other meal components such as calcium and plant peptides may reduce heme iron bioavail-ability. The absorption of both heme and non-heme iron is increased as an adaptive response in people who are iron deficient or have increased iron requirements. It should be noted that iron bioavail-ability studies have not been undertaken on special groups such as athletes. The general assumption is that observations of iron absorption characteristics can be applied across populations of healthy people. Assessment of total dietary iron intake is not necessarily a good predictor of iron status. After all, the mixing and matching of foods at meals plays an important role by determining the bioavailability of dietary iron intake. In a mixed diet, where lean meats are consumed regularly, heme iron may provide around half of the absorbable iron. However in many Western countries, cereal products such as bread and breakfast cereals are the single greatest source of total dietary iron due to the fortification of these products with additional iron and the frequency with which they are consumed.

Minerals of special interest to athletes: calcium

Bone is a dynamic tissue, continually undergoing remodeling through the simultaneous processes of bone resorption and rebuilding. Osteoporosis, or low bone density, is now widely recognized as a problem for both men and women, and an increased bone mineral content is one of the benefits of participation in an exercise program. Regular exercise results in increased mineralization of those bones subjected to stress and an increased peak bone mass may delay the onset of osteoporotic fractures. Exercise may also delay the rate of bone loss. The specificity of this effect is demonstrated by the increase in forearm bone density observed in the dominant arm of tennis players. Calcium plays a permissive role in bone status, meaning that an inadequate calcium intake can interfere with optimal bone health, while high calcium intakes do not stimulate additional bone growth.

Interest in the calcium status of female athletes has intensified with recent studies reporting low bone density and an increased risk of stress fractures in various groups. However, these problems do not simply arise from inadequate calcium intake. Rather, there is a complex interrelationship between hormonal status, particularly of the female sex hormone estrogen, and bone health. Athletes often experience disturbances to regular menstrual function. Secondary amenorrhea (cessation of the normal menstrual cycle) is the most widely publicized form, but primary amenorrhea (failure to start menstruating) is commonly encountered in sports such as gymnastics where girls train intensively from early ages. Alterations in the luteal phase of the menstrual cycle may precede secondary amenorrhea and may also cause significant disruption to hormonal patterns. Since this will not be noticed unless blood tests are taken, the female athlete may not be aware of the early signs of menstrual dysfunction.

The prevalence of menstrual dysfunction in female athletes is uncertain as it is hard to compare reports that have studied athletes of different caliber, or that have used different definitions to describe menstrual dysfunction. Nevertheless, it appears that problems occur more frequently than in the general female population, and that athletes in "weight-conscious" sports are most at risk. Despite a number of interesting hypotheses, there is no single cause that can explain menstrual disturbances in athletes. Low body fat levels *per se* do not seem to predict amenorrhea, as was originally proposed. Many athletes are able to maintain regular cycles while at low body fat levels, while other athletes and non-athlete counterparts may become amenorrheic at relatively higher body fat levels. Rather, a number of risk factors seem to be involved and individual athletes may be susceptible to certain factors or combinations of these factors. A more complex scenario involving a cluster of proposed risk factors is the "energy drain" syndrome. This syndrome describes the female athlete who consumes a diet that is restricted in energy intake and variety, while undertaking a heavy exercise load. This athlete is exposed to a chronic energy deficit, psychological stress and/or perhaps a struggle to achieve or maintain body fat below the level that is genetically determined as "natural" for them.

Of course, observations of impaired menstrual function in female athletes are not new. In fact, they have been reported for at least 30 years. However, it is only recently that the negative outcome of altered menstrual function has been recognized: the alteration of steroid hormone profiles in female athletes has a detrimental effect on bone health.

Education is needed to raise the awareness of athletes about the problems associated with amenorrhea or other forms of menstrual dysfunction. Many athletes, particularly female endurance athletes, consider amenorrhea to be a "normal" condition for heavily training athletes. Although it might be "normal" in the sense that it is widely prevalent among some athletic groups, it is clearly not a healthy or desirable state. As part of this education process, sports medicine experts have described the syndrome as the "female athlete triad". This describes the common presentation of disordered eating, menstrual dysfunction, and reduced bone health among female athletes. Of course, each of these problems is multifactorial, and does not always occur in the presence of the other problems.

Nevertheless, the female athlete triad has drawn the attention of doctors, coaches, and athletes towards the importance of early intervention and management of any symptoms. Reduced bone density in athletes or failure to optimize peak bone mass may be a risk factor for the development of stress fractures during their athletic career, and more importantly, the earlier onset, or increased risk of osteoporosis in later life.

In the case of stress fractures, many factors can combine to cause excessive loading on the bone. The role of reduced bone density in athletes in later osteoporosis remains speculative since it will take extensive longitudinal studies into middle age and beyond to determine its significance.

Of course, factors other than hormonal status and exercise can affect bone mineral status. These include dietary factors, such as intakes of calcium, protein, and phosphorus, as well as genetic or familial predisposition, and smoking. Population guidelines for calcium intake recognize increased calcium requirements during periods of growth, as well as during pregnancy and breastfeeding. The recommended intakes proposed by some countries also include increased calcium intake for post-menopausal women, recognizing that higher calcium intakes are needed to maintain calcium balance in a lower estrogen state. Note that some calcium balance studies suggest that calcium intakes of 1500 mg $\cdot day^{-1}$ might be needed in such situations. Presumably the recommended dietary intake guidelines for postmenopausal women should be extended to athletes who have developed a low estrogen status as evidenced by menstrual dysfunction.

Typically, dairy products provide around 50-70% of the calcium intake in Western diets. In many dietary surveys of female athletes, it has been reported that they consume significantly less calcium than the recommended intakes. Dietary restriction or disordered eating may not only be a risk factor for the development of menstrual dysfunction, but is also likely to be associated with suboptimal intakes of calcium. Restriction of energy intake is a common cause of inadequate consumption of calcium. Many athletes also restrict their intake of dairy foods because of false beliefs that these foods are fattening, or cause "allergies" or "mucus". It is rare to find true situations where all dairy foods must be avoided on medical grounds. Some athletes have cultural, religious, or environmental beliefs that prevent th from consuming dairy foods. In this case, fortified soy products provide an alternative source of calcium; moderate sources of calcium include canned fish eaten with bones, and some vegetables. It is useful to provide dietary advice for athletes in which high calcium eating is matched with other dietary goals*a*for example, finding low-fat calcium choices, or mixing a calcium-rich food into a high-carbohydrate meal.

It is often difficult to work with athletes who suffer from disordered eating, amenorrhea, impaired bone status, or combinations of these problems, and there is no single management plan. Rather, these athletes need individualized assessment and therapy, involving input from appropriate experts. Assessment is necessary to determine the factors underlying each problem, and the overall threat to the athlete's health and performance. Ideally, the athlete should aim to return to menstrual health and an optimum diet, even though this may not be possible, at least in the short term. The role of estrogen replacement therapy and calcium supplementation as interim or long-term interventions requires further research. There is some doubt about the degree of reversibility of bone loss, and in particular the restoration of strong bone formation, particularly in cases of long-term loss. Early intervention and prevention are clearly the preferred options.

SUMMARY

Vitamins and minerals play a key role in optimizing the health and performance of the athlete. In many cases there may be an increased requirement for a particular micronutrient, arising from the commitment to a regular exercise schedule. However, there are no fixed guidelines for recommended intakes of vitamins and minerals by athletes. Rather, it is suggested that a moderate to high energy intake, coupled with a variety of nutrient-rich food choices, will enable the athlete to achieve intakes of vitamins and minerals that are in excess of both the population recommended dietary intakes, and their increased requirements. Studies fail to provide evidence that vitamin supplementation enhances exercise performance, except in cases where there was a pre-existing deficiency. Nevertheless, there is interest in the possible role of antioxidant vitamins in the prevention of damage arising from excessive production of free oxygen radicals. With regard to minerals, some athletes are at risk of suboptimal intakes of iron and calcium, which may have detrimental effects on either immediate performance or long-term health. The prevention and management of such problems requires input from experts in sports medicine and nutrition.

12

Fluids and Electrolytes

INTRODUCTION

Most athletes and coaches are aware that dehydration*a*a reduction in the body's water content— will result in a loss of performance. It is equally clear, however, that this knowledge does not always translate into behaviors designed to prevent or limit the risk of dehydration. Many recent major sports events*a*the 2002 Soccer World Cup, the 1996 Olympic Games, the 1998 Commonwealth Games *a*have been held in hot humid climates; these events are often organized in the summer months, and are often scheduled for the hottest part of the day. There no longer remains any doubt that exercise performance is impaired in most types of activity in these conditions, yet the athlete has no choice but to compete. All athletes will be affected, but the athlete who has prepared by a period of acclimatization to these conditions, and who has a clear rehydration strategy, is likely to be least affected. Although these preparations are not a substitute for talent, training, or motivation, they are prerequisites if the individual is to realize his or her potential.

DAILY FLUID NEEDS

Water is often referred to as the "silent nutrient", reflecting the extent to which its presence and availability are taken for granted. As with all nutrients, however, a regular intake of water is required for the body to maintain health, and both deficiency symptoms and overdosage symptoms can be observed. Water is the largest single component of the normal human body, accounting for about 50-60% of total body mass. Lean body tissues contain a constant fraction about 75%*a*of water by mass, whereas adipose tissue has little water content. The fraction of body mass that is accounted for by fat therefore largely determines the normal body water content: the higher the body fat level, the lower the fraction of total mass that is accounted for by water. For a healthy lean young male with a body mass of 70 kg, total body water will be about 42 l. The turnover rate of water exceeds that of most other body components: for the sedentary individual living in a temperate climate, daily water turnover is about 2-4 l, or about 5-10% of the total body water content. In spite of its abundance, however, there is a need to maintain the body water content within narrow limits, and the body is much less able to cope with restriction of water intake than with restriction of food intake. In the absence of strenuous exercise, a few days of total fasting has little impact on functional capacity, provided fluids are allowed, and even longer periods of abstinence from food are well tolerated. In contrast, except in exceptional circumstances, cessation of water intake results in serious debilitation after times ranging from only an hour or two to a few days at most.

Several factors will influence the body's water losses and thus determine the requirement for fluid intake. Among the most important of these are the ambient climatic conditions and the level of physical activity. Body size is, of course, also important: both body composition and volume, which is closely related to body mass and which defines the amount of metabolically active tissue, and body surface area, which is a function of the square of body mass and which represents the surface available for heat exchange with the environment, are important. There also appears to be a large interindividual variability in water intake and loss even after accounting for body size, but the reasons for this have not been thoroughly studied. All of these factors will combine to determine the physiological requirement for water.

The requirement for water is set by the total water losses occurring by various routes, for in all cases except the very short term, the water intake must equal the loss. The only significant additional factor influencing the water requirement is the electrolyte content, and to a lesser extent the protein content, of the diet, which will influence the volume of urine that must be excreted. The water formed by the oxidation of foodstuffs will make some small contribution to meeting the daily water losses, but water in drinks and in foods will meet most of the demand. The water losses from the body are highly variable and include a number of significant losses as well as a number of minor ones. Losses in urine, feces, sweat, expired air and through the skin are the major avenues of water loss; smaller losses occur through blood loss, and in semen, tears, etc., but these are normally trivial.

The regulation of body water and electrolyte concentrations involves a number of neural and hormonal mechanisms which influence both intake and loss. Superimposed on these physiological control mechanisms are the various social and other factors that act to increase or restrict fluid intake.

Basal water requirements

The extent of the daily water loss and intake will vary from individual to individual, but a general example for a sedentary individual. Body size is clearly a factor having a major influence on water turnover, but the total body water content will also be markedly affected by the body composition. It is expected therefore that there will be differences between men and women and between adults and children. Unless otherwise specified, the values given here will relate to the average 70-kg male with a moderate body fat content.

Environmental conditions will affect an individual's water requirements by altering the losses that occur by the various routes. Water requirements for sedentary individuals living in the heat may be two- or threefold higher than the requirement when living in a temperate climate, even when this is not accompanied by pronounced sweating. Transcutaneous and respiratory losses will be markedly influenced by the humidity of the ambient air, and this may be a more important factor than the ambient temperature. Respiratory water losses are incurred because of the humidification of the inspired air. These losses are relatively small in the resting individual in a warm, moist environment (amounting to about 200 ml per day), but will be increased approximately twofold in regions of low humidity, and may be as high as 1500 ml $\cdot$day^{-1} during periods of hard work in the cold dry air at altitude. To these losses must be added insensible loss through the skin (about 600 ml $\cdot$day^{-1}) and urine loss, which will not usually be less than about 800 ml $\cdot$day^{-1}.

The water content of food ingested will also be influenced greatly by the nature of the diet, and water associated with food may make a major contribution to the total fluid intake. Some additional water is obtained from the oxidation of nutrients, and this will depend on the total metabolic rate, but will also be influenced to a lesser extent by the nature of the substrate being oxidized. If we assume an energy expenditure of 3000 kcal$\cdot$day^{-1}, composed of 50% carbohydrate, 35% fat, and 15% protein, this will give about 400 ml of water per day. Reducing the energy expenditure to 2000 kcal but keeping the same diet composition will give about 275 ml of water. The contribution of water of oxidation to water requirements is thus appreciable when water turnover is low, but becomes a rather insignificant fraction of the total when water losses are high.

Control of water balance

Water intake and excretion are driven by a complex interaction of neural and hormonal factors which respond to a number of different inputs. Under normal conditions, the blood volume and the osmolal-ity of the extracellular fluid are maintained within narrow limits: a rise or fall of about 5 mosmol$\cdot$l^{-1} in the plasma osmolality is sufficient to switch the kidney from maximum conservation of water to maximum urine output. Sodium, as the major ion of the extracellular space, accounts for about 50% of the total plasma osmolality, with the result that maintenance of osmotic balance is closely coupled to the intake and excretion of both sodium and water. The profound diuresis that ensues when plasma osmolality falls normally prevents water overload, but cases of hyponatremia (low plasma sodium levels) have been reported. These normally occur when a conscious effort is made to override the physiological signals and ingest large volumes of plain water or other low-electrolyte fluids. Some degree of hyponatremia may be a normal accompaniment of the consumption of large volumes of beer, which is essentially sodium free.

The kidneys can conserve water or electrolytes by reducing the rate of loss, but can do nothing to restore a deficit, which can only be corrected by fluid intake. The subjective sensation of thirst initiates the desire to drink and hence plays a key role in the control of fluid balance. Thirst, whether measured as a perceived response or as the outcome (i.e. the volume of fluid consumed), appears to be relatively insensitive to acute changes in hydration status in humans, but the overall stability of the total water volume of an individual indicates that the desire to drink is a powerful regulatory factor over the long term. The absence of a sensation of thirst should not be taken as an indication that the body is fully hydrated.

Thirst may not be a direct consequence of the physiological need for water intake, but can be initiated by a number of unrelated factors, including habit, ritual, taste or desire for nutrients, stimulants, or a warm or cooling effect. A number of the sensations associated with thirst are learned, with drinking behavior being initiated by signals such as dryness of the mouth or throat, while distention of the stomach can stop ingestion before a fluid deficit has been restored. However, the underlying regulation of thirst is controlled separately by both the osmotic pressure and the volume of the body fluids, and as such is regulated by the same mechanisms that affect water and solute reabsorption in the kidneys and control central blood pressure.

The thirst control centers in the brain play a key role in the regulation of both thirst and diuresis. Receptors in these centers respond directly to changes in plasma osmolality and blood pressure and volume, while others are stimulated by the fluid balance hormones which also regulate renal excretion. The level of neural activity in the thirst control centers regulates the relative sensations of thirst and satiety, and can also influence urine output. Input from the higher centers of the brain, however, can override these physiological mechanisms. A rise of between 2 and 3% in plasma osmolality from the normal level of about 285-290 mosmol l^{-1} is sufficient to evoke a profound sensation of thirst coupled with an increase in the circulating concentration of antidiuretic hormone (ADH). The mechanisms that respond to changes in intravascular volume and pressure are less sensitive, reflecting the large variations in blood volume and pressure that occur during normal daily activity.

When a water deficit has been incurred, the normal drinking response in humans involves a period of rapid ingestion during which 50% or more of the total intake is consumed, followed by a longer period during which intermittent consumption of relatively small volumes of drink occurs. The initial alleviation of thirst occurs before significant amounts of the beverage have been absorbed and entered the body pools. This indicates a role for receptors in the mouth, esophagus, and stomach, which are thought to respond to the volume of fluid ingested; distension of the stomach also tends to reduce the perception of thirst. These preabsorptive signals appear to be behavioral, learned responses and may be subject to disruption in situations which are essentially novel to the individual.

This may partly explain the inappropriate voluntary fluid intake in individuals exposed to an acute increase in environmental temperature or to exercise-induced dehydration. In the longer term, a fall in plasma osmolality and increase in the extracellular volume inhibit the sensation of thirst.

IMPACT OF PHYSICAL ACTIVITY ON WATER BALANCE

Exercise elevates the metabolic rate, and only about 25% of the energy made available by the metabolic pathways is used to perform external work, with the remainder being dissipated as heat. When the energy demand is high, as occurs during exercise, this results in high rates of heat production. The normal resting oxygen consumption is about 4 ml $\cdot$kg body mass^{-1} min^{-1}: for a 70-kg individual, this gives a resting rate of heat production of about 60-70 W (the equivalent of a small electric light bulb). Running a marathon in 2 h 30 min requires an oxygen consumption of about 4 l min^{-1} to be sustained throughout the race for the average runner with a body mass of 70 kg. The accompanying rate of heat production is now about 1100 W (1.1 kW), and body temperature begins to rise rapidly.

To limit the potentially harmful rise in core temperature, the rate of heat loss must be increased accordingly. Maintenance of a high skin temperature will facilitate heat loss by radiation and convection, but these mechanisms are effective only when the ambient temperature is low and the rate of air movement over the skin is high.

At high ambient temperatures (above about 35°C), skin temperature will be below ambient temperature, and the only mechanism by which heat can be lost from the body is evaporation. Evaporation of 1 l of water from the skin will remove 2.4 MJ (580 kcal) of heat from the body. For the 2 h 30 min marathon runner with a body mass of 70 kg to balance the rate of metabolic heat production by evaporative loss alone would therefore require sweat to be evaporated from the skin at a rate of about 1.6 l$\cdot$h^{-1}; at such high sweat rates, an appreciable fraction drips from the skin without evaporating, and a sweat secretion rate of about 2 $l \cdot h^{-1}$ is likely to be necessary to achieve this rate of evaporative heat loss. This is possible, but would result in the loss of 5 l of body water, corresponding to a loss of more than 7% of body weight for a 70-kg runner. Water will also be lost by evaporation from the respiratory tract. During hard exercise in a hot dry environment, this can amount to a significant water loss, although it is not generally considered to be a major heat loss mechanism in humans.

In most activities, the energy demand varies continuously: average sweat losses for various sporting activities are well categorized, but average values often conceal the responses at the extremes of the range. Even at low ambient temperatures high sweat rates are sometimes observed when the energy demand is high as in marathon running, so it cannot be concluded that dehydration is a problem only when the ambient temperature and humidity are high. The sweat loss is, however, closely related to the environmental conditions, and substantial fluid deficits are much more common in the summer months and in tropical climates. Body mass losses of 6 l or more are reported for marathon runners in warm weather competition. This corresponds to a water deficit of about 8% of body mass, or about 12-15% of total body water. In spite of the large variation between individuals, sweating rate has been found to be related to running speed in a heterogeneous group of marathon runners; there was, however, no relationship between total sweat loss and running speed.

It is well established that women tend to sweat less than men under standardized conditions, even after a period of acclimatization. It is likely, however, that a large part of the apparent sex difference can be accounted for by differences in training and acclimatization status.

There is a limited amount of information on the effects of age on the sweating response, and again levels of fitness and acclimatization are confounding factors, but the sweating response to a standardized challenge generally decreases with age. These observations should not, however, be interpreted as suggesting an inability to exercise in the heat, nor should they be taken to indicate a decreased need for women or older individuals to pay attention to fluid intake during exposure to heat stress.

Table: Rates of sweat loss measured in different sports and exercise activities. These average values do not reveal the large variability between individuals (data taken from Rehrer & Burke 1996).

Sport	Gender	Environment (°C)	Sweat loss (ml-h~¹)
10-km run	F	19-24	1490
10-km run	M	19-24	1830
Marathon	M	6-24	540-1520
40-km cycle	F	19-25	750
40-km cycle	M	19-25	1140
Soccer	M	10	1000
		25	1200
Soccer	F	26	800
Netbal	F	16-22	900-1000
Basketball	F	20-25	900
	M	20-25	1600
Rowing	F	10	780
		32	1390
	M	10	1165
		30	1980
Rugby	M	18-23	1600–2200
Cricket	M	23	500
		33	700-1400

There are some differences between children and adults in the sweating response to exercise and in sweat composition. The sweating capacity of children is low, when expressed per unit surface area, and the sweat electrolyte content is low relative to that of adults, but the need for fluid and electrolyte replacement is no less important than in adults. Indeed, in view of the evidence that core temperature increases to a greater extent in children than in adults at a given level of dehydration, the need for fluid replacement may well be greater in children.

Dehydration is harmful to athletic performance, and both endurance sports and high-intensity events are adversely affected.

It is commonly stated that exercise performance is impaired when an individual is dehydrated by as little as 2% of body mass, and that losses in excess of 5% of body mass can decrease the capacity for work by about 30%. An examination of the original data (derived from a total of 13 trials involving three subjects) on which this statement was based, however, shows that the conclusion is much less robust than it might appear: there was no good relationship between the extent of dehydration incurred by sauna exposure and the degree of impairment of the capacity to perform a high-intensity exercise test lasting about 6 min, and a large variation in response between and within individuals was observed. Nonetheless, there is convincing evidence that prior dehydration will impair the capacity to perform high-intensity exercise as well as endurance activities. It has been shown that prolonged exercise, which resulted in a loss of fluid corresponding to 2.5% of body weight, resulted in a 45% fall in the capacity to perform high-intensity exercise. There is equally convincing evidence the prevention of dehydration by administration of fluids can improve exercise performance, and the evidence to support this will be discussed later.

Fluid losses are distributed in varying proportions among the plasma, extracellular water, and intra-cellular water. The decrease in plasma volume which accompanies dehydration may be of particular importance in influencing work capacity; blood flow to the muscles must be maintained at a high level to supply oxygen and substrates, but a high blood flow to the skin is also necessary to convect heat to the body surface where it can be dissipated. When the ambient temperature is high and blood volume has been decreased by sweat loss during prolonged exercise, there may be difficulty in meeting the requirement for a high blood flow to both these tissues. In this situation, skin blood flow is likely to be compromised, allowing central venous pressure and muscle blood flow to be maintained but reducing heat loss and causing body temperature to rise.

The preferential loss of water from the extracellular space reflects the relatively high sodium and chloride concentration in sweat. Electrolyte losses in sweat are a function of sweating rate and sweat composition, and both of these vary over time as well as being substantially influenced by the exercise intensity, the environmental conditions, and the physiology of the individual.

Added to this variability is the difficulty in obtaining a reliable estimate of sweat composition, and these methodological problems have contributed at least in part to the diversity of the results reported in the literature. In spite of the variability in the composition of sweat, however, it is invariably isotonic with respect to plasma, and the major electrolytes are sodium and chloride, as in the extracellular space. It is usual to present the composition in mmol $\cdot l^{-1}$, and the extent of the sodium losses in relation to daily dietary intake, which is usually expressed in grams, is not widely appreciated. Loss of 1 l of sweat with a sodium content of 50 mmol $\cdot l^{-1}$ represents a loss of 2.9 g of sodium chloride; the athlete who sweats 5 l in a daily training session will therefore lose almost 15 g of salt. Even allowing for a reduced sweat sodium concentration and a decreased urinary output when sodium losses in sweat are large, this amount is large in comparison to the reported normal intakes, and it is clear that the salt balance of individuals exercising in the heat is likely to be precarious. The possible need for supplementary salt intake in extreme conditions is something that the athlete training hard in warm conditions must consider.

Table: Concentration (mmol $\cdot l^{-1}$) of the major electrolytes in sweat, plasma, and intracellular water. These values are taken from a variety of sources.

	Sweat	Plasma	Intracellular
Sodium	20-80	130-155	10
Potassium	4-8	3.2-5.5	150
Calcium	0-1	2.1-2.9	0
Magnesium	< 0.2	0.7-1.5	15
Chloride	20-60	96-110	8

It was mentioned earlier that there appear to be few reliable measurements of water turnover in normal healthy individuals. There are formidable obstacles that tend to confound the results of measurements of the various components of water intake and water loss. Intake is usually estimated from weighed or measured food and fluid intake diaries, but the data are complicated by uncertainties in the water content of foodstuffs, and are subject to the usual reliability issues. Measurement of the various avenues of water loss is beset by similar problems. Advances in the application of isotopic tracer methodology have recently permitted the non-invasive measurement of water turnover, using deuterium as a tracer for body water. The principle of the measurement and the practicalities are both relatively straightforward. Body water is labeled with deuterium, and the water turnover is measured over a period of a few days from the rate of decrease in the tracer concentration in body water. The measurement can be made conveniently on blood or urine samples. Collection of 24-h urine output allows non-renal losses (consisting mainly of sweat and transcutaneous losses, respiratory water loss, and fecal loss) to be calculated by difference.

Application of this method to two groups of subjects, including runners and matched sedentary individuals, showed a higher rate of water turnover in the exercising group. Both groups had a similar total body water content, but the average daily water turnover over the 7-day measurement period in the active group was about 4.7 l per day, which was higher than that of the sedentary subjects (about 3.3 $l \cdot day^{-1}$). It might have been expected that the runners would have a greater daily sweat loss than the sedentary group, but there was no significant difference between the groups in non-renal water losses. These results seem surprising, but may reflect the relatively low total exercise load of the runners and the temperate climate at the time of the study. The results also suggest that the runners were habituated to drinking a volume of fluid in excess of that required to match the sweat loss incurred during exercise, perhaps because they were conscious of the need for an increased water intake in active individuals. When the same methodology was applied to another physically active group, in this case cyclists covering an average daily distance of 50 km in training for competition, and another matched sedentary group, the water turnover rate was again higher in the cyclists than in the sedentary individuals. In this study, however, there was no difference between the groups in the daily urine output, indicating that the difference in water intake was largely accounted for by an increased sweat loss.

MEASURES OF HYDRATION STATUS

Dehydration generally has a negative effect on physical performance as well as on overall health. A reliable marker of hydration status may therefore be of benefit to many individuals in many situations. A body water deficit of as little as 1-2% of total body water impairs exercise performance, so any marker that is to be of use in this situation would have to be capable of indicating such a deficit. Acute changes in body mass during exercise will generally be due to loss of body water in the form of sweat; respiratory water loss and substrate oxidation are relatively small. A 1-g change in mass represents a 1-ml change in water status. Over the course of a single bout of exercise, a reduction in body mass, measured nude and with skin toweled dry before and after exercise, will indicate a state of dehydration.

However, food or fluid consumed during the exercise will confuse the picture. Urinary indices, including the volume, color, protein content, specific gravity, and osmolality of the urine, have been investigated as hydration status markers. Urine color, estimated from a color chart, has been demonstrated to provide a reasonable "in the field" estimate of hydration status in association with exercise.

Bloodborne indices, including hemoglobin and hematocrit, plasma osmolality and sodium concentration, plasma testosterone, adrenaline, norad-renaline, cortisol, and atrial natriuretic peptide, have been investigated as hydration status markers. These bloodborne indices have the disadvantage of being more invasive than many of the other measures described, and in an exercise setting some respond not only to hydration stresses but to exercise stresses too. Bioelectrical impedance analysis can give a rapid estimate of total body water, and its cellular divisions if a multifrequency device is utilized. Changes in hydration status may be detected if the procedure is carefully standardized in many ways but the precision and sensitivity of the method remain to be established.

Alterations in the response of pulse rate and systolic blood pressure to postural change have been demonstrated in clinical settings of dehydration and rehydration. However, these measures may not be sensitive enough to be of value in an exercise situation. A wide variety of indices have been investigated to establish their effectiveness as markers of hydration status in an exercise situation. An individual's choice of hydration status marker will be influenced by the sensitivity and accuracy with which they need to establish hydration status, together with the technical and time requirements and expense involved.

Water replacement in exercise

The major issues in fluid replacement are the optimization of hydration status prior to exercise, the provision of fluid and substrate (and possibly also other nutrients) during exercise, and rehydration and recovery after exercise. The kidneys effectively prevent attempts to increase the body water content prior to exercise, and although the addition of osmotically active substances such as glycerol to ingested fluids can decrease the fraction of ingested fluid that appears promptly in the urine, the effectiveness of this procedure in affecting the physiological responses to exercise is unclear.

Dilute glucose-electrolyte solutions are the most effective way of replacing water losses when rapid rehydration is desired: variations on this formulation are the basis of oral rehydration solutions for the treatment of infectious diarrhea and of sports drinks. The rate of gastric emptying of such solutions is slowed in proportion to the carbohydrate content, and concentrated solutions will be unable to deliver water at high rates. Intestinal water absorption is driven by osmotic gradients and by solvent drag resulting from active absorption of solute, especially glucose and sodium which are cotrans-ported by an ATP-dependent mechanism. Hypotonic (200-250 mosmol $\cdot kg^{-1}$) solutions containing glucose and sodium will maximize the rate of water absorption, but hypertonic solutions will cause a temporary secretion of water into the intestinal lumen, exacerbating any existing dehydration.

The ingestion of water or carbohydrate-electrolyte sports drinks during exercise has been shown to help reduce the fall in plasma volume that normally occurs: this in turn helps to maintain cardiac output by maintaining stroke volume and increases the skin blood flow, which helps promote heat loss and limit the rise in core temperature. Although ingestion of plain water can help to improve exercise performance, further benefits are observed if glucose or glucose plus electrolytes are added.

Rehydration is a vital part of the recovery process after exercise which has resulted in sweat loss. The usual recommendation to ensure adequate fluid replacement after exercise is to replace each kilogram of weight lost during exercise with 1 liter of fluid, but there is now compelling evidence, that it is necessary to ingest at least 50% more volume than the volume of sweat lost if euhydration is to be achieved. It is also essential to replace the electrolytes lost in sweat if the ingested fluid is to be retained rather than being lost in the urine.

ELECTROLYTES

Variations in the amount and type of food eaten have some effect on water requirements because of the resulting demand for excretion of excess electrolytes and the products of metabolism. An intake of electrolytes in excess of the amounts lost (primarily in sweat and feces) must be corrected by excretion in the urine, with a corresponding increase in the volume and osmolality of urine formed. The daily intake of electrolytes is subject to wide variation between individuals, with strong trends for differences between different geographical regions. Daily dietary salt (sodium chloride) intakes for 95% of the young male UK population fall between 3.8 and 14.3 g with a mean of 8.4 g; the corresponding values for young women are 2.8-9.4 g, with a mean value of 6.0 g. For the same population, mean urinary sodium losses were reported to account for about 175 mmol $\cdot day^{-1}$, which is equivalent to about 10.2 g of sodium chloride.

There are also large differences between countries in the recommended intake of salt: the British advice is for a maximum of 6 $g \cdot day^{-1}$, but in Germany, a maximum of 10 $g \cdot day^{-1}$ is recommended. In contrast, Sweden recommends a maximum of 2 $g \cdot day^{-1}$, and Poland recommends a minimum of 1.4 $g \cdot day^{-1}$. These differences in the recommendations by different expert committees reflect in part different interpretations with regard to the evidence linking salt intake and health, but also reflect regional consumption patterns. Water intake will reflect rather closely the patterns of salt intake. A high-protein diet also requires a greater urine output to allow excretion of water-soluble nitrogenous waste: this effect is relatively small compared with other losses, but becomes meaningful when water availability is limited.

Salt losses in sweat can be significant. The sweat that is secreted onto the skin contains a wide variety of organic and inorganic solutes, and significant losses of some of these components will occur where large volumes of sweat are produced. The electrolyte composition of sweat is variable, and the concentration of individual electrolytes as well as the total sweat volume will influence the extent of losses. A number of factors contribute to the variability in the composition of sweat; methodological problems in the collection procedure, including evaporative loss, incomplete collection, and contamination with skin cells, account for at least part of the variability, but there is also a large biological variability.

The sweat composition undoubtedly varies between individuals, but can also vary within the same individual depending on the rate of secretion, the state of training, and the state of heat acclimatization. In response to a standard heat stress, the sweat rate increases with training and acclimatization and the electrolyte content decreases. These adaptations are generally considered to allow improved thermoregulation while conserving electrolytes. There are, however, some puzzling aspects: where the sweat rate is sufficient to keep the skin wet, further increases in the sweat rate will increase the amount of water which drips from the skin without evaporation but will not further increase the rate of evaporative heat loss.

In spite of the variations which do occur, the major electrolytes in sweat, as in the extracellular fluid, are sodium and chloride, although the sweat concentrations of these ions are invariably lower than those in plasma. Contrary to what might be expected, there is some evidence that the concentration of sodium and chloride in sweat increases with increased flow, as a result of a reduced opportunity for reabsorption in the sweat duct. Acclimatization studies have shown that elevated sweating rates are accompanied by a decrease in the concentration of sodium and chloride in sweat in spite of the increased flow rate. The potassium content of sweat appears to be relatively unaffected by the sweat rate, and the magnesium content is also unchanged or perhaps decreases slightly.

These apparently conflicting results demonstrate some of the difficulties in interpreting the literature in this area. Differences between studies may be due to differences in the training status and degree of acclimatization of the subjects used, as well as difference in methodology: some studies have used whole body washdown techniques to collect sweat, whereas others have examined local sweating responses using ventilated capsules or collection bags. There may be differences between the composition of sweat from a specific region, such as the hand and forearm, and the whole body sweat. The use of improved sweat collection techniques will begin to resolve these issues.

Because sweat is hypotonic with respect to body fluids, the effect of prolonged sweating is to increase the plasma osmolality, which may have a significant effect on the ability to maintain body temperature. A direct relationship between plasma osmolality and body temperature has been demonstrated during exercise. Hyperosmolality of plasma, induced prior to exercise, has been shown to result in a decreased ability to regulate body temperature; the threshold for sweating is elevated and the flow of warm blood to the skin is reduced. In short-term (30-min) exercise, however, the cardiovascular and thermoregulatory response appears to be independent of changes in osmolality induced during the exercise period. The changes in the concentration of individual electrolytes are more variable, but an increase in the plasma sodium and chloride concentrations is generally observed in response to both running and cycling exercise. Exceptions to this are rare and occur only when excessively large volumes of drinks low in electrolytes are consumed over long time periods.

The plasma potassium concentration has been reported to remain constant after marathon running, although others have reported small increases, irrespective of whether drinks containing large amounts of potassium or no electrolytes were given. Much of the inconsistency in the literature relating to changes in the circulating potassium concentration can be explained by the variable time taken to obtain blood samples after exercise under field conditions; the plasma potassium concentration rapidly returns to normal in the postexercise period. Laboratory studies where an indwelling catheter can be used to obtain blood samples during exercise commonly show an increase in the circulating potassium concentration in the later stages of prolonged exercise. The potassium concentration of extracellular fluid (4-5 mmol $\cdot l^{-1}$) is small relative to the intracellular concentration (150-160 mmol $\cdot l^{-1}$), and release of potassium from liver, muscle, and red blood cells will tend to elevate plasma potassium levels during exercise in spite of the losses in sweat.

The blood magnesium concentration is usually reported to be unchanged after prolonged moderate-intensity exercise, but a 20% fall in the serum magnesium concentration has been observed after a marathon race. A larger fall in the serum magnesium concentration has been observed during exercise in the heat than at neutral temperatures, supporting the idea that losses in sweat may be responsible. There are, however, reports that the fall in plasma magnesium concentration that occurs during prolonged exercise is a consequence of redistribution between tissues, with uptake of magnesium by red blood cells, active muscle, or adipose tissue, rather than a net loss from the body. Although the concentration of potassium and magnesium in sweat is high relative to that in the plasma, the plasma content of these ions represents only a small fraction of the whole body stores; only about 1% of the body stores of these electrolytes is lost when individuals are dehydrated by about 5-6% of body weight.

PRACTICAL IMPLICATIONS FOR THE ATHLETE

Although the basic principles that govern fluid replacement strategies for athletes are well established, there are some real difficulties in putting these into practice. Athletes and their advisers want a prescription for the composition, amount, and timing of fluid intake that will cover all situations. Even within a single event, however, the requirement will vary so much between individuals, depending on the physiological and biochemical characteristics of the individual as well as on the training load and on other factors such as taste preference, that such recommendations can only be made on an individual basis. When the possible effects of different climatic conditions and different training and competition schedules are added, the problems in making a simple recommendation are multiplied.

These difficulties are immediately apparent when any of the published guidelines for fluid intake during exercise are examined. These guidelines are generally formulated to include the needs of most individuals in most situations, with the results that the outer limits become so wide as to be at best meaningless, and at worst positively harmful. The guidelines of the American College of Sports Medicine, expressed in their 1984 Position Statement on the prevention of heat illness in distance running, were an attempt to give athletes some indication of the amount of fluid they might need. The recommendation for marathon runners was for an intake of 100-200 ml every 2-3 km, giving a total intake of 1400-4200 ml at the extremes. Taking these extreme values, it is unlikely that the elite runners, who take only a little over 2 h to complete the distance, could tolerate a rate of intake of about $2\ l \cdot h^{-1}$, and equally unlikely that an intake of $250\ ml \cdot h^{-1}$ would be adequate for the slowest competitors except perhaps when the ambient temperature was low. These same guidelines also recommended that the best fluid to drink during prolonged exercise is cool water: in view of the accumulated evidence, this recommendation seems even less acceptable now than it was in 1984.

Because of the difficulty in making specific recommendations that will meet the needs of all individuals in all situations, the only possible way forward is to formulate some general guidelines and to indicate how these should be modified in different circumstances. Assuming that athletes are willing and able to take fluids during training, the recommendations for fluid use in training will not be very different for training and competition, except in events of very short duration.

The sprinter or pursuit cyclist, whose event lasts a few seconds or minutes, has no opportunity or need for fluid intake during competition, but should take fluids during training sessions which may stretch over 2 h or more.

All athletes should aim to ensure that they begin exercise fully hydrated, and this includes those who may have had to meet weight categories and have undergone fluid restriction practices to do so. Attempts to overhydrate by the ingestion of saline or glycerol solutions have met with limited success, but the negative effects of beginning exercise in a state of fluid deficit are clear. The most effective drinks to be consumed during exercise will vary greatly between individuals, as will the amounts and timing of intake. In general, the aim should be to replace a substantial fraction of the fluid loss and to limit the extent of dehydration to no more than 1-2% of the pre-exercise body mass. The sweat rate can vary from a few hundred ml to more than 3 l per hour, depending on the climatic and exercise conditions and on the acclimatization status and physiological characteristics of the individual. Only by self-monitoring in the conditions of training and competition can athletes learn how much fluid they need and how much they can tolerate.

Fluids should contain some carbohydrate, and also some electrolytes, of which sodium is the main requirement. Although the optimum formulation of a sports drink will depend on the conditions, it is important that athletes choose a drink that is palatable under the conditions in which they will perform.

Practicing drinking in training is an important skill that is often neglected.

SUMMARY

Dehydration impairs performance and increases the risk of heat illness during exercise. Daily fluid losses are small in temperate conditions when no physical activity is performed, but sweat losses increase with ambient temperature and humidity and are greatly increased during hard exercise. Replacing losses by ingesting fluid during exercise improves performance and adding carbohydrate further improves performance. Sweat contains variable amounts of electrolytes, but sodium is the primary electrolyte lost. High sodium intakes may be necessary to replace losses in sweat. Carbohydrate and sodium should be added to drinks ingested during exercise, but the optimum formulation will depend on the exercise conditions and on the relative needs for carbohydrate supply and rehydration.

13

Alcohol and Sport

INTRODUCTION

Alcohol and sport are closely linked through sponsorship and advertising, with many sporting organizations, teams, and events being supported by companies who make beer and other alcoholic drinks. While a small number of athletes drink alcohol in the belief that it may improve their sports performance, alcohol consumption by athletes generally occurs in a social environment. However, these social occasions are often embedded in the culture that surrounds participation in sport. This chapter will review the effect of alcohol on sports performance, particularly binge drinking patterns that typify the alcohol intake of many athletes, and will provide some guidelines for sensible use of alcohol by sportspeople.

Alcohol use by athletes

How many athletes regularly consume alcohol and how much do these athletes drink? It is hard to find reliable answers to these questions. First, because alcohol intake typically provides only a minor contribution to daily energy intake (usually less than 5% of the total energy intake of adults), it is often excluded or forgotten in the results of dietary surveys of athletes. Second, experts in dietary survey research tell us that what people report about their use of alcohol is particularly unreliable. Athletes may either under-report their true use of alcohol if they feel they will be judged poorly because of it, or they may exaggerate their intake if they feel it is something to brag about.

In general, dietary surveys of athletes which include information about alcohol intake suggest that it contributes 0-5% of total energy intake in the everyday diet. However, these figures may provide a misleading view of the drinking habits of athletes. After all, many athletes only consume alcohol on a few occasions each week or month, but they consume it in large amounts at these times. This pattern was demonstrated in a dietary survey of Australian Football players whose mean daily intake of alcohol was reported to be a modest 20 g or two standard drinks. However, almost all this intake occurred during postmatch celebrations or commiserations, with the mean intake in this situation being 120 g (range 27-368 g), and alcohol providing a mean contribution of 19% of total energy intake on match day (range 3-43% of total energy intake). These self-reports of excessive alcohol intake after the game were confirmed when blood alcohol levels (BALs) were estimated at a training session on the morning after a game: 34% of players registered a positive BAL, with 10% of players showing a level above the legal limit for driving a motor vehicle. Binge drinking episodes are frequently the topic of stories or media reports about the off-field exploits of athletes. These appear to occur most often after a session of sport, at sport-related social events, or in the company of other athletes. Post-exercise drinking is subject to many rationalizations and justifications by athletes including "everyone is doing it", "I only drink once a week" and "I can run/ sauna it off the next morning". In some cases these episodes are romanticized and the drinking prowess of the athletes is admired.

Whether total alcohol intake, or episodes of heavy alcohol intake, by athletes are different from those of the general population is not known. Various theories have been proposed to explain likely associations between sport and alcohol use. On one hand it has been suggested that athletes might have a lower intake due to increased self-esteem, a more rigid lifestyle, and greater interest in their health and performance. Alternatively, alcohol has been associated with the rituals of relaxation and celebration in sport, and with risk taking, which may be higher among athletes. Several studies in different countries have reported that athletes report greater intakes of alcohol than sedentary people, with team sport players recording higher intakes than other types of athletes.

While there is some evidence that many athletes consume alcohol in excessive amounts, on at least some occasions, further studies are needed to fully determine the alcohol intake and patterns of use by athletes. Information on the attitudes and beliefs of athletes about alcohol is also desirable, since it would allow education programs to specifically target current drinking practices that are detrimental to the athlete's performance or health.

METABOLISM OF ALCOHOL

Table: A standard drink contains approximately 10 g of alcohol.

Drink	Amount (ml)
Standard beer (4% alcohol)	250
Low-alcohol beer (2% alcohol)	500
Cider, wine coolers, alcoholic soft drinks	250
Wine	100
Champagne	100
Fortified wines, sherry, port	60
Spirits	30

The NADH formed in these reactions must be re-oxidized within the mitochondria, but transfer of the hydrogen atoms into the mitochondria might be a limiting process that can interfere with carbohydrate metabolism. If the liver glycogen stores are low because of a combination of exercise and a low carbohydrate intake, the liver will be unable to maintain the circulating glucose concentration, leading to hypoglycemia.

Acetaldehyde, which is thought to be responsible for many of the adverse effects of alcohol, is metabolized within the liver. The rate at which ethanol is cleared by the liver varies widely between individuals, and the response of the individual will depend on the amount of ethanol consumed in relation to their habitual intake. There is conflicting information about whether the rate of metabolism of alcohol is increased by exercise. Table 6.1 summarizes the amount of alcohol contained in some standard servings of alcohol drinks.

The metabolism of alcohol (ethanol) occurs primarily in the liver, where it is oxidized first to acetaldehyde and then to acetate. The first step is catalysed by a number of hepatic enzymes, the most important of which is the NAD-dependent alcohol dehydrogenase:

$$CH_3CH_2OH + NAD^+ \rightarrow CH_3CHO + NADH + H^+$$

Aldehyde dehydrogenase catalyses the further oxidation of acetaldehyde to acetate:

$$CH3CHO + NADH+ + H_2O \rightarrow$$
$$CH_3COO^- + NADH + 2H^+$$

Effects of acute alcohol ingestion on exercise

In previous times, some athletes deliberately consumed alcohol immediately before or during an event in the hope of improving their performance. Alcohol was believed to decrease sensitivity to pain and increase confidence. Additional effects on the cardiovascular system were thought to reduce tremor and stress-induced emotional arousal, important issues during fine motor control sports. For this reason, although alcohol is no longer on the general doping list of the International Olympic Committee (IOC), it is still considered a banned substance in some sports such as shooting and fencing.

In modern sports practice, few athletes would intentionally consume alcohol during exercise as a performance aid. Even in sports like darts and billiards where participants popularly drink during competition, this practice is probably a reflection of the culture of games that are usually played in a hotel environment. Similarly, some people may undertake recreational exercise, such as snow- or water-skiing, with a positive blood alcohol level as a result of social activities between sessions of exercise. For these reasons it is useful to examine the effects of alcohol on exercise metabolism and performance. However such outcomes are hard to determine since alcohol has a variety of effects on different body tissues and there is great variability in individual responses to alcohol intake.

A position stand released in 1982 by the American College of Sports Medicine reviewed the acute effects of alcohol ingestion on metabolism and performance of exercise. The conclusion was that alcohol does not contribute significantly to energy stores used for exercise, and in situations of prolonged exercise it may increase the risk of hypoglycemia due to the suppression of glucose production by the liver. Increased heat loss may be associated with this hypoglycemia, as well as the cutaneous vasodilatation caused by exercise, causing an impairment of temperature regulation in cold environments.

Studies of the effects of alcohol on cardiovascular, respiratory, and muscular function have provided conflicting results. The outcomes vary according to the dose of alcohol consumed and there is considerable variability in the responses of different subjects. It is difficult to conduct alcohol studies according to the ideal protocols for scientific research since it is hard to provide a suitable placebo treatment people can generally tell when they have consumed large amounts of alcohol, and their beliefs may bias their performance.

Ethics committees are also reluctant to approve studies that may appear to encourage individuals to consume alcohol. Nevertheless, it has been generally concluded that the acute ingestion of alcohol has no beneficial effects on muscle function, and alcohol may actually produce detrimental effects on exercise performance when consumed in large doses.

Studies of alcohol and fine motor control and skill show a detrimental effect of small to moderate amounts of alcohol on reaction time, hand-eye coordination, accuracy, balance, and complex skilled tasks. In fact there is no evidence to support the proposed beneficial effects of reduced muscle tremor. However, alcohol intake may result in a greater feeling of self-confidence in athletes, and this may, in turn improve performance, or the perception of performance, in some situations. There is good reason for the legal bans on driving motor vehicles after having consumed moderate to large amounts of alcohol since this will interfere with the judgement and skill involved in this activity. Skilled performance in sport is not so different in this respect from driving a motor car.

EFFECTS OF ACUTE ALCOHOL INGESTION ON POSTEXERCISE RECOVERY

Alcohol intake and binge drinking seem particularly linked with postcompetition activities, and perhaps even the social rituals following training or practice sessions in some sports. Athletes are likely to be dehydrated and to have eaten little on the day of competition. Therefore, alcohol consumed after exercise is more quickly absorbed and likely to have greater effects than under normal circumstances. It is important to examine the effects of alcohol on processes that are important in the recovery from exercise, and on the performance of subsequent exercise bouts.

Rehydration

Rehydration is an important component of post-exercise recovery. The restoration of the fluid deficit caused by exercise is a balance between the amount of fluid that the athlete will drink after exercise, and their ongoing fluid losses.

The palatability of drinks provided after exercise will help to determine total fluid intake, while replacement of sodium losses is a major determinant of the success in retaining this fluid. It has been suggested that beer may be an acceptable postexercise beverage since athletes will voluntarily consume it in large volume! However, beer does not provide a substantial sodium content (unless it is accompanied by the intake of salty foods). Furthermore, alcohol is known to have a diuretic action that is likely to promote increased urine losses.

A study by Susan Shirreffs and Ron Maughan examined the effect of alcohol on postexercise rehy-dration after subjects had lost fluid equivalent to 2% of body mass (BM). Subjects replaced 150% of this volume of fluid by consuming drinks containing 0, 1, 2, or 4% alcohol.

The study found that total volume of urine produced during the 6 h of recovery was positively related to the alcohol content of the fluid. In the case of the 4% alcohol drink, subjects were still dehydrated at the end of the recovery period, despite having consumed 1.5 times the volume of their fluid deficit. Although individual variability must be taken into account, this study suggests that the intake of significant amounts of alcohol will interfere with rehydration.

In practical terms, low-alcohol beers (< 2% alcohol) or beer "shandies" (beer mixed in equal proportions with lemonade, to dilute the alcohol content and provide some carbohydrate) may not be detrimental to rehydration. In fact, these drinks might be useful in encouraging large fluid intakes in dehydrated athletes and the carbohydrate content of the lemonade may be useful for the replenishment of glycogen stores. However, wine and spirits with a more concentrated alcohol content are not advised, since effective fluid replacement will be reduced by the combination of a smaller fluid volume and a greater alcohol intake When rapid rehydration is required, the athlete should stick to a well-considered fluid intake plan that includes replacement of sodium.

Glycogen storage

Since alcohol has a number of effects on carbohydrate metabolism, it is possible that postexercise intake might impair the restoration of depleted glycogen stores. In the absence of carbohydrate intake, alcohol intake is known to impair the liver carbohydrate stores. Alcohol intake has been reported to impair muscle glycogen storage in rats following depletion by fasting or exercise; however, the effect in humans is not clear. Burke and colleagues undertook an investigation of the effects of alcohol intake on muscle glycogen storage in humans over 8 h and 24 h of recovery from a prolonged cycling bout. In these studies, athletes undertook three different diets following their glycogen-depleting exercise: a high-carbohydrate diet, an alcohol displacement diet (reduced carbohydrate + ~ 120 g alcohol) and an alcohol plus carbohydrate diet (~ 120 g alcohol added to the high-carbohydrate diet). Muscle glycogen storage was significantly reduced on the alcohol displacement diets when inadequate amounts of carbohydrate were consumed. On the other hand, when the high-carbohydrate diet was eaten, there was no clear evidence that alcohol intake caused a reduction in muscle glycogen storage. However, this may have been masked by the variability of the responses of different subjects.

The most important message of this study is that alcohol intake often has an indirect effect on postexercise refueling. Binge drinking is likely to prevent the athlete from consuming adequate carbohydrate intake after all, athletes do not often eat much food or make good choices of high-carbohydrate food on such an occasion. Food intake may also be affected over the next day as the athlete sleeps off his or her hangover.

Other effects

Many sporting activities are associated with muscle damage and soft tissue injuries, either as a direct consequence of the exercise, or as a result of accidents or the tackling and collisions involved in contact sports. Standard medical practice is to treat soft tissue injuries with vasoconstrictive techniques (e.g. rest, ice, compression, elevation). Since alcohol causes blood vessels to dilate it has been suggested that the intake of large amounts of alcohol might cause or increase undesirable swelling around damaged sites, and might impede repair processes. The evidence for this is mainly based on case studies and the subjective evaluation of physiotherapists who treat injured athletes, and there is a need for carefully controlled studies to investigate these observations. Until such studies are undertaken, it seems sensible for players who have suffered considerable muscle damage and soft tissue injuries to avoid any intake of alcohol in the immediate recovery phase (e.g. for 24 h after the event).

Since heat loss from the skin is another effect of cutaneous vasodilatation, athletes who consume large quantities of alcohol in cold environments may have problems with thermoregulation. An increased risk of hypothermia may be found in sports or recreational activities undertaken in cold weather, particularly hiking or skiing, where alcohol intake is an integral part of "après ski" activities.

However, it is likely that the major effect of excessive alcohol intake comes from the athlete's failure to follow guidelines for optimal recovery. The intoxicated athlete may fail to undertake sensible injury management practices or to report for treatment. In cold environments they may fail to seek suitable clothing or shelter, or to notice early signs of hypothermia. Studies which measure the direct effect of alcohol on thermoregulation and soft tissue damage are encouraged.

ACCIDENTS AND HIGH-RISK BEHAVIOR

Alcohol impairs judgement and reduces inhibitions. As a result, intoxicated athletes frequently undertake high-risk behavior, leading to an increased risk of accidents that may lead to injury and an inability to train or compete. Alcohol consumption is a major factor in road accidents, and is frequently involved with drowning accidents, spinal injuries, and other problems in recreational water activities.

As outlined in Expert Comment 1, athletes are not immune to the social and behavioral problems following excess alcohol intake. Further research is needed to investigate whether athletes, or some groups of athletes, are more likely to drink excessively or suffer a greater risk of alcohol-related problems. However, it appears that athletes should at least be included in population education programs related to drink-driving and other high-risk behavior.

Effect of previous day's intake (hangover) on performance

Some athletes will be required to train (or even compete again) on the day after a competition and its post-event drinking binge. In some cases, athletes may choose to drink heavily the night before a competition, as a general part of their social activities, or in the belief that this will help to "relax" them prior to the event. The effect of an "alcohol hangover" on performance is widely discussed by athletes, but has not been well studied. Two studies have looked at "next day" performance in athletes who consumed large amounts of alcohol. Although the study design was not ideal in either study, they reported a reduction in some but not all aspects of exercise performance in the hungover athletes. Research in other areas of industrial work (e.g. machine handling and flying) suggests that impairment of psychomotor skills may continue during the hangover phase. This is likely to be an issue in team and court sports that demand tactical play and a high skill level.

Effects of chronic alcohol intake on issues of sports performance

Athletes who frequently consume large amounts of alcohol face the large number of health and social problems associated with problem drinking. Early problems to affect sports performance include inadequate nutrition and a generally poor lifestyle (e.g. inadequate sleep and recovery). Since alcohol is an energy-dense nutrient (providing 7 kcal or 27 kJ per gram), weight gain is a typical problem arising from frequent episodes of heavy alcohol intake. The accompanying factors of erratic eating patterns and choice of high-fat foods can lead to excess energy consumption. A common story, particularly in team sports, is that athletes gain significant amounts of body fat during the off season due to increased alcohol intake coupled with reduced exercise expenditure. Many players need to spend a significant part of their preseason (and even early season) conditioning to reverse the problems of being overfat and unfit. Clearly this is a disadvantage to performance and to the longevity of a sports career.

Guidelines for sensible use of alcohol by athletes

It is important for athletes to set themselves a sensible plan regarding alcohol intake. The following guidelines are suggested.

1 It is an athlete's personal decision about whether to consume alcohol or not. Alcohol is not an essential component of a diet. However, there is no evidence of impairments to health and performance when alcohol is used sensibly.

2 Community guidelines in various countries provide messages about intakes of alcohol that are "safe and healthy". In general, they suggest that mean daily intake of alcohol intake should be less than 40-50 g (4-5 standard glasses) for males, and perhaps 20-30 g (2-3 standard glasses) for females. Binge drinking is discouraged. Since individual tolerance to alcohol is variable, it is difficult to set a precise definition of "heavy" intake or an alcohol "binge". However, intakes of about 80-100 g (8-10 standard glasses) at a single sitting are likely to constitute a heavy intake for most people.

3 Alcohol is a high-energy (and nutrient-poor) food and should be restricted when the athlete is attempting to reduce body fat.

4 Drinking large amounts of alcohol on the night before competition is unwise. However, it appears unlikely that the intake of one or two standard drinks will have negative effects in most athletes.

5 The intake of alcohol immediately before or during exercise does not enhance performance. In many athletes it may impair performance, particularly of psychomotor skills and judgement. Therefore the athlete should not consume alcohol deliberately to aid performance, and should be wary of exercise that is conducted in conjunction with the social intake of alcohol.

6 Excess intake of alcohol is likely to interfere with recovery after exercise. It may directly impair rehydration, glycogen recovery, and repair of soft tissue damage. More importantly, the athlete is unlikely to remember to undertake strategies for optimal recovery when they are intoxicated. Therefore, the athlete should attend to these strategies first before any alcohol is consumed. In the case of the athlete who has suffered a substantial soft tissue

injury, no alcohol should be consumed for 24 h after the event.

7 The athlete should rehydrate with appropriate fluids in volumes that are greater than their existing fluid deficit. Low-alcohol beers and beer-soft drink mixes may be suitable and seem to encourage large volume intakes. However, drinks containing more than 2% alcohol are not recommended during rehydration. Better choices include sports drinks, fruit juices, soft drinks (all containing carbohydrate), and water (when refueling is not a major issue). Sodium replacement via sports drinks, oral rehydration solutions, or salt-containing foods is also important to encourage the retention of these rehydration fluids.

8 Before consuming any alcohol after exercise, the athlete should consume a high-carbohydrate meal or snack to aid muscle glycogen recovery. Food intake will also help to reduce the rate of alcohol absorption and thus reduce the rate of intoxication.

9 Once postexercise recovery priorities have been addressed, the athlete who chooses to drink is encouraged to do so "in moderation". Drink-driving education messages in various countries provide guidelines for sensible and well-paced drinking.

10 Athletes who drink heavily after competition or at other times should take care to avoid driving and other high-risk activities.

11 It is difficult to change the attitudes and behaviors of athletes with regard to alcohol. However, coaches, managers, and sports medicine staff can encourage guidelines such as these. Importantly, they should reinforce these messages with an infrastructure that promotes sensible drinking practices. For example, alcohol should be banned from locker rooms, and replaced with snacks or meals appropriate to postexercise recovery strategies. In many cases, athletes drink in a peer group situation and it may be easier to change the environment in which this occurs than the immediate attitudes of the athletes.

SUMMARY

Alcohol is strongly linked with modern sport. The alcohol intakes and drinking patterns of athletes are not well studied, but it appears that some athletes undertake binge drinking practices, often associated with postcompetition socializing. There is no evidence that alcohol improves sports performance; in fact there is evidence that intake during or immediately before exercise, or large amounts consumed the night before exercise, may actually impair performance. There are considerable differences in the individual responses to alcohol intake. Recovery after exercise is likely to be impaired, particularly by the failure of the intoxicated athlete to follow guidelines for optimum recovery. Athletes are not immune to alcohol-related problems, including the greatly increased risk of motor vehicle accidents following excess alcohol intake. Not only should athletes be targeted for education about sensible drinking practices, they might also be used as spokespeople for community education messages.

Athletes are admired in the community and may be effective educators in this area. Alcohol is consumed in greater or lesser amounts by the vast majority of adults around the world, and merits education messages about how it might be used to enhance lifestyle rather than detract from health and performance.

14

Preparation for Competition

INTRODUCTION

The goal of competition nutrition strategies is to combat factors that would otherwise cause fatigue or loss of performance during an event. Factors that can stop the athlete from performing optimally include depletion of glycogen stores in the active muscle, hypoglycemia (low levels of blood glucose) and other mechanisms of "central fatigue" involving neurotransmitters, hyperthermia, dehydration, hyponatremia (low levels of blood sodium), and gastrointestinal discomfort and upset. These factors vary according to the duration and intensity of the exercise, the environmental conditions, and the athlete's individual characteristics including their nutritional and training status. Competition nutrition includes special eating strategies undertaken before, during, and in the recovery from the event. In this chapter we will review the strategies undertaken in the hours or days prior to competition to prepare the athlete to perform at his or her best. Ideally, these will form part of a total nutrition plan that is developed to meet the challenges of the event within the practical opportunities provided to the athlete.

Hydrating before the event

Dehydration poses one of the most common nutritional problems occurring in sport. Since some degree of dehydration during exercise is commonly experienced, it is critical for the athlete to start the session as well hydrated as possible. Therefore, athletes must ensure that they have fully replaced any previous fluid deficits, such as the dehydration incurred during a previous exercise session or in an attempt to "make weight" in a weight division sport. Sometimes the challenge comes simply from the fluid losses incurred as a result of living in a hot environment. The athlete needs to recognize such fluid deficits and drink appropriately during the hours leading up to the event to ensure that fluid balance is achieved prior to the start of the new event.

Some athletes attempt to "hyperhydrate" prior to a competition, especially when they expect that conditions in the event will lead to an inevitable and detrimental fluid deficit. Such dehydration can occur when an athlete's sweat rate is extremely high, when there is little opportunity to drink during the event, or when these factors are combined. However, even if the athlete is not aiming to "fluid overload", there can be good reasons to drink just before exercise. Effective rehydration during exercise depends on maximizing the rate of fluid delivery from the stomach to the intestine for absorption, with gastric stretching arising from the volume of stomach contents being one of the factors that stimulates high rates of gastric emptying.

An effective way to optimize fluid delivery during exercise is to begin the session with a comfortable volume of fluid in the stomach, then adopt a pattern of periodic fluid intake during exercise to replace the partially emptied gastric contents. Obviously the athlete will need to experiment to determine what is a comfortable volume with which to prime gastric volume, and in particular how comfortable this feels once exercise has commenced. However, as a general rule of thumb, most athletes can tolerate a bolus of about 300-400 ml of fluid immediately before the event starts. Waiting to become dehydrated before beginning to drink is a recipe for disaster.

Fueling up for the event

Depletion of body carbohydrate (CHO) stores is a major cause of fatigue during prolonged exercise, so pre-event nutrition strategies should focus on optimizing CHO stores in the muscle and liver. Early studies using muscle biopsy techniques, combined with new techniques involving nuclear magnetic resonance spectroscopy, have enabled sports scientists to investigate the factors that enhance or impair storage of muscle glycogen. Typically, the resting values for muscle glycogen in trained muscle are 100-120 mmol·kg wet weight $(ww)^{-1}$, and this will fall to a greater or lesser extent during each training session, depending primarily on the duration and intensity of the session. In the absence of muscle damage, muscle glycogen stores can be normalized by 24 h of rest and an adequate intake of CHO: 7-10 g per kilogram body mass (BM). Such stores appear adequate for the muscle fuel needs of events of less than 60-90 min in duration; at least, studies in which muscle glycogen stores have been supercompensated have generally failed to show a performance enhancement for events of this type.

For many athletes, normalizing muscle glycogen stores prior to competition might be as simple as scheduling a day of rest or light training before the event, while continuing to follow high CHO eating patterns. However, not all athletes eat sufficient CHO in their typical or everyday diets to maximize glycogen storage. This applies particularly to female athletes who restrict their total energy intake to control body fat levels. These athletes may need education or encouragement to temporarily increase their energy intakes to make fueling up the chief dietary goal on the day before competition. Similarly, some athletes may need to reorganize their training programs to allow lighter training sessions on the day prior to their event. In particular, the athlete should avoid training sessions that cause significant muscle damage on the day before competition, since glycogen storage is impaired by this damage.

Carbohydrate loading for endurance events

Carbohydrate loading refers to practices that aim to maximize or supercompensate muscle glycogen stores prior to a competitive event that would otherwise deplete these fuel reserves. CHO loading protocols may elevate muscle glycogen stores to ~ 150-250 mmol·kg ww^{-1}*a*up to twice the normal level. This will be an important strategy for events lasting more than 90 min, which would otherwise be limited by the depletion of muscle glycogen stores. CHO loading protocols were an outcome of the first studies to use biopsy techniques to directly measure glycogen concentrations in the muscle.

In a series of now classic studies undertaken in the 1960s, Scandinavian sports scientists showed that the capacity for prolonged moderate-intensity exercise was determined by the size of the pre-exercise muscle glycogen stores. Several days of low-CHO eating combined with regular training were found to deplete muscle glycogen stores, leading to a reduction in cycling endurance compared to that achieved on a normal CHO diet. However, the subsequent intake of a high-CHO diet for a few days caused a supercompensation of glycogen stores in the muscle that had previously been depleted, and an increase in the time to exhaustion during sub-maximal cycling. The activity of the glycogen synthase enzyme was identified as an important factor in glycogen synthesis. As a result of these studies, the sports world was introduced to the "classical" 7-day model of CHO loading, involving a 3-4-day "depletion" phase of hard training and low CHO intake, and finishing with a 3-4-day "loading" phase of high CHO eating and exercise taper. Early field studies of prolonged running events showed that CHO loading enhanced performance, not by allowing the athlete to run faster, but by prolonging the time that race pace could be maintained.

In the 1980s, sports scientists produced a "modified" CHO loading strategy after finding that well-trained athletes were able to supercompensate muscle glycogen stores without a depletion or 'glycogen-stripping" phase. Runners were found to be able to elevate their muscle glycogen stores with 3 days of taper and high CHO intake, regardless of whether this was preceded by a depletion phase or a more typical diet and training preparation. For well-trained athletes at least, CHO loading may be seen as an extended period (3-4 days) of "fueling up". This modified CHO loading protocol offers a more practical strategy for competition preparation, by avoiding the fatigue and complexity of extreme diet and training requirements associated with the previous depletion phase. However, although CHO loading is so well known that it has entered everyday language, even in its simplified form it seems difficult for athletes to master. At least one study has shown that in real life, athletes may not have the knowledge to plan a suitable exercise taper; furthermore, they fail to reach the daily CHO intake targets of 7-10 g·kg BM^{-1} needed to maximize glycogen storage.

Theoretically, CHO loading could enhance the performance of exercise or sporting events that would otherwise be limited by glycogen depletion. An increase in pre-event glycogen stores can prolong the duration for which moderate-intensity exercise can be undertaken before fatiguing. In fact, a review of available literature on CHO loading found that it typically postpones fatigue and extends the duration of steady-state exercise by ~ 20%. CHO loading may also enhance the performance of a set amount of work (i.e. a set distance) by preventing the decline in pace or work output that would otherwise occur as glycogen stores decline towards the end of the task. Again, the literature suggests that a performance improvement of 2-3% is achieved by CHO loading. Such an intervention would provide a substantial improvement in most simple endurance events such as marathons, prolonged cycling and triathlon races, and crosscountry skiing events. However, shorter events of 45-90-min duration do not generally show significant performance benefits from CHO loading.

While it is relatively easy to measure performance in a predictable event like a marathon, complex and variable events such as tennis matches or football matches that last for 90 min or more of playing time are harder to study. These sports, mixing prolonged duration and intermittent high-intensity exercise, which is associated with an increased rate of glycogen utilization, might be expected to result in muscle glycogen depletion. Intuitively, super-compensation of muscle glycogen stores prior to the event should lead to enhanced performance. Some studies have shown that CHO loading strategies are of benefit to the performance of the movement patterns in a soccer-simulated trial, an indoor soccer match, and a real-life ice hockey game. However, other studies have failed to show significant improvement in the performance of skill-based tasks in a simulation of a soccer match.

It is likely that benefits of CHO loading are specific not only to the sport, but to the individual athlete, depending on the requirements of their position or style of play. Of course, the logistics of competition in many of these sports, where games may be played twice a week or even more frequently, prevent the athlete from undertaking a full CHO loading preparation before each event. Nevertheless, athletes in these sports should fuel up prior to each competition as completely as is practical, and should perhaps experiment with an extended preparation before the most important games, such as the final of a tournament.

It should be remembered that most studies of glycogen storage or CHO loading have been undertaken in male subjects. It is assumed that the findings of these studies also apply to female athletes, although one study reported that female athletes are less responsive to a CHO loading protocol; they failed to supercompensate muscle glycogen stores or show a performance benefit compared to male subjects. However, it is difficult to undertake gender comparison studies due to problems in matching males and females for important parameters such as aerobic capacity (relative vs. absolute values), and to control for the phase of the menstrual cycle in females. One of the confounding issues in studies of female athletes is their intake of smaller amounts of dietary CHO as a result of restricted energy intake. Although females may increase CHO intake to achieve a similar relative energy contribution, total CHO intake will be restricted if total energy intake is low. Without a substantial increase in the intake of substrate, a female athlete could not expect to increase muscle fuel stores nor gain the potential performance enhancement arising from increased fuel availability.

Gender differences in substrate utilization and storage are still being investigated. There is some evidence that the menstrual status of female athletes affects glycogen storage, with greater storage occurring during the luteal phase rather than the follicular phase. One study of CHO loading undertaken with well-trained female athletes during the luteal phase of their menstrual cycle found an increase in muscle glycogen stores compared with storage on a moderate CHO intake, and increased time to exhaustion during submaximal cycling. Other studies have shown that females are equally able to increase muscle glycogen stores with an increase in dietary CHO intake, provided that total energy intake is adequate. It is likely that inadequate CHO intake is a common cause of suboptimal fuel stores in athletes who are driven by body fat and body mass concerns.

The pre-event meal (1-4 hours pre-event)

The goals of the pre-event meal are to:

1. continue to fuel muscle glycogen stores if they have not been fully restored or loaded since the last exercise session;
2. restore liver glycogen content, especially for events undertaken in the morning where liver stores are depleted from an overnight fast;
3. ensure that the athlete is well hydrated;
4. prevent hunger, yet avoid the gastrointestinal discomfort and upset often experienced during exercise; and

5 include foods and practices that are important to the athlete's psychology or superstitions.

A CHO-rich meal consumed 4 h before exercise significantly increases the glycogen content of muscle and liver that has been depleted by previous exercise or an overnight fast. Compared to results achieved after an overnight fast, the intake of a substantial amount of CHO (~ 200-300 g) in the 2-4 h before exercise has been shown to prolong cycling endurance and to enhance performance of time trial undertaken at the end of a standardized cycling task. CHO availability is enhanced by increasing muscle and liver glycogen stores, as well as providing a later release of glucose from the gastrointestinal space. Since liver glycogen stores are labile and may be substantially depleted by an overnight fast, CHO intake on the morning of an event may be important for maintaining blood glucose levels via hepatic glucose output during the latter stages of prolonged exercise.

Thus, the pre-event menu should include CHO-rich foods and drinks, especially in situations where body CHO stores are still suboptimal, or where the event is of a sufficient duration and intensity to challenge these stores. In the field, it is not always possible to consume a substantial amount of CHO in the 4 h before a sporting event. For example, it is unlikely that an athlete will want to sacrifice sleep to eat a large meal before an early morning race start. An alternative plan is to consume a lighter meal or snack before the event, and consume CHO throughout the event to balance missed fueling opportunities. This strategy may also make sense for athletes who are at risk of gastrointestinal discomfort from an excessive volume of food intake. Foods with a low fat, low fiber, and low to moderate protein content are the preferred choice for the pre-event menu since they are less prone to cause gastrointestinal upsets. Liquid meal supplements or CHO-containing drinks and bars are also useful for athletes who suffer from pre-event nerves. Above all, the athlete should practice their pre-event eating strategies during training and in less important competitions, and fine-tune a plan to meet their individual situation.

Is it bad to consume CHO in the hour before exercise?

Theoretically, CHO intake prior to exercise could provide a disadvantage rather than an advantage for exercise metabolism and performance. The elevation of plasma insulin concentrations following pre-exercise CHO feedings suppresses the release of fatty acids from adipose cells and thus decreases fat utilization, causing an increase in CHO oxidation and a decline in plasma glucose concentrations at the onset of exercise. These metabolic alterations have been observed even when CHO was consumed 4 h before exercise, and persisted despite the normalization of plasma glucose and insulin concentrations at the onset of exercise. However, they might be of greater magnitude if exercise is undertaken in the hour after eating a CHO-rich snack, and insulin is still elevated at the onset of the session.

Warnings to avoid CHO intake during the hour prior to endurance exercise became sports nutrition dogma following the results of a couple of studies published in the late 1970s. One investigation in particular found that athletes who consumed 75 g of glucose 30 min prior to exercise had a performance impairment in comparison to a trial undertaken after an overnight fast. The researchers observed a rapid drop in blood glucose concentration during the first 10 min of exercise after subjects had been fed CHO, but noted that this response was transient and was not associated with fatigue. Instead they attributed the reduction in endurance following CHO feeding to an accelerated utilization of muscle glycogen, although muscle glycogen content was not actually determined. However, reviews of the literature reveal that this is the only study to find a reduction in performance capacity after the ingestion of CHO in the hour before exercise. This must be balanced against the large number of other investigations of pre-exercise CHO feeding where the effect on performance has ranged from neutral to a significant improvement. In most cases, the decline in blood glucose observed during the first 20 min of exercise is self-corrected with no apparent effects on the athlete.

Nevertheless, it seems that there are a few athletes who have a negative response to CHO feedings in the hour before exercise. These athletes experience an exaggerated CHO oxidation and decrease in blood glucose concentrations at the start of exercise, suffering a rapid onset of fatigue and symptoms of hypoglycemia. Why some athletes experience such an extreme reaction is not known. One study found that risk factors for this problem include the intake of small amounts of CHO (< 50 g), increased sensitivity to insulin, a lower sympathetic-induced counter-regulation, and exercise intensity of low to moderate workload. Not all athletes who experience a major decline in blood glucose concentrations experience hypoglycemic symptoms; these is some evidence that sensitization to low glucose levels may adapt the athlete to an increased threshold before symptoms are reported.

Nevertheless, these effects are so clear-cut that athletes at risk are easily identified. Preventative action includes a number of options such as experimenting to find the critical time before exercise that CHO intake should be avoided and ensuring that the pre-event snack/meal provides a substantial amount of CHO (> 70 g). The choice of low glycemic index (GI) CHO-rich options in the pre-event menu, which have an attenuated and sustained blood glucose and insulin response, may also be useful for some athletes, although a universal benefit is not supported. Athletes may also find it helpful to include some high-intensity sprints during the warm-up to the event to stimulate hepatic glucose output. To many sprints will reduce the muscle glycogen content so some care is necessary. Finally, the intake of CHO during the event should prevent any problems of hypoglycemia as well as providing an important strategy for the promotion of performance.

SUMMARY

The importance of pre-event eating strategies will depend on the range and severity of physiological challenges that are likely to limit performance in the athlete's individual event. This is determined by characteristics of the event itself, as well as the degree to which the athlete has been able to recover since his or her last workout or competition event. Pre-event preparation should consider fluid balance, with strategies to rehydrate from previous dehydration associated with exercise or weight-making activities, as well as the potential for hyperhydra-tion in preparation for events in which a large fluid deficit is unavoidable. Nutrition strategies should also include an increase in dietary CHO during the day or days prior to the event, as well as the extended fueling up known as CHO loading, which has been shown to enhance endurance and the performance of prolonged exercise events. The pre-event meal also provides an opportunity to refuel muscle and liver glycogen stores.

There is some concern that pre-exercise CHO feedings may increase CHO utilization during exercise, but the intake of substantial amounts of CHO can offset the increased rate of substrate use. The choice of low GI CHO-rich foods in the pre-event menu may also sustain the delivery of CHO during exercise; however, this does not provide a guaranteed performance advantage, especially when additional CHO is consumed during the event. A variety of eating practices can be chosen by athletes to meet their competition preparation goals. These need to consider the practical aspects of nutrition such as gastrointestinal comfort, the athlete's likes and dislikes, and food availability. Above all, athletes should experiment with their pre-event nutrition practices to find and fine-tune strategies that are successful.

15

Eating and Drinking

INTRODUCTION

Ingestion of food and fluid during exercise has the potential to improve performance by influencing one or more of the factors that limit exercise performance. Prolonged hard exercise is associated with an increased body temperature, a decrease in body water content due to sweat loss, and a fall in the body's liver and muscle carbohydrate (CHO) stores. All of these factors can impair performance by reducing exercise capacity and, in some circumstances, by bringing about an impairment of skilled movements and of decision making. Ingestion of CHO and fluids before and during competition can improve performance, but athletes prone to gastrointestinal problems often avoid any solid or liquid intake for some hours before, and also during, competition. The demands of travel, precompetition preparation, and frequent competitions may also limit the opportunities for eating and drinking. The choice of food and fluids to be consumed during an event will be influenced by a variety of factors, including the nature and duration of the event, the climatic conditions, the pre-event nutritional status, and the physiological and biochemical characteristics of the individual.

Food and fluid consumed during competition are part of a specific short-term nutritional strategy aimed at maximizing performance at that particular time. There is no need to take account of long-term nutritional goals, except perhaps, and even then only to a limited extent, in extreme endurance events such as the Tour de France or in multiday running events. A balanced nutrient composition is therefore not necessary and intake is targeted at minimizing the impact of those factors that are responsible for fatigue and impaired performance. The primary considerations for food and fluid intake during exercise are to supplement the body's limited carbohydrate stores, and to provide water, and in some situations also electrolytes, to replace sweat losses. There is good evidence that CHO metabolism is central to the athlete's ability to perform well in competition. In warm environments, however, fatigue occurs while substantial CHO stores remain, and performance is limited more by thermoregulatory failure and dehydration. These observations point clearly to the nutritional strategies that the athlete should adopt to improve performance.

CHO supplementation during exercise

CHO ingested during exercise will enter the blood glucose pool at a rate that will be dictated by the rates of gastric emptying and absorption from the intestine; if this exogenous CHO can substitute for the body's limited endogenous glycogen stores, then exercise capacity should be increased in situations where liver or muscle glycogen availability limits endurance. Several studies have shown that the ingestion of even modest amounts of glucose during prolonged exercise will maintain or raise the circulating glucose concentration. Glucose can be replaced by a variety of other sugars, including sucrose, glucose polymers, and mixtures of sugars, without markedly affecting this response.

In well-trained marathoners running at racing pace, the rate of CHO oxidation can be about 3-4 g min^{-1}, but if this was sustained the available CHO stores would be depleted long before the finish line was reached. Certainly in cycling, and perhaps also in running, the point of fatigue in prolonged exercise carried out in cool or temperate conditions coincides closely with the depletion of glycogen in the exercising muscles. Increasing muscle glycogen stores prior to exercise can improve performance in both cycling and running, and performance is closely related to the size of the pre-exercise glycogen stores. Improvements in performance have also been reported in cycling time trials carried out in the laboratory, and in a variety of running models, including intermittent shuttle running tests. A laboratory study showed that ingestion of 1l of a glucose polymer-sucrose (50 g l^{-1}) solution did not increase the total distance covered in a 2-h treadmill run, but subjects ran faster over the last 30 min of exercise when CHO was given compared with a placebo trial. A similar effect was seen when a CHO solution (50 g of glucose-glucose polymer, or 50 g of fructose-glucose polymer) or water was given in a 30-km treadmill time trial. The running speed decreased over the last 10 km of the water trial, but was maintained on the other two runs; there was no significant difference between the three trials in the time taken to cover the total distance. This ergogenic effect was initially attributed to a sparing of the body's limited muscle glycogen stores by the oxidation of the ingested CHO, but other studies have failed to show a glycogen-sparing effect of CHO ingested during prolonged exercise. The current consensus view seems to be that there is probably little or no sparing of muscle glycogen utilization in cycling exercise but there is good evidence for muscle glycogen sparing in running.

Tracer studies have shown that a substantial part of the CHO ingested during exercise is available for oxidation, but there appears to be an upper limit of about 1 g min^{-1} to the rate at which ingested CHO can be oxidized, even when much larger amounts are ingested. This has been used as an argument to suggest that CHO should not be ingested at rates of more than 1 g min^{-1}, but these high rates of oxidation will not be achieved unless the amount ingested is in excess of this. Based on the feeding protocols used in studies that show performance enhancements, it has been suggested that carbohydrate should be ingested at a rate of about 30-60 g per hour.

Studies in field situations, or in laboratory settings simulating competition, have shown that CHO ingestion during team and racquet games sometimes, but not always, enhances measures of mental and physical skill by reducing the impairment seen with fatigue. A growing number of studies report benefits of CHO ingestion during high-intensity exercise lasting about 1 h. In these situations, the intake of a CHO drink was shown to enhance the performance of running and cycling time trials (lasting about 10 min) undertaken at the end of about 50-60 min of exercise, or cycling time trials lasting 1 h. CHO availability to the muscle is not considered to be limiting in the performance of such exercise, and further research is needed to confirm and explain these effects. It is possible that benefits to "central performance", involving the brain and nervous system, are involved. In most sports, practical considerations dictate the timing and frequency of CHO (and fluid) intake during the event. Intake is generally much less in running than in cycling events of comparable duration, as few runners are able to tolerate solid food, even when the exercise intensity is low. Intake during competition may be limited by consideration of the time lost in stopping or slowing down to consume food or fluid, or the impact of such ingestion on gastrointestinal discomfort. In other events, such as team sports, formal and informal pauses in play provide opportunities to consume CHO or fluid. Effects of hyperthermia and dehydration on performance

The perception of effort is increased, and exercise capacity reduced, in hot climates. In a laboratory study, exercise capacity was greatly reduced at 31°C (55 min) compared to 11°C (93 min): exercise time was also reduced (to 81 min) at the comparatively modest temperature of 21°C. Other studies have shown similar effects and also showed that muscle glycogen was not depleted at the point of fatigue at high ambient temperature (40°C). Dehydration can compromise performance in high-intensity exercise as well as endurance activities. Although sweat losses during brief exercise are small, prior dehydration (by as much as 10% of body mass) is common in weight category sports. Prolonged exercise resulting in a loss of fluid corresponding to 2.5% of body weight was found to result in a 45% fall in the capacity to perform high-intensity exercise. Even very small fluid deficits may impair performance, but the methods used are not sufficiently sensitive to detect small changes.

The mechanisms responsible for the reduced exercise performance in the heat are not entirely clear, but it has been proposed that the high core temperature itself is involved. This proposition was based on the observation that a period of heat acclimatization was successful in delaying the point of fatigue, but that this occurred at the same core temperature. The primary effect of acclimatization was to lower the resting core temperature, and the rate of rise of temperature was the same on all trials. This observation is further supported by numerous studies which show that manipulation of the body heat content prior to exercise can alter exercise capacity: performance is extended by prior immersion in cold water and reduced by prior immersion in hot water. This, of course, immediately raises questions about the "warming up" strategies that should be adopted before exercise in hot climates.

ELECTROLYTE LOSS AND REPLACEMENT

The sweat loss that accompanies prolonged exercise leads to a loss of electrolytes and water from the body. Sodium is the most abundant cation of the extracellular space, and is the major electrolyte lost in plasma; chloride, which is also mainly located in the extracellular space, is the major anion. The greatest fraction of fluid loss is therefore derived from the extracellular space, including the plasma. Although the composition of sweat is highly variable, sweat is always hypotonic with regard to body fluids, and the net effect of sweat loss is an increase in plasma osmolality. The plasma concentration of sodium and potassium also generally increases, suggesting that replacement of these electrolytes during exercise may not be necessary.

When the exercise duration is very prolonged and when excessively large volumes of low-sodium drinks (such as plain water or cola drinks) are taken during exercise, hyponatremia has been reported to occur. Hyperthermia and hypernatremia associated with dehydration are commonly encountered in athletes requiring medical attention at the end of long-distance races, and the symptoms usually resolve on treatment with oral rehydration solutions. A small number of individuals at the end of very prolonged events may be suffering from hyponatremia in conjunction with either hyper-hydration or dehydration. Most of the cases have occurred in events lasting in excess of 8 h, and there are few reports of cases where the exercise duration is less than 4 h. Supplementation with sodium may be required where large sweat losses occur and where it is possible to consume large volumes of fluid. Most competitors, however, will be hypohydrated and hypernatremic.

Fluid replacement and exercise performance

Only a few studies have investigated the effects of plain water or of CHO-free electrolyte solutions on performance. In prolonged exercise at low intensity, water may be as effective as dilute saline solutions or nutrient-electrolyte solutions in maintaining cardiovascular and thermoregulat-ory function: when subjects ingested plain water (100 ml every 10 min) median exercise time was longer (93 min) than when no drink was given (81 min). Subjects also completed trials where dilute CHO-electrolyte drinks were given and these also extended exercise time compared to the no-drink trial. In a prolonged (90-min) intermittent high-intensity shuttle running test designed to simulate the demands of competitive soccer, ingestion of flavored water was found to prevent a decline in performance of a soccer-specific skilled task: when no fluid was given, performance deteriorated.

The effects of providing fluid and CHO were investigated in a study where subjects performed 50 min of exercise at about 80% of ^O_{2max} followed by a time trial where a set amount of work had to be completed as fast as possible. During the initial 50 min of exercise, subjects were given either a small volume (200 ml) of water, a small volume of water with added CHO (40% solution, 79 g of maltodex-trin), a large volume (1330 ml) of flavored water, or a large volume of water with the same amount of CHO as in the other CHO trial (as a 6% solution). Water ingestion was found to be effective in improving performance; exercise time was 11.34 min on the placebo trial and 10.51 min on the water trial. Exercise time on the CHO trial was 10.55 min, indicating that CHO provision during exercise acted independently to improve performance, and the effects were found to be additive, with the shortest time (9.93 min) when the 6% CHO drink was given.

The results of these and other studies suggest that fluid replacement is effective in improving exercise performance in a variety of different situations, and that an additional benefit is gained by the addition of CHO, and possibly also of electrolytes, to fluids ingested during exercise. The optimum formulation of drinks for use in different exercise situations has not, however, been clearly established at the present time.

Guidelines for replacing fluid and CHO during exercise

As well as providing an energy substrate for the working muscles, CHO added to ingested drinks can promote water absorption in the small intestine. Because of the role of sugars and sodium in promoting water uptake in the small intestine, it is sometimes difficult to separate the effects of water replacement from those of substrate and electrolyte replacement when CHO-electrolyte solutions are ingested. It was shown in the study mentioned above that ingestion of CHO and water have separate and additive effects on exercise performance, and it might be concluded from this that ingestion of dilute CHO solutions would optimize performance. Most reviews of the available literature have come to the same conclusion. The optimum concentration of CHO to be added to a sports drink will depend on individual circumstances. High CHO concentrations will delay gastric emptying, reducing the amount of fluid that is available for absorption, but will increase the rate of CHO delivery. If the concentration is high enough to result in a markedly hypertonic solution, net secretion of water into the intestine will result, and this will actually increase the danger of dehydration. Dilute glucose-electrolyte solutions may be as effective as, or even more effective than, more concentrated solutions in improving performance, and adding as little as 90 mmol l^{-1} (about 16 g l^{-1}) glucose may improve endurance performance. The consequences of severe dehydration and hyper-thermia are serious and potentially fatal, but the symptoms of CHO depletion are usually nothing more than severe fatigue. It seems sensible to focus on fluid replacement and to favor low-CHO, high-sodium drinks when training or competing in warm weather.

CHO-electrolyte sports drinks are often referred to as isotonic drinks, as though tonicity were their most important characteristic. The osmolality of ingested fluids is important as this can influence the rates both of gastric emptying and of intestinal water flux. Both of these processes together will determine the effectiveness of rehydration fluids at delivering water for rehydration and substrate for oxidation. Ingestion of strongly hypertonic drinks will promote net secretion of water into the intestine and, although this effect is transient, it will result in a temporary exacerbation of the extent of dehydration. The composition of the drinks, and the nature of the solutes is, however, of greater importance than the osmolality itself. Most of the popular sports drinks are formulated to have as osmolality close to that of body fluids, and are promoted as isotonic drinks, but there is good evidence that hypotonic solutions are more effective when rapid rehydration is desired.

Electrolyte composition and concentration

The available evidence indicates that the only electrolyte that should be added to drinks consumed during exercise is sodium, which may be added in the form of sodium chloride or sodium citrate (the latter helps regulate the acidity of the drink). Sodium will stimulate sugar and water uptake in the small intestine and will help to maintain extracellular fluid volume. The optimum sodium concentration is unclear, and equilibration may occur so rapidly in the upper part of the small intestine that addition of high concentrations of sodium is not necessary. Most soft drinks of the cola or lemonade variety contain virtually no sodium (1-2 mmol $\cdot l^{-1}$), but sports drinks commonly contain about 10-30 mmol $\cdot l^{-1}$ sodium. A high sodium content may stimulate absorption of glucose and water in the upper part of the small intestine, but too much can make drinks unpalatable. Drinks intended for ingestion during or after exercise should have a pleasant taste in order to stimulate consumption. Specialist sports drinks are generally formulated to strike a balance between the twin aims of efficacy and palatability.

Taste

The thirst mechanism is rather insensitive and does not stimulate drinking behavior until some degree of dehydration has been incurred. This absence of a drive to drink is reflected in the rather small volumes of fluid that are typically consumed during exercise. In endurance running events, voluntary intake seldom exceeds about 0.5 L $\cdot h^{-1}$, and seems to be largely unrelated to the sweating rate. Because the sweat losses normally exceed this, even in cool conditions, a fluid deficit is almost inevitable whenever prolonged exercise is performed. Anything that stimulates drinking behavior is therefore likely to be advantageous, and palatability is clearly important. Several factors will influence palatability, and the addition of a variety of flavors has been shown to increase fluid intake relative to that ingested when only plain water is available. The addition of flavorings can result in an increased consumption (by about 50%) of fluid during prolonged exercise. Athletes and coaches should recognize that relying on the thirst mechanism to prompt drinking will not result in an adequate intake: a conscious effort is necessary to prevent dehydration.

ADDITION OF OTHER NUTRIENTS AND INGREDIENTS

Many commercial sports drinks and energy products for athletes contain a wide range of added vitamins, minerals, and other ingredients. There is, however, no compelling evidence for a beneficial effect of any of these additives. The athlete's normal diet should supply the essential nutrients and, except in a few extremely unusual situations, food and fluid ingested during exercise will not make a significant contribution to an athlete's total energy or nutrient intake.

Gastrointestinal disturbances during exercise

Disturbances of both the upper and lower gastrointestinal tract may occur during exercise, with problems including reflux, burping, gastritis, and vomiting (upper), and cramp, irritable bowel, and diarrhea (lower). These problems not only cause distress or embarrassment to the athlete, but may exacerbate the performance and health impairments caused by dehydration or low carbohydrate availability during exercise. After all, symptoms such as vomiting and diarrhea cause the further loss of fluids and electrolytes from the body, as well as impeding the potential for replacement of fluid, electrolytes, and carbohydrate during the exercise session. Exercise can be a direct cause of gastrointestinal problems or it may simply exacerbate underlying problems in individual athletes. Factors that seem to be involved in the development of problems include high-intensity exercise, exercise involving "joggling" of the gut (e.g. running), moderate to severe levels of dehydration, and the intake of inappropriate amounts or types of foods and fluids before or during exercise. Dietary factors that can be modified include the timing and volume of food consumed before exercise, and the presence of large amounts of fiber, fat, protein, fructose, or lactose in pre-event meals. Factors that may cause problems during exercise include dehydration (i.e. waiting too long before attempting to replace fluids during the session), and the intake of fluids or foods that are too highly concentrated, or have an excessive amount of fructose or fiber. Females appear to be at greater risk of gut disturbances, and training appears to reduce the frequency of symptoms. Athletes who experience gut problems should seek the advice of a sports doctor, and be prepared to experiment with their pre-event and during-event nutrition strategies.

SUMMARY

The intake of fluid and CHO offers benefits to the performance of most sports events and exercise activities. The effects of dehydration on performance are now well known, with the penalties ranging from subtle, but often important, decrements in performance at low levels of fluid deficit, to the severe health risks associated with substantial fluid losses during exercise in the heat. Beneficial effects of CHO intake during exercise appear to occur across a variety of activities, ranging from high-intensity sessions lasting about 1 h to more prolonged sessions of moderate-intensity, or intermittent high-intensity work. Optimal strategies for CHO and fluid intake during exercise are yet to be fine-tuned, and ultimately will be determined by practical issues such as the opportunity to eat or drink during an event, and gastrointestinal comfort.

16

Post-event Recovery

INTRODUCTION

In the world of sport, success is often determined by the athlete's ability to recover between one exercise bout and the next. In sports such as track and field or swimming, athletes compete in a program of brief races heats, semifinals, and finals often performing more than once each day. In cycling stage races, and tennis or team sport tournaments, the schedule consists of one or more lengthy events each day, with the competition extending for 1-3 weeks. Even where teams compete in a weekly fixture, the athlete must train between matches or races to maintain fitness.

Perhaps even more importantly, the daily training program for many sports, even at a recreational level, involves one or more workouts, with less than 24 h separating each session. The ability to recover between training sessions and to maintain quality training without succumbing to the effects of cumulative fatigue and injury is a key characteristic of the top athletes. To meet these challenges, an athlete must practice special recovery strategies between sessions.

Recovery encompasses a complex range of nutrition-related issues including:

- restoration of muscle and liver glycogen stores;
- replacement of fluid and electrolytes lost in sweat; and
- regeneration, repair, and adaptation processes following the catabolic stress and damage caused by the exercise.

This chapter will provide an overview of the well-defined issues of postexercise refueling and rehydra-tion. The biochemical and physiological events that make up the regeneration and repair processes remain somewhat nebulous, and involve activities ranging from the synthesis of protein (muscle cells, enzymes, etc.) to the activities of the antioxidant defense systems and the immune system. At present, we are unable to make definite recommendations on strategies to optimize all the recovery processes. However, it seems prudent to promote a varied intake of nutrients in postexercise eating strategies. Such variety will help to meet the needs of recovery processes that are yet to be well defined.

Postexercise refueling

There is a strong drive to restore glycogen levels in a muscle whose carbohydrate stores have been depleted by exercise, with muscle glycogen storage taking priority over the restoration of liver glycogen content. The rate of synthesis is determined by factors that regulate glucose transport into the cell (for example, glucose supply and glucose uptake) as well as glucose disposal (for example, the activity of glycogen synthase enzyme). Brief periods of high-intensity exercise resulting in high postexercise levels of lactate are associated with rapid recovery of muscle glycogen stores, even in the absence of carbohydrate intake after exercise. In the case of prolonged moderate-intensity exercise, however, muscle glycogen synthesis is largely dependent on the postexercise carbohydrate supply. In the absence of dietary intake of carbohydrate, synthesis occurs at a low rate (1-2 mmol per kg wet weight (ww) of muscle per hour), with some of the substrate being provided through gluconeogenesis. Glycogen storage follows a two-phase timescale: a very rapid synthesis during the first hour after exercise, followed by a slower restoration phase that is under the influence of factors such as insulin. When optimal amounts of carbohydrate are consumed, maximal rates of postexercise muscle glycogen storage during the first 12 h of recovery are within the range of 5-10 $mmol \cdot kg\ ww^{-1} \cdot h^{-1}$ and gradually decline as restoration continues. In the face of substantial glycogen depletion, 20-24 h of well-fed recovery are required for the restoration of muscle glycogen stores.

Liver glycogen stores are more labile than muscle glycogen stores, and may be depleted by an overnight fast as well as a prolonged bout of exercise. Strategies to enhance the restoration of liver glycogen store have been less well studied due to practical problems in obtaining liver biopsy samples. However, it is considered that liver glycogen is restored by a single carbohydrate-rich meal.

Dietary factors that can impair or enhance the refueling of muscle glycogen stores will be reviewed in greater detail below.

AMOUNT OF CARBOHYDRATE

The most important dietary factor affecting muscle glycogen storage is the amount of carbohydrate consumed. There is a direct relationship between the quantity of dietary carbohydrate and the rate of postexercise glycogen storage, at least until the muscle storage capacity or threshold has been reached. Studies suggest that the threshold varies between individual athletes but generally occurs within the intake of 7-10 g carbohydrate per kg body mass (BM). Maximal refueling during the first 0-6 h of recovery is achieved when foods or drink providing a carbohydrate intake of about 1 $g \cdot kg^{-1}$ are consumed during the first hour, and repeated every 2 h until the normal meal pattern can be resumed.

These figures form the basis of carbohydrate intake guidelines for athletes who desire to optimize muscle glycogen recovery within a busy training or competition schedule. However, total carbohydrate intake recommendations or requirements may be higher in some situations.

For example, athletes who undertake strenuous daily competition may need to meet the fuel requirements of their continued exercise in addition to postexercise recovery needs. For example, cyclists undertaking prolonged daily training sessions or stage races may need to consume carbohydrate intakes of more than 12 $g \cdot kg\ BM^{-1}$. In fact, the ingestion of substantial amounts of carbohydrate during low to moderate intensity exercise has been reported to cause a net glycogen storage during the session, particularly within non-active muscle fibers that have been previously depleted. Increased carbohydrate intake may also be useful in the case of muscle damage (e.g. following eccentric exercise or substantial contact injuries), which typically impairs the rate of postexercise glycogen resynthesis. In this case, low rates of glycogen restoration in damaged muscles may be partially overcome by increased amounts of carbohydrate intake during the first 24 h of recovery.

Timing of carbohydrate intake

The highest sustained rates of glycogen storage occur during the first few hours after exercise. In addition to the activation of the glycogen synthase enzyme, early postexercise recovery is marked by an exercise-induced permeability of the muscle cell membrane to glucose and an increased muscle sensitivity to insulin. Carbohydrate feeding during these early stages appears to accentuate these effects by increasing blood glucose and insulin concentrations. The intake of carbohydrate immediately after prolonged exercise has been shown to result in higher rates of glycogen storage (~ 8 mmol kg $ww^{-1} \cdot h^{-1}$) during the first 2 hours of recovery, slowing thereafter to the more typical rates of storage (~ 4 mmol $\cdot$kg $ww^{-1} \cdot h^{-1}$). However, failure to consume carbohydrate in the immediate postexercise phase of recovery leads to very low rates of glycogen restoration (1-2 mmol $\cdot$kg $ww^{-1} \cdot h^{-1}$) until feeding occurs. If ingestion of carbohydrate is delayed for 2 h or more, this phase of very rapid carbohydrate synthesis is missed. Thus the importance of early intake of carbohydrate following strenuous exercise is to start effective refueling by ensuring the provision of substrate to the muscle cell. This strategy is most important when there is only 4-8 h of recovery between exercise sessions, but may be of less significance when there is a longer recovery time (24 or more hours).

Overall it appears that when the interval between exercise sessions is short, the athlete should maximize the effective recovery time by beginning carbohydrate intake as soon as possible. However, when longer recovery periods are available, the athlete can choose their preferred eating schedule as long as total carbohydrate intake goals are achieved. It is not always practical or enjoyable to consume substantial meals or snacks immediately after the finish of a strenuous workout.

Whether carbohydrate is best consumed in large meals or as a series of snacks is of practical interest to athletes. One study has shown that very high rates of glycogen synthesis can be achieved during the first couple of hours after exercise when substantial amounts of carbohydrate are consumed every 15 min during recovery. However, these rates were simply compared with the values reported in other studies rather than being directly measured against a different eating schedule. This finding needs to be confirmed by other studies. In terms of long-term refueling (24 h of recovery), several studies have reported that as long as total carbohydrate is adequate, the rate of muscle glycogen synthesis appears unaffected by the frequency of intake. One benefit of small frequent meals may be in overcoming the gastric discomfort often associated with eating large amounts of bulky high-carbohydrate foods. It is also possible that when total carbohydrate intake is limited, there may be some advantage in altering the pattern of intake to promote greater blood glucose and insulin profiles at key times.

TYPE OF CARBOHYDRATE INTAKE

Different types of carbohydrate and carbohydrate-rich foods appear to have different effects on rates of muscle glycogen synthesis. Studies using feedings of simple sugars have found that glucose and sucrose feedings produce similar rates of muscle glycogen recovery after exercise, whereas the intake of fructose produces a lower rate of glycogen storage in the exercised muscles. However, these studies are of little practical relevance to athletes who need to eat real food to achieve their everyday nutrition goals.

Since glycogen storage is influenced by both insulin and a rapid supply of glucose substrate, it has been proposed that dietary carbohydrates designated as high glycemic index (GI) might enhance postexercise refueling. The GI system classifies carbohydrate-rich foods according to actual measurements of blood glucose levels following the intake of each food. Older studies investigating the effect of different types of carbohydrate-rich foods on glycogen storage failed to find consistent results, most probably because they used the confusing system of classifying carbohydrate foods as "simple" or "complex". However this system does not truly differentiate the effects of different carbohydrate-rich foods on glucose and insulin responses.

One study supports the benefits of refueling with high GI carbohydrate-rich foods, observing greater glycogen storage during 24 h of postexercise recovery on a diet based on high GI carbohydrate-rich foods compared to a diet based on low GI carbohydrate sources. However, the magnitude of increase in glycogen storage (~ 30%) with the high GI carbohydrate trial was far greater than the increase in 24-h blood glucose and insulin concentrations following the high GI trial. In other words, while the outcome of the study was as predicted, it could not be explained in terms of alteration of glucose and insulin responses. The cause of reduced glycogen storage with low GI carbohydrate foods is unclear, but may be in part due to the relatively poor digestibility of many of these foods. A diet or meals based on indigestible carbohydrate foods may overestimate the real amount of carbohydrate that is available for glycogen storage by the muscle. This issue needs to be further studied.

Form of carbohydrate feeding

Solid and liquid forms of carbohydrate appear to be equally effective in providing substrate for muscle glycogen synthesis. Practical issues such as compactness and appetite appeal may be important in choosing a menu that meets the athlete's total carbohydrate intake goals. Liquid forms of carbohydrate or carbohydrate foods with a high fluid content may be particularly appealing in hot weather or to athletes who are too fatigued to eat bulky foods.

Co-ingestion of protein

It is possible that other macronutrients present in carbohydrate-rich foods or simultaneously ingested at a meal may influence muscle glycogen storage for example, by affecting digestion, insulin secretion, or the satiety of meals. The effect of adding protein to a carbohydrate-rich meal or snack has been the focus of attention because of the suggestion that it achieves a greater postmeal insulin response, which might in turn stimulate glycogen synthesis. Indeed, one well-quoted study reported that the 2-hourly feedings of protein (40 g) and carbohydrate (112 g) achieved a greater rate of muscle glycogen storage during 4 h of recovery than the carbohydrate alone. More recent versions of this type of study involve the comparison of concentrated carbohydrate-protein sports supplements to sports drinks.

Unfortunately, studies of this type are flawed by the failure to match the energy content of the diets it is impossible to know whether additional glycogen storage is due to the protein *per se*, or the extra energy consumed by the subjects. Although it is a good marketing ploy by the manufacturers of various sports supplements, it is unfair to compare equal volumes of a concentrated (e.g. 20% carbohydrate) drink with a dilute (e.g. 6%

carbohydrate) drink. In fact, in several recent studies of postexercise refueling in which carbohydrate and carbohydrate-protein mixtures of equal energy value have been compared, identical rates of glycogen storage have been seen. Nevertheless, snacks or meals providing substantial amounts of carbohydrate and protein may be useful for achieving other recovery goals in particular, promotion of protein synthesis or retention during and after exercise.

In general it appears that the addition of fat and protein to carbohydrate foods and meals does not affect glycogen storage as long as targets for carbohydrate intake are met. However, it should be remembered that the presence of large amounts of protein and fat can displace carbohydrate foods within the athlete's energy requirements and gastric comfort, thereby indirectly interfering with glyco-gen storage by promoting inadequate carbohydrate intake.

Issues in postexercise rehydration

Ideally, an athlete should aim to fully restore fluid losses between exercise sessions so that the new event or workout can be commenced in a euhy-drated state. In normal healthy people, the daily replacement of fluid losses and maintenance of fluid balance are well regulated by thirst and urine losses. However, under conditions of stress (e.g. exercise, environmental heat and cold, altitude) thirst may not be a sufficient stimulus for maintaining fluid balance. Furthermore, there may be a considerable lag of 4-24 h before body fluid levels are restored following moderate to severe hypohydration.

Studies of voluntary fluid intake patterns across a range of sports show that athletes typically replace only 30-70% of the sweat losses incurred during exercise. As a result, most athletes can expect to finish training or competition sessions with a mild to moderate level of hypohydration. After exercise, people fail to drink sufficient volumes of fluid to restore fluid balance, even when drinks are made freely available*a*this effect was first described in the 1940s and termed "voluntary dehydration". More recently, the name has been changed to "involuntary dehydration" to recognize that the dehydrated individual has no desire to rehydrate even when fluids and opportunity are available.

An additional challenge to postexercise rehydration is that the athlete may continue to lose fluid during this phase, partly due to continued sweat losses, but principally due to urination. The success of postexercise rehydration ultimately depends on the balance between fluid intake and ongoing fluid losses.

In summary, although hydration is generally well maintained in the long term, special attention is needed for an acute situation of a moderate to high degree of hypohydration (i.e. fluid deficit of 2-5% BM or greater) and a recovery interval of less than 6-8 h. Optimal rehydration requires a scheduled plan of fluid intake, to overcome both physiological challenges such as inadequate thirst, and practical problems such as poor access to fluids. A number of factors affecting postexercise rehydration have been identified and will now be discussed.

Palatability of fluid

Numerous studies have reported that the palatability of a drink affects how much a person will voluntarily consume, and this probably becomes more important when very large volumes must be consumed. Flavor and temperature are two important characteristics determining the drink palatability. It should be noted that most studies of rehydration in athletes have been undertaken *during* moderate-intensity exercise rather than *after* exercise, so it is uncertain whether the findings apply directly to postexercise recovery.

However, some studies show that an athlete's perception of what tastes good to drink may change according to the environmental conditions, their body temperature, and their degree of dehydration. In some situations palatability may not always determine the total intake of a rehydration fluid. For example, while a person who is hot and thirsty may regard very cold water (0°C) as the most desirable drink, it is easier to drink larger quantities of cool water (15°C).

Flavoring of drinks has also been considered to contribute to voluntary fluid intake, with studies reporting greater fluid intake during postexercise recovery with sweetened drinks than with plain water. Further research is needed to differentiate whether subjects are responding to a sweet flavor or to energy replacement. Drinks that are too sweet may reduce voluntary intake, and there is some evidence of "flavor fatigue" *a*that after several hours of drinking, people tire of drinking things they initially preferred.

Replacement of electrolytes

Drinking water following dehydration leads to a dilution of plasma osmolality and sodium content, which in turn causes an increased diuresis (urine production) and reduction of thirst. Therefore, water is an ineffective rehydration fluid since it is likely to inhibit fluid intake and stimulate urine lossesaeven while the athlete is still dehydrated. By contrast, when sodium is replaced in conjunction with fluid, there is a greater voluntary intake of fluid and a lower urine output, leading to faster restoration of plasma volume. Sodium can be replaced in the drink itself, or by simultaneously eating sodium-containing foods or meals with added salt. Varying the sodium content of rehydration fluids has effects on both the taste of the fluids (affecting voluntary intake) and the degree of fluid retention. Sports drinks provide a source of sodium, but this is less than the amount present in the specially formulated oral rehydration solutions used in the medical treatment of dehydration (e.g. for diarrhea and gastrointestinal upsets). This lower sodium content reflects the needs for these drinks to have a well-accepted taste that will lead to wide commercial appeal. Studies show that even low sodium concentrations have a mild advantage over plain water in terms of restoration of plasma volume. However, when this effect is added to the improved palatability of the drink, it appears that sports drinks may confer some rehydration advantages over plain water. The composition of the postexercise recovery drink is discussed in greater detail in Expert Comment 2.

Volume and pattern of drinking

Since sweat and urine losses occur during recovery, an athlete must drink a volume greater than the postexercise fluid deficit to restore total fluid balance Typically, studies show that replacement of fluid in volumes equal to the deficit results in only a 50-70% fluid restoration over 2-4 h of recovery (based on body weight restoration). However, forced rehydration with greater volumes of fluid will not achieve fluid balance unless sodium losses are simultaneously replaced. In general, a volume of fluid equal to 150% of the fluid deficit will be required to restore fluid balance in conjunction with sodium replacement.

There is little information about the preferred drinking patternafor example comparing the effect of a large volume consumed immediately after exercise with a pattern of frequent small drinks throughout the recovery period. However issues such as gastric comfort must also be considered, especially if the athlete has to undertake another exercise session within a short period.

Caffeine and alcohol—potential diuretics

Urine losses are required to get rid of waste material. However, urine production is further stimulated by dilution of blood osmolality and by the action of pharmacological agents including caffeine and alcohol. These constituents are frequently found in beverages consumed after exercise. A study comparing the postexercise consumption of a diet cola drink containing caffeine with water and sports drink found less effective restoration of body fluid losses with the cola drink than with the other fluids. In fact, although subjects consumed volumes of fluid equal to their sweat losses in all trials, the cola drink resulted in a net restoration of only 54% of body mass. Compared to the other drinks, there were substantially greater urine losses and a small but significantly greater loss of fluid through continued sweating. The balance of evidence, however, suggests that the amount of caffeine present in cola-type drinks and in tea or coffee does not have a strong diuretic effect, especially in those who habitually consume these drinks. There are likely to be more problems from avoiding these drinks than from consuming them in moderation.

Alcohol consumption has also been shown to increase urinary losses during postexercise recovery. Subjects consuming drinks containing 4% alcohol showed slightly greater urinary losses than when drinks containing 0, 1, or 2% alcohol were consumed. Therefore drinks containing alcohol at concentrations of more than 2-3% (e.g. full-strength beer, wine, coolers, spirits) are not considered good rehydration drinks. Excessive intake of alcohol may have other detrimental effects on recovery and health.

SUMMARY

Recovery after exercise poses an important challenge to the modern athlete. Important nutrition goals include resynthesis of glycogen stores in the muscle and liver, as well as the replacement of fluid and electrolytes lost in sweat. Effective recovery of muscle glycogen stores occurs with the intake of carbohydratewith targets of at least 1 g·kg BM^{-1} during the first 2 h of recovery and a daily total of 7-10 g·kg BM^{-1}. Rapid refueling, beginning with the intake of carbohydrate as soon as possible after the session, may be important for the athlete who has less than 8 h between lengthy exercise sessions. As long as the athlete consumes enough carbohydrate, it appears that the frequency of intake, the form (liquid vs. solid) and the presence of other macronutrients do not appear to affect the rate of glycogen storage. Practical considerations such as the availability and appetite appeal of foods or drinks and gastrointestinal comfort may determine ideal carbohydrate choices and the pattern of intake. Rehydration requires a special fluid intake plan since thirst and voluntary intake will not provide for full restoration of sweat losses in the acute phase (0-6 h) of recovery. Steps should be taken to ensure that a supply of palatable drinks is available after exercise. Cool sweetened drinks are generally preferred and can contribute towards achieving carbohydrate intake goals. Replacement of the sodium lost in sweat is important in maximizing the retention of ingested fluids. Beverages containing large amounts of caffeine and alcohol are not ideal rehydration fluids since they promote an increased rate of diuresis. It may be necessary to consume 150% of fluid losses to allow for complete fluid restoration.

17

Assessing Nutritional and Needs

INTRODUCTION

Athletes often expect precise information and feedback to guide them in their sporting pursuits. After all, they are used to following a strict training prescription and to receiving detailed information about their training and competition performances, and they are generally more impressed if measurements are made to several decimal places. It is understandable that an athlete might want clear guidelines about when and what to eat, and from time to time, a precise assessment of how well they are meeting their dietary goals. In this chapter, issues related to setting and assessing the achievement of nutritional goals will be addressed.

Assessment of nutritional status

Although alternative practitioners often advertise that they can do a complete nutritional and medical assessment via a single technique such as hair analysis or iridology (examining the eyes), in fact, the assessment of nutritional status is complex and often inexact. No single technique or piece of information can tell the full story. Instead, an assessment is made by piecing together information from a variety of sources.

Many serious athletes undertake a complete screening that includes a variety of medical, physiological, and psychological measures at critical times of their competitive year for example, at the beginning of a new season, and perhaps around competition peaks (to gain a picture of measurements that are consistent with optimal performance). Some of these assessments might be usefully repeated to distinguish the causes of sub-optimal health or performance if they occur.

Components of a complete screening include a medical check-up, a musculoskeletal screening by a physiotherapist, physiological testing in the laboratory, and a psychological assessment. A complete nutritional screening should include a dietary evaluation (an overview of what the athlete is eating), biochemical and hematological testing of blood and perhaps urine, anthropometric testing to assess body composition, and a clinical assessment of the athlete's appearance and well-being. In previous chapters we discussed that many parameters cannot be assessed as optimal or suboptimal in isolation. Occasionally a reading is found to be clearly suboptimal, but the usual situation is that readings need to be compared to information previously collected from the same athlete and interpreted in conjunction with other data. For example, in Chapter 4 we saw that a diagnosis of iron deficiency required an examination for clinical signs of fatigue and pallor, indications of suboptimal intake of dietary iron, and a clear reduction in biochemical and hematological measures of iron status. Since an evaluation of the dietary patterns of the athlete provides a key piece of the puzzle, it is important to understand what is involved and how the information should be used in light of the limitations of the various methods of evaluation.

Assessment of dietary intake

A complete evaluation of an athlete's dietary patterns is time-consuming and requires special expertise. Throughout this book, case histories of different athletes have been included to illustrate various nutritional challenges and issues arising in sport. Each has included a brief summary of key findings in the nutritional assessment of the athlete or athletes involved, without the opportunity to discuss how the information was collected or interpreted. In fact, there are a number of methods that can be used to monitor dietary intake; each has specific advantages and disadvantages and each adds a typical bias to the information collected. The dietary survey method chosen to monitor the intake of an individual athlete or group of athletes will depend on the type of information that is sought, and the resources and opportunities available. When assessing the intake of an individual athlete, most sports dietitians use several techniques in combination, using one method to cross-check the results of another technique. For example, the results of an athlete's food diary may be compared with the information collected using a dietary history protocol.

It is important to underpin all the information provided by dietary recalls or records with an appreciation of the athlete's lifestyle and commitments, and their interest in and understanding of nutrition. After all, issues such as motivation, finances, food availability, nutrition beliefs, domestic skills, and time will influence the athlete's present dietary patterns and their ability to make changes. Therefore, the primary contact with the athlete should include a thorough interview to collect information such as where they live, who cooks their meals, how often they travel, how and why they have chosen their present eating patterns, what supplements they take, and how their time is spent in a typical day. Against this background, the athlete's eating patterns can then be monitored and assessed. The following techniques for monitoring dietary intake collect information about the athlete's typical consumption of food and drinks. Sometimes, this information is compared directly against dietary benchmarks, while on other occasions an assessment is made of the typical nutrient intake provided by these foods and fluids.

Techniques for monitoring dietary intake fall into two major categories: "retrospective" or "recall" techniques that monitor behavior in the past or immediate past, and "prospective" techniques that monitor ongoing behavior. Popular retrospective techniques include dietary history, diet recall, and food frequency questionnaires (FFQs).

Retrospective or recall techniques

The technique that is generally called a dietary history (and is actually a shorter modified version of the original technique) asks the athlete to describe their food intake during a typical day over recent times. A skilled interviewer, using prompts and probing questions, ascertains the athlete's whereabouts and activities over each section of the day, and the food and drink that is usually consumed. Ideally, the athlete will be assisted to build up a composite of their usual eating patterns, including descriptions of serving sizes of various items as well as a summary of how different options might be chosen weekly, monthly, or seasonally. Aids such as food models may help the athlete to accurately describe their usual portion sizes. The dietary history is usually cross-checked against a brief FFQ. The advantages of the dietary history are that it focuses on usual intake, is relatively quick, and places relatively little burden on the athlete. On the other hand, it requires a skilled interviewer and assumes that the athlete can provide an accurate (and truthful) recall of their intake. An athlete who has a chaotic lifestyle and erratic eating habits, or a poor memory or insight into their eating patterns, will not necessarily be able to provide an objective account of a typical day.

The dietary recall technique involves questioning about actual intake of foods and fluids on a previous occasion, usually the last 24 h. Again, a skilled interviewer is needed and should use prompts and aids to stimulate the athlete to provide accurate information about the type and amounts of foods and drinks consumed. Although most subjects will find it easier to remember what they ate yesterday, rather than create an overview of what is typically eaten, a major disadvantage of this technique is that it does not provide a picture of usual intake. After all, we eat differently from day to day, and the athlete may have followed a totally unrepresentative eating plan the day before their interview. The 24-h recall is often used in dietary surveys of large groups where a number of accounts of a day's eating can build up a picture of the typical eating habits of a population. Alternatively, it may be undertaken on a number of separate occasions in the same individual to build up a picture of the daily or weekly changes in their intake.

A food frequency questionnaire (FFQ) takes the form of a checklist of commonly eaten foods and drinks, with each item requiring one response denoting the size of the serving that the athlete typically consumes, and another response listing the frequency of consumption of this item. This list is often supplemented with questions on other foods eaten by the respondent but not on the list, and questions about food preparation, supplement use, and other food-related behaviors. FFQs can be undertaken by interview, or as a self-administered questionnaire. In its early form, the FFQ was designed as a qualitative method, seeking information on the frequency of consumption of specific food items without specification of the actual serving or portion sizes usually consumed. More recent versions of FFQs focus on portion sizes so that a quantitative determination of food and nutrient intake can be achieved. The accuracy of FFQs is dependent on how well the checklist has been prepared to include the foods and drinks consumed by the athlete, and how well and accurately the athlete can summarize his or her usual intake. Many FFQs are developed to focus on the intake of a specific nutrient (e.g. carbohydrate or calcium), and are validated against the results achieved by other dietary survey techniques. A particular advantage of the FFQ is that it is relatively quick and easy for both the athlete and the interviewer.

In general, all recall or retrospective techniques are limited by the athlete's memory, insight, and cooperation. Research shows that young and adolescent subjects have limited insight into their food intake, and that a "typical" day is difficult to picture in an erratic and chaotic lifestyle. Furthermore, people deliberately or unconsciously "rewrite" their usual food intake to downplay the foods they see as undesirable (e.g. snacks and sweets) and increase their stated intake of foods seen as desirable (e.g. fruit). Many athletes give biased responses either in fear of revealing inappropriate dietary behavior to a coach or investigator, or to impress the investigator. Many studies have shown that people have poor skills in recalling portion sizes of foods and fluids. In general, retrospective methods of assessing food and nutrient intake tend to overestimate true intake, although they may underestimate the true intake of large eaters.

PROSPECTIVE MONITORING TECHNIQUES

The duplicate portion method is an old technique that was sometimes used to monitor the ongoing dietary intake of an individual in the era before extensive food composition tables were available. To undertake this technique, the athlete would collect a duplicate sample of all food and drinks consumed over a specified period of time; this collection would then be thoroughly homogenized and a chemical analysis of the energy and nutrient content would be undertaken. Clearly, such a method is time-consuming and expensive and is very rarely used in modern times.

The most popular method of dietary survey work is the food diary or food record, in which a completed account of all food and fluid intake is kept over a specified period of time, either by the subject, or in special cases (such as the monitoring of children or athletes in extreme competition such as a cycling tour) by the designated food handler. As in all dietary survey methods, accuracy in describing the type and amount of food and fluid intake is critical. In some food record protocols, the athlete is required to use scales to weigh all food and drinks, whereas other techniques ask the athlete to estimate portion sizes using a combinations of household measures and grids. The weighed food record is sometimes considered the "gold standard" of dietary survey techniques, but although this protocol improves the accuracy of the quantification of the athlete's intake, it may be a source of other errors if increased demands on the athlete lead to reduced compliance or distortion of their true intake.

In general, all dietary surveys are hampered by errors of validity (how well they measure the subject's actual intake), and reliability (how closely the period of monitoring reflects the athlete's usual intake). Prospective techniques carry a disadvantage in that athletes may deliberately or subconsciously alter their eating habits during the period of recording so that it no longer reflects their usual intake. This may happen, as in the case of recall techniques, because the athlete is embarrassed about their true intake and wants to appear to "eat better" than they usually do. On the other hand, the requirement to record all intake is intrusive and time-consuming, and the athlete may subconsciously try to simplify the demands by choosing to eat foods that are easier to record, or by omitting to eat or record the consumption of meals or snacks altogether if it is inconvenient.

Extensive study of the accuracy of food diaries in the general population shows a bias towards widespread and significant under-reporting of true intake; comparison of energy intakes estimated from food diaries and other techniques such as doubly labeled water show that records typically underestimate intake by about 20%. However, not all subjects under-report, and studies have identified that some individuals under-report to an even greater extent. This latter population includes those who are overfat and those who are dissatisfied with their body mass and body image. Under-reporting errors can be divided into under-eating (reducing food intake during the period of recording), and under-recording (failing to record all food consumed during the observation period), but few studies have tried to measure the relative contribution of each aspect to the total error. Several sophisticated energy balance studies have also been carried out on athletes and most, but not all, have found discrepancies between reported energy intakes and energy requirements, particularly among female athletes and those in weight-conscious sports. It is not known whether the under-reporting of all nutrients mirrors the underreporting of energy intake.

Typically, food records are kept for periods of 1-7 days, although there have been rare studies which have monitored food intake over several years. The duration of the food diary is important both for the reliability of the estimate of energy or nutrient intake (a longer period of recording reduces the variability in estimation of daily intakes) and for the compliance of the subject (longer periods reduce the attention and compliance of the subject). In the general population, a 3-4-day record is considered a reasonable compromise, although it is limited in being able to accurately estimate typical intakes of only the stable dietary components such as energy and carbohydrate. Other more variable nutrients such as vitamin A and cholesterol may require up to 3-4 weeks of recording to accurately estimate the daily intake of an individual to within 95% of true intake. In athletic populations, where individuals are highly motivated and familiar with regimented assessment of other aspects of their preparation, many researchers and clinicians like to use a 7-day food diary, since this usually represents a complete microcycle in the athlete's training program.

An alternative method to increase the reliability of monitoring is to have the athlete complete a number of food diaries over shorter periods (e.g. 4-day food diaries completed two or three times over a period of training). If 3-4-day food diaries are used, they should be undertaken over a period that is representative of the different influences on food intake (for example, 1 weekend day and 3 weekdays, or 3 heavy training days and 1 light day or rest day). In summary, although food records offer advantages as a dietary survey tool, these must be balanced against the disadvantages such as an increased burden on the subject, and the time involved (initial interview to train the athlete about recording, the daily recording commitment, and the processing of the completed diary). Most athletes are likely to under-report or underconsume their usual intakes when undertaking dietary records, and those who are weight or physique conscious or dissatisfied with their body image are at highest risk of significant underestimation errors. Reporting errors can be minimized where athletes are motivated to receive a true dietary assessment, and where training to enhance record-keeping skills has been undertaken. Nevertheless, researchers and practitioners should be cautious in their interpretation of the results of self-reported assessments of dietary intake.

Problems in converting information about food intake into nutrient intake

Dietary surveys collect information about the food intake of athletes, which is often then analysed quantitatively, in terms of intake of energy and nutrients. The conversion of food into nutrients is a major source of error in dietary surveys and is a reflection of the skills and knowledge of the researcher, the method of data collection, and the available food composition database. Errors arise from the lack of specificity in the description of food or quantities consumed, insufficient knowledge about common preparation methods, differences in handling situations which are not instantly matched by the food composition database, and simple mistakes in coding and data entry. Food composition databases do not contain all of the large number of different foods consumed, so appropriate food substitutes, omission of foods, and guesswork must be used. The importance of defining a standard protocol for coding and entering data, and for handling food substitutions is crucial for minimizing error when analysing food record data. When interpreting nutrient data derived from food composition tables, the following limitations should be recognized. Food composition data are only estimates of the average nutrient composition of foods, are specific to the country of origin, and suffer from incomplete information on many nutrients and on many commonly eaten foods. The common portions of foods documented in software programs are not necessarily the serving sizes consumed by people, especially athletes who have extremes in energy requirements.

Benchmarks for assessing or setting dietary intake

There are various sources of information against which dietary intake can be monitored or a new dietary plan can be developed. These vary from qualitative messages about food use to quantitative benchmarks for nutrient intake. Most are aimed at the nutrition of the general population, although some guidelines have been prepared especially for athletes.

Nutritional guidelines for athletes and physically active people

Over the past two decades, recognition of the specialized nutritional needs of athletes and the importance of nutrition in determining sports performance has led to the release by expert bodies of position stands on sports nutrition. These have attempted to provide a state of the art summary of current thinking, either over the broad spectrum of nutrition and exercise performance, or on a special issue such as alcohol and exercise, creatine supplementation, or acute techniques of weight loss by athletes. Expert bodies that have issued position stands, either individually or as joint commentaries, include professional organizations representing sports medicine and science or nutrition and dietetics as well as the international governing bodies of sport. The evolution in knowledge of sports nutrition has meant that new position stands often have to be issued to update, or even contradict, the recommendations made in previous statements. However, in general, these position stands can provide a valuable reference for athletes.

Guidelines can be found for principles of meeting the nutritional goals of training and competition, ranging from recommendations guiding the selection of the type and timing of meals and snacks, to guidelines for nutrient intakes especially adapted for athletes undertaking a heavy exercise program. Even though the expert bodies in most countries have failed to take the special needs of exercise into account in formulating official daily reference intakes, in the case of some nutrients (e.g. protein and carbohydrate), there is sufficient evidence to provide reasonably precise guidance to athletes at various levels of performance and training commitment.

Qualitative benchmarks: dietary guidelines and food guides

The nutrition and health experts in many countries have developed a series of dietary guidelines which provide a set of qualitative recommendations for ways in which the typical dietary patterns of the population should be modified to fit the model of healthy eating. The goals of such eating are to achieve nutrient requirements in the short term, as well as to minimize eating behaviors associated with risks for the development of long-term health problems. In some countries such as Australia, separate dietary guidelines have been prepared for adults, children and adolescents, and the aged. The education messages contained in dietary guidelines are generally similar across countries for example, eat more cereals, fruits, and vegetables, or reduce the intake of fats, particularly saturated fats. However, the ways in which these guidelines are expressed can differ between countries. For example, while the dietary guidelines for Australia and America encourage people to "eat a variety of nutritious foods", the Japanese dietary guidelines are more specific in recommending that "30 or more different foods" should be eaten each day. These messages are appropriate for nutrition education of athletes and are used by sports dietitians in combination with other qualitative guides to assess and advise athletes about food choice. Other qualitative education tools include "food pyramids", "food plates", and "rainbows" that provide a pictorial representation of the proportion in which foods should be chosen to make up meals and diets.

Food guides are nutrition education tools to assist children and adults to plan and select nutritionally desirable diets consistent with the dietary guidelines. Most countries have devised food selection guides specific to the food supply, nutrient recommendations, and cultural needs of their population. These food guides translate dietary standards and recommendations into suggested servings of foods from groups that can be easily understood and used by people who have little formal training in nutrition. Examples of food guides include "The Core Food Group" and "CSIRO 12345+ Food and Nutrition Plan" (Australia), "Four Food Groups Guide" (USA), and "Food Guide for Healthy Eating" (Canada).

Food guides categorize food into groups that are usually based on similar nutrient content, and make recommendations about the number of servings from each group that should be consumed daily so that requirements for key nutrients are probably achieved. In many countries, specific recommendations are given according to gender, age, or special nutritional need (e.g. pregnancy and breastfeeding). A quick way of assessing nutrient intakes is to check if the recommended number of foods from each group is represented in a day's dietary intake. Such an achievement is by no means a foolproof or precise assessment of dietary adequacy, and will not meet the energy requirements for most people, especially athletes. Athletes need to increase the number of servings to meet their energy and nutrient requirements. Nevertheless, food guides can provide a baseline tool for assessing dietary intake.

Recommended nutrient intakes

All major countries have a set of recommended intakes for energy, protein, and micronutrients for use in their populations. These recommendations vary in name from country to country, and include recommended nutrient intakes (RNIs) (UK), recommended dietary intakes (RDIs) (Australia) and the recommended dietary allowances (RDAs), which are in the process of evolving into the dietary reference intakes (DRIs) (USA). The original use of these recommendations (hereafter, simply referred to as RNIs) was to set a standard for an adequate diet for different groups of the population. Their use has spread so that they have become the basic unit of nutrition education, a benchmark for planning therapeutic diets and food programs, and a benchmark for food enrichment and food labeling programs. Their use as a tool for assessing the dietary intakes of individuals has also become widespread, although this is a purpose for which they were not designed.

In each country, expert committees in nutrition and health set RNIs from a mathematical treatment of information about requirements for individual nutrients. These requirements are generally derived from studies that have identified the lowest levels of intake that are consistent with the absence of evidence of a nutrient deficiency or with maintenance of the body pool. RNIs are extrapolated and interpolated from these data, taking into account the distribution of values around the mean value for the minimum requirement (i.e. adding 2 x SD to the mean value so that it theoretically encompasses the needs of 99% of a population). The special needs of different groups within the population, and factors of dietary quality or nutrient absorption are also taken into account. The final RNI value is meant to represent the intake of a nutrient that should meet the requirements of nearly all members of a community. The DRIs that are currently being issued in the USA are broader in scope and application than RNIs, encompassing a family of markers for nutrient intakes ranging from estimated average requirements to an upper limit that takes into account problems of excessive intake or toxicity. It is interesting to note that values for RNIs differ between countries, based on the way that their expert committees have interpreted the available data on nutrient requirements and the priority that is given to simply avoiding symptoms of deficiency vs. consuming an intake that might promote optimal health.

The use of RNIs to assess the adequacy of the dietary intake of an individual is problematic, since these standards are recommendations for the average daily amounts of nutrients that population groups should consume over a period of time, rather than requirements for a specific individual. Differences in the nutrient requirements of individuals are unknown, and by definition the RNI values overestimate the real nutrient needs of most of the population. RNIs should be considered a general assessment tool that assesses the likelihood that an individual is meeting his or her requirements for various nutrients. By convention, nutrient intakes that are below two-thirds of the RDI are considered to be at high risk of being inadequate. However, the accuracy of the assessment of nutrient intake must also be taken into account when comparing such values to RNIs.

Although very few countries have included special RNIs for athletes, or contemplated any changes to nutrient requirements arising from a heavy exercise program, the RNIs are generally considered suitable for use with athletic populations. In the case of some micronutrients, there is recognition that requirements are related to energy requirements, so that an athlete with a high turnover of energy would also have an increased requirement for those micronutrients (e.g. some of the B group vitamins). Nevertheless, some elite athletes may not fit within the range of these "average" population values on which nutrient standards are based. Evidence for a slightly higher requirement for protein and carbohydrate than the general population is well documented in some groups of athletes. Recent evidence supports a slight increase in micronutrient needs in physically active people to compensate for losses in sweat, urine, and perhaps feces, and for an increase in free radical formation. However, this evidence is based on biochemical and physiological indices of micronutrients, which are highly variable among athletes and difficult to interpret. More research is needed on large groups of athletes participating in different sports to allow micronutrient recommendations to be quantified; however, for the present time, RNIs are considered to be satisfactory for use by the majority of athletes.

SUMMARY

The collection of nutritional status measures in sports people is critical to our understanding of the association between nutrition, health, and sports performance, and is information that is often requested by the athlete or coach. A complete nutritional screening should include a dietary evaluation, biochemical and hematological testing of blood and perhaps urine, anthropometric testing to assess body composition, and a clinical assessment of the athlete's appearance and well-being. Many of these parameters cannot be assessed as optimal or suboptimal in isolation. Occasionally a reading is found to be clearly suboptimal, but the usual situation is that readings need to be compared to information previously collected from the same athlete and interpreted in conjunction with other data. Collection of information about the dietary intakes of athletes requires highly trained people who are familiar with limitations and bias in collecting and interpreting these data.

18

Changing Size and Composition

INTRODUCTION

Many athletes want to know what their ideal body size and composition is, so that they can work towards achieving this. This is particularly common in sports where the athlete's body weight, muscle mass, or body fat level have an effect on performance. However, other athletes are motivated to lose body fat or gain muscle mass for their appearance or for health reasons. Optimum body weight and body fat levels vary from sport to sport, and even with team positions or specific events within the same sport. In some sports, athletes commonly set their body weight and body fat goals below a level that is "natural" or "healthy" for many of the individuals concerned. There is some evidence that this is most likely to involve female athletes. This chapter will discuss issues in deciding on body weight and body composition goals, and eating strategies that underpin changes in body fat or lean body mass.

Measurement of lean body mass and body fat levels in athletes

Athletes come in a range of sizes and shapes from the 40-kg gymnast to the 200-kg sumo wrestler. Contributions of lean body mass and body fat to the athlete's total body mass also vary widely. Although body mass (weight) does not distinguish between muscle mass or body fatness, many athletes, like sedentary people, rely on regular measurements of body weight to judge the suitability of their size and body composition. This is often a source of misinformation and frustration. Changes in body weight over the long term (a week or more) can sometimes be used to monitor energy balance, but changes in body mass are often difficult to interpret. Instead, the most valuable use of weighing scales is to determine acute body weight changes during a training or competition session, and thus estimate the sweat losses that must be replaced.

Assessment of body composition, particularly muscularity and fatness, is valuable for monitoring the characteristics that promote good performance in certain sports. Often these measurements are made on elite athletes, and it is assumed that mean values, or the values of the best athletes, provide a template that all aspiring athletes should attempt to achieve. However, it should be realized that even at the elite level there is some variety in size and shape, and there are too many exceptions to make all but the broadest generalizations about what is desirable. In fact, the most valuable use of body composition assessments is to sequentially monitor the same athlete, looking for changes that occur with growth and maturation, training or dietary manipulations, and stages of the competition season. Over a period of time, this information can be used to determine the athlete's body weight and body fat goals, and their success in achieving them. "Ideal" body mass and composition (i.e. body fatness, muscle mass) should only be determined for the individual athlete after consideration of the factors that are consistent with good performance and good health in the long term. The picture is further complicated by the wide variety of different methods used to assess body composition. Not all will give the same answers for an individual, even though the average values for a group may be the same, so athletes and those who advise them must be aware of the need for selection of an appropriate method.

Criteria for choosing a technique for measuring body composition in athletes include validity and reliability of the technique and the ease of access within the athlete's lifestyle. Techniques such as underwater weighing (hydrodensitometry) or dual-energy X-ray absorptiometry (DEXA) are generally considered to be the "gold standard" protocols for assessing body composition. However, these techniques are relatively expensive and are not available to many athletes, especially for use in the field or for sequential monitoring. Other methods which may be more portable or less expensive such as TOBEC (total body electrical conductivity), bioelectrical impedance analysis, and infrared spectrophotometry all need to be validated on athletic populations before absolute accuracy can be guaranteed. In surveys of large populations, the body mass index (BMI) may be used to give an estimate of fatness. This is calculated as the body mass (in kg) divided by the height (in m) squared. This measure is reasonable for the general population but should not be used with athletes as it will be misleading when the muscle mass is high.

In the field, the measurement of anthropometric data, such as girths, circumferences, and subcutaneous fat levels (via skinfold calipers) remains the most practical, simple, and inexpensive technique for the estimation of body fatness and muscularity of athletes.

Measurements of skinfold fat thickness, often together with other anthropometric data, can be used to estimate percentage body fat levels and lean body mass by means of prediction equations. However, these equations are only considered accurate and reliable when they have been derived from the specific group of athletes on which they will then be applied. Therefore, many sports scientists use anthropometric data as a direct measure on which feedback can be provided. For example a "sum of skinfolds" (the sum of measurements of subcutaneous fat from a number of standard sites) can be used as an absolute indication of body fat levels, and the athlete can be counseled about desirable levels or desirable changes in levels based on comparisons to previous determinations of this measure. Regardless of which anthropometric information is collected for the sequential monitoring of individual athletes, it is important that technical errors in collecting data are minimized. Strategies include the expert training of anthropometrists, the use of the same anthropometrist in sequential monitoring, consistency in following a set protocol and well-defined landmarks for choosing sites, and the use of standard equipment.

Effect of body mass and body fat levels on sports performance

An athlete's muscle mass and body fat levels are determined by both genetics and the changes achieved through the conditioning effect of high-level training and diet. These characteristics exert a range of effects on performance, and different values will be more likely to bring success in different sports. As a result, successful sportspeople tend to fall into some predictable patterns of body weight and body fat levels according to the demands of their sport.

In sports that are essentially based on skill (e.g. golf, archery, bowling), performance is largely independent of body size and fatness. Since the level of physical activity in these sports, however lengthy, is low to moderate in terms of energy expenditure, participation does not contribute significantly to energy balance. Both selection and conditioning factors tend to allow higher body fat levels to occur in these sports in some cases, elite athletes may have body fat levels that are considered obese by normal community standards. Often, strategies to reduce body fat are undertaken for improvements in health, general fitness, and appearance, rather than as a direct benefit to performance.

By contrast, low body mass, and in particular, low body fat levels, are considered important for performance across a number of sports. A small body size decreases the energy cost of activity, and allows the athlete to achieve tight movements like turns and twists in a restricted space (e.g. diving, gymnastics). The advantages of low body fat levels include physical and mechanical gains, for example, an increased "power to weight" ratio or simply a reduced amount of "dead weight" that must be moved by the athlete. This is a particular advantage in sports such as distance running, triathlon, and road cycling where the athlete transports his or her body mass over long distances, and in hill cycling and jumping for height or distance, where the athlete must move vertically against greater gravity effects. However, low body fat levels are often also important for reasons of aesthetics and appearance in sports such as gymnastics, diving, figure skating, and bodybuilding.

In other sports, competition takes place in specific weight divisions that are intended to match opponents of similar size and strength and therefore promote fair competition. Such sports include weightlifting, boxing, amateur wrestling, lightweight rowing, and horse racing. However, in these sports, most competitors attempt to compete in a weight division that is below their typical training weight, trying to gain an advantage over a smaller, lighter opponent. Athletes in these sports often show large and frequent fluctuations in body weight, and pursue weight loss even when they are already very lean.

Finally, in sports in which power and momentum are important, athletes are interested to increase body mass, primarily though an increase in muscle mass. In some of these sports (e.g. throwing events and heavyweight division lifting events), athletes are not necessarily penalized by also having high levels of body fat. However, in the case of athletes who must also possess speed and agility (e.g. track sprinters and mobile players in rugby and the various codes of football), low levels of body fat are typical.

Although some athletes easily achieve a body weight and composition suited to their sport, others may need to manipulate characteristics such as muscle mass or body fatness through changes in diet or training. It is important that the athlete can identify suitable and realistic goals, take appropriate measures to achieve them, and have a suitable means of monitoring progress. The optimal body fat level for an athlete should be obtained from their individual history and should meet the following criteria:

1 be associated with (consistent) good performances;

2 promote good health in the athlete including the absence of evidence of "underweight" or overtraining; and

3 allow the athlete to consume a diet providing adequate energy and nutrients to meet all nutritional goals and to remain reasonably free of food-related stress.

STRATEGIES TO REDUCE BODY FAT IN SPORT

Although most sedentary people may find it hard to imagine, many athletes consider themselves to be overfat. In fact, a desire to lose body fat is one of the most common reasons for an athlete to seek dietary advice from a sports doctor or dietitian. Weight loss counseling for athletes shares many features with counseling for the general community. Athletes have the same misconceptions about body composition, and about safe and long-term methods of reducing body fat. However, they may need specialized help to identify and achieve their individual ideal body weight and body fat levels. Sports-specific knowledge and empathy are important to combat the misconceptions and unsafe weight loss practices that become entrenched within many sports.

There are common situations, at both elite and recreational levels of sports participation, in which energy mismatches have caused the athlete to become overfat. Athletes in skill-based sports that have low energy expenditure may be considered essentially sedentary, especially if their sporting commitments prevent them from having other active hobbies or pursuits. A rapid gain of body fat is a common experience for highly active athletes who suddenly reduce or cease their training or competition activities. Athletes who are injured or are in the off season of their sport, are often unable or unwilling to regulate their energy intake to their lower energy needs.

As a result they resume their sports activities with substantially increased body fat levels. Other lifestyle issues associated with some sports interfere with the achievement of optimum nutritional goals. Athletes with irregular lifestyles (e.g. travel commitments) and without a settled domestic routine (e.g. living outside a family environment) may have erratic eating patterns and rely on high-fat food choices from restaurants and fast food outlets. Young athletes pursuing a sports career are often required to move away from home before they have accumulated adequate nutrition knowledge or food preparation skills. Financial constraints may also limit food choices. Practical nutrition advice will be important in weight loss counseling for these athletes.

Athletes with "aesthetic" requirements for a low body fat level often find their goals and energy expenditure mismatched. Although typical training commitments for elite performers may be in the order of 20-40 h per week, these activities generally involve strength, skill, and flexibility exercises, with only short bursts of high-intensity work.

Therefore, training activities do not assist the athlete to achieve the energy deficit required to reduce body fat easily. While athletes in high energy expenditure sports may be assisted by both selection and conditioning to achieve low levels of body fatness, many individuals still consider themselves overfat and wish to further reduce body fat levels. At present it is fashionable among some athletic groups to try to achieve the lowest possible body fat levels. However, statistical evidence that reduced body fat correlates with improved performance cannot always be applied to individual cases. There are many examples of athletes who achieve world-class performance with atypical body physiques, including body fat levels that are at the high end of (or even above) the typical range for that sport. There are also many case histories to show that short-term improvements in performance following substantial loss of body fat are soon compromised by long-term health and injury problems.

Problems of setting goals for very low body fat levels

Many athletes set unrealistic weight loss goals either seeking to reach an unnecessarily and harmfully low body fat level, or to achieve body fat loss in an unacceptably short timescale. The pressure to set these goals may come from a number of sources. Athletes at least most of the successful ›nes are, by nature, compulsive and focused. The same trait· that encourage good sports performance in many athletes p‹ fectionism, dedication, ability to work hard and withstand discomfort may lead to false expectations and preoccupation with body fat levels. Parents, trainers, coaches, and other athletes are often guilty of providing pressure and misguided expectations. Many people do not understand that "natural" or "healthy" standards of weight and body fat are an individual characteristic. Instead they focus on the lowest possible body fat levels, or the very low body fat levels of another successful competitor. The situation appears worse for female athletes, perhaps reflecting the general dissatisfaction of females in the community with their body shape and the biological predisposition for female athletes to have higher levels of body fat than their male counterparts, despite undertaking similar training.

Surveys of athletes involved in sports in which body fat levels are considered important, and female athletes in general, often report problems with eating disorders and disordered eating behaviors and body perceptions. Pathogenic weight control techniques include fasting or very low energy diets, dehydration techniques (saunas, diuretics, exercise in the heat), excessive training, self-induced vomiting, and the use of appetite suppressants or laxatives. These strategies may have detrimental effects on health and well-being as well as on exercise performance. Such problems appear to occur at a higher rate than seen in the general community or in sports in which weight or fatness is not an issue. The extent of eating disorders among athletes remains unknown, but should be seen as a continuum that includes clinical cases of anorexia and bulimia nervosa at one end, to food-related stress and unhealthy eating practices at the other. Eating disorders also occur among male athletes, although at a lower rate, and require special consideration and treatment.

It should be noted that many of the athletes reporting the use of abnormal eating and training practices do not appear to have classical eating disorders. Some athletes use these techniques simply as a method of achieving their weight and body fat goals, and are supported by the similar practices and beliefs of their peers. Indeed, we applaud other examples of extreme behavior in the athlete's lifestyle (e.g. rising very early in the morning to train, minimizing normal social and leisure activities to concentrate on sports goals). Some studies have reported that unhealthy weight control behaviors and preoccupation with weight and body fat levels do not persist in the off season in the majority of these athletes.

However, even in these groups, the potential problems associated with extreme dieting and achieving unnaturally low body fat levels should be recognized. Very low energy diets and specific low-carbohydrate diets will result in low muscle (and perhaps liver) glycogen stores in athletes, and are likely to cause fatigue and poor performance in athletes undertaking strenuous daily training. Rapid weight loss may also lead to loss of muscle mass, which will also adversely affect sports performance. In the longer term, frequent periods of dieting may place the athlete at risk of an inadequate intake of protein and micronutrients. There is speculation that hormonal and metabolic function may be compromised, including impairment of growth and development in young athletes. Psychological distress, including anxiety, isolation and depression, is also common.

The disadvantages of very low body fat levels *per se* include loss of body insulation and cushioning, but these effects are hard to separate from the indirect consequences of the techniques used to achieve them. Some racial groups and some individuals appear to have naturally low levels of body fat, or at least to be better able to tolerate low body fat levels. However, there is accumulating evidence that individuals who chronically restrict energy availability to reduce body fat below the natural level that their body wishes to defend may induce complex metabolic and hormonal changes. This work remains speculative, and offers no real cure for affected athletes other than to encourage them to reassess their body fat goals. The present emphasis on the prevention of this problem may be best achieved by safe and conservative methods of body fat loss.

The special case of "making weight"

The tradition of "making weight" to meet a competition

division in weight category sports has been well described among jockeys, lightweight rowers, wrestlers, and weightlifters. Body builders are also known to "cut up" immediately prior to competition, although their intention is not directly related to body weight. Instead they claim to increase muscle definition by minimizing the subcutaneous fat cover or dehydrating themselves in the hope of making skin tissue "paper thin". Rapid and short-term weight loss is typically achieved over the days leading up to an event using techniques such as dehydration, food restriction, self-induced vomiting, and the use of diuretics and laxatives. Competition may occur in these sports from once or more a week (e.g. lightweight rowers, wrestlers, and jockeys), to once or twice a year (body builders, professional boxers). Weight loss and gain will cycle between these periods. The interval between weigh-in and competition varies from 1 to 12 h, and generally leaves little time to overturn the effects of rapid weight loss strategies.

Techniques of "making weight" can threaten health as well as athletic performance. The seriousness of the effects will be greatest in athletes who are required to lose the greatest amounts of weight and in sports where this is repeated most often. The acute and chronic effects of restricted eating have already been discussed. The effect of dehydration will vary according to the degree of fluid deficit, the method by which it was induced (e.g. thermal stress, exercise, or diuretics) and the type of exercise that is performed. Nevertheless, the outcome may vary from reduced performance to severe health risks, including death from hyperthermia or renal failure.

"Making weight" practices exist in most weight category sports in spite of the continued attention of medical, educational, and research bodies. It appears that the traditions, however negative, have become part of the culture of these sports and are resistant to change. Coaches and athletes are also convinced that performance benefits result from competing in the lowest possible weight category, in spite of the acknowledged performance decrement that results from the procedures that are used to make this possible. It is unlikely that sound nutrition and weight loss education will be embraced by athletes in weight category sports without additional reinforcement from the governing bodies in these sports. In some sports considerable discussion has led to proposals for rule modifications that might discourage weight cutting. These include certification of athletes at a weight division at the beginning of a season, measuring the level of hydration in competitors before an event, redistributing weight divisions to better match the normal weight distribution in the sports population, and making weigh-in closer to the event to prevent the reliance on post-weigh-in recovery.

Education programs for athletes and coaches should target the need for the athlete to make informed decisions about the weight category in which they compete. The core advice should be to achieve any desired weight loss through safe and realistic changes to body fat levels well in advance of competition. Minor adjustment of body mass (e.g. loss of 1-2 kg) in the week leading up to the event might be achieved by light dehydration and a low-residue diet to reduce gastrointestinal contents.

The female athlete triad: disordered eating, menstrual dysfunction, and reduced bone density

Disturbed menstrual function, including amenorrhea (absence of periods), is commonly reported in athletic groups, particularly in sports where body weight and body fat levels are considered important. Although low body fat levels *per se* have not been implicated as the cause of impaired menstrual function, there is evidence that restrained or disordered eating practices present a risk factor in some individuals. Studies have shown that practices which reduce energy availability below a critical threshold cause metabolic and hormonal adaptations. These changes may be mediated, at least in part, by the hormone leptin.

Whatever the underlying cause, menstrual dysfunction presents a concern for the bone health of young women and adolescents. In contrast to the protective effects of weight-bearing exercise on bone health, menstrual dysfunction is associated with reduced bone mass, perhaps as a result of low levels of the sex hormone, estrogen. Bone health is influenced by a complex array of factors, and athletes with menstrual disturbances seem at risk of suffering a reduction in bone mass or a failure to gain optimal bone mass during their early adult years. This may increase the risks of developing stress fractures in the short term, as well as an earlier onset of osteoporosis in later life. Of course, for the athlete who is concerned about their sporting career, the problem of chronic injury is the most immediate concern. The interrelationship and frequent coexistence of disordered eating, menstrual dysfunction, and poor bone health including stress fractures have led to the identification of the "female triad" syndrome. This is discussed in more detail in Chapter 4, with consideration of calcium intake as another issue in bone health.

Awareness of the female triad and associated problems may help to alert athletes to the need to avoid dangerous eating/ training practices and to seek assistance as soon as problems do occur. It may also help sports medicine to develop early identification and treatment programs. However, it is important to remember that each of these problems can occur independently, and the athletes with problems should receive comprehensive and individualized attention, rather than expecting a simple cure. The treatment should attend to symptoms, but must also address the underlying causes. Intensive therapy from a team involving the athlete's coach, family, doctor, psychologist or psychiatrist, dietitian, and other members is typically required. The athlete may need to address her training load, eating practices, and body fat goals.

Guidelines for safe and effective weight (fat) loss by athletes

Few studies have systematically investigated the effects of various body fat levels, or the safety and effectiveness of weight loss techniques, on sports performance. Therefore we are left to develop general guidelines for weight loss in athletes based on common sense rather than rigorous scientific research. A clear role for the sports dietitian or sports nutrition expert exists at all levels of this plan. Services provided by these professionals may include:

1 monitoring and counseling of individual athletes;

2 screening of athletes at high risk of developing disordered eating and eating disorders;

3 developing programs to incorporate sound nutrition practices into the plans of sports groups, clubs, or teams;

4 developing nutrition education resources based on safe and effective strategies for management of weight and body fat in specific sports; and

5 providing input into the programs underpinning the management and development of each specific sport (e.g. development of the coaching syllabus, rule changes to

discourage unsafe weight loss practices such as "making weight").

SUMMARY

Athletes require access to simple and inexpensive techniques to identify body fat and body weight goals and to monitor changes that occur with training, growth, and maturation. The physique characteristics of elite athletes might be used to provide general guidelines for the range of body fat levels that are consistent with good performance in a sport. However, they should not be used to provide rigid body fat prescriptions for individual athletes. The optimal weight and body fat level for an athlete should be obtained from their individual history and should consider a range of goals including good performance and good health over the long term. Athletes in sports in which low body fat levels are deemed necessary for optimal performance, and in particular, female athletes in these sports, should be considered at high risk for the development of disordered eating. These sports may benefit from education programs promoting safe and effective weight loss strategies, and from screening techniques to identify athletes in the early stages of developing disordered eating and body image problems.

19

Dietary Supplements Ergogenic AIDS

INTRODUCTION

The sports world is filled with products that claim to prolong endurance, enhance recovery, reduce body fat, increase muscle mass, minimize the risk of illness, or achieve other characteristics that enhance sports performance. Athletes are major consumers of supplements, and an important target group for the multibillion dollar supplement industry. The distinction between a supplement and a sports food is sometimes arbitrary. If the distinction is based on the form of the product, we might consider supplements to exist in the form of pills, potions, capsules, or powders, whereas sports foods would take a more traditional form of energy-containing bars, drinks, and other edible products.

However, the definitions differ between countries according to the way that food and pharmaceutical products are regulated. This distinction can have important practical implications for the way that these products are manufactured and marketed. This chapter will review the range of products that are currently available, noting items that have true value as part of the athlete's nutrition program and compounds that have been proven by rigorous scientific testing to be ergogenic (work enhancing). Issues that should be considered in contemplating the use of a supplement include, first, the effectiveness of the product; the amount and timing of supplementation and the specific exercise conditions under which its effects may be optimized must be considered. A second concern relates to whether there is a possibility of contravening the antidoping code imposed by the governing bodies of sport, as this might lead to suspension from competition. Thirdly, and perhaps most importantly of all, the question of safety of supplementation must be considered. This should perhaps be the primary concern, but the use by athletes of pharmaceuticals with well-recognized harmful side-effects shows that this is often not the case.

As a general principle, it is safe to assume that most supplements that offer a direct performance-enhancing effect are against the rules of sport: this category includes drugs and hormones. Most substances that are not banned are not effective: this includes most of the vitamin and mineral supplements as well as the herbal products sold in health food shops. There are, however, some exceptions to these generalizations: substances in this category might include creatine, bicarbonate as well as an-tioxidant nutrients. There are also grey areas, sometimes referred to as "nutraceuticals", and including compounds such as caffeine, that may be classified as foods but which are consumed for their pharmacological action. Of course, we will also see that many sports foods are effective when used by the athlete to meet a special nutritional goal for training or competition.

SUPPLEMENTS

Supplement use is widespread in sport. Reviews of the published literature suggest that the use of supplements is more prevalent in athletes (about 50%) than in the general population (35-40%), while among elite athletes almost 60% report supplement use. All these surveys find that the overall prevalence and the types of supplements used vary with the nature of the sport, the sex of the athletes, and the level of competition. In some surveys, 100% of bodybuilding and strength-training athletes use some form of nutritional supplementation.

It is not possible to review all of the nutritional supplements used by athletes, nor to consider in any detail the evidence relating to more than a few. However, consideration of some specific examples will illustrate the general principles that determine usage, and the evaluation that ought to be applied to these supplements.

CREATINE

Creatine supplementation has been practiced by many successful athletes, particularly in track and field athletics, but also now in many, if not most, other sports. Some indication of the extent of its use is gained from the fact that the estimated sales of creatine to athletes in the US alone in 1997 amounted to over 300 000 kg. This represents a remarkable growth, as its use first became popular in sport after the 1992 Olympic Games in Barcelona. What distinguishes creatine from most other ergog-enic aids is that it seems to be effective in improving performance. More significantly, perhaps, its use is not prohibited by the governing bodies of sport, and there appear to be no harmful side-effects even when very large doses are taken, at least in the quantities that are necessary to produce an ergogenic effect. Issues relating to the use of creatine will be considered in some depth as these highlight the questions that relate to all supplement use.

Creatine metabolism

Creatine phosphate (CP) itself is present in resting muscle in a concentration approximately 3-4 times that of ATP, the immediate energy source for muscle contraction. The amount of ATP in muscle cells is small, and only a fraction of this can be viewed as an energy store: when the cellular ATP concentration falls too far, fatigue ensues. Muscle ATP content rarely falls by more than about 25-30% at the point of fatigue in high-intensity exercise.

Regeneration of ATP at a rate close to that of ATP hydrolysis is essential if fatigue is to be delayed. Transfer of the phosphate group from CP to ADP is catalysed by the enzyme creatine kinase, resulting in the restoration of ATP and the release of free creatine (C). The situation during intense muscle contraction can be represented as follows:

$$ATP \rightarrow ADP + Pi$$

$$CP + ADP \rightarrow ATP + C.$$

The rate of ATP hydrolysis is set by the power output of the muscle, and can exceed 10 mmol·kg dry muscle^{-1} in maximum efforts. The resting ATP content of muscle is about 24 mmol·kg^{-1}, but this cannot fall by more than about 30%, so the need for rephosphorylation of the ADP formed during contraction is obvious. This reaction is extremely rapid, and since the muscle CP concentration can fall to almost zero, it can make a significant contribution to the energy supply necessary for brief bursts of very high intensity exercise. The CP store is also limited, however, and increasing the CP content of muscle ought to allow a greater amount of work to be done using this energy source. During the recovery process after exercise, the creatine kinase reaction is reversed, using energy made available by oxidative metabolism that occurs within the mitochondria:

$$C + ATP \rightarrow CP + ADP$$

$$ADP + Pi + \text{metabolism} \rightarrow ATP.$$

In high-intensity exercise, glycolysis will result in the formation of pyruvate at a rate higher than that at which it can be removed by oxidative metabolism, leading to an accumulation of lactate within the muscle. The hydrogen ions associated with anaerobic glycolysis cause muscle pH to fall, and this increasing acidity is a factor in the fatigue process. A number of buffers within the cell resist changes in pH, and the breakdown of CP is such a mechanism. The creatine kinase reaction can be rewritten to take account of the charges involved:

$$CP^{2-} + ADP^{3-} + H^{+} \rightarrow ATP^{4-} + C.$$

An increased availability of CP for breakdown has the potential to increase the intramuscular buffering capacity, delaying the point at which pH reaches a critically low level.

CP has been reported to play another role within the muscle cell, which is to transfer ATP equivalents from within the mitochondria, where ATP is generated by oxidative phosphorylation, to the cytoplasm where it is required. There is, however, no evidence from studies of human skeletal muscle that this process is limited by the availability of creatine. The apparent failure of creatine supplementation to influence the metabolic response to exercise of moderate intensities or performance in this type of exercise also argues against an important*a*or at least limiting*a*role for this shuttle.

Creatine supplementation and muscle CP concentration

Creatine is an amino acid (methylguanidine-acetic acid) which occurs naturally in the diet, being present in meat: 1 kg of fresh steak contains about 5 g of creatine. The normal daily intake is less than 1 g, but the estimated daily requirement for the average individual is about 2 g. The body has a limited capacity to synthesize creatine in the liver, kidney, pancreas, and other tissues, but the primary site of synthesis in humans is the kidney. This supplies the amount required in excess of the dietary intake, and is also the only way in which vegetarians can meet their requirement. Synthesis occurs from amino acid precursors (methionine, arginine, and glycine), but the synthetic pathway is suppressed when the dietary creatine intake is high.

Studies of resting human skeletal muscle have shown the CP concentration to be about 75 mmol kg dry weight^{-1} and the free creatine concentration to be about 50 mmol $\cdot$kg^{-1}. There is, however, quite a large range of values reported in the literature, and it seems clear that there is considerable interindi-vidual variability. The first studies of creatine supplementation in the 1990s showed that taking creatine (5 g four times per day) over a period of 4-5 days resulted in a marked increase in the total creatine content of the quadriceps femoris muscle. An increase in muscle creatine content was apparent within 2 days of starting this regimen, and the increase was greatest in those with a low initial level: in some cases an increase of 50% was observed. Approximately 20% of the increase in total muscle creatine content was accounted for by creatine phosphate.

More recent studies show that creatine supplementation of ~ 3 g $\cdot$day^{-1} will result in similarly increased muscle creatine concentrations, but it may take 3 weeks to reach the creatine storage threshold. Once creatine loading has been achieved, a continued daily intake of 1-2 g of creatine will maintain the increased muscle creatine content, whereas cessation of all supplemental intake will cause muscle creatine concentrations to gradually return to presupplementation levels over 3-4 weeks. Since coingestion of creatine with carbohydrate (75-100 g) enhances the uptake of creatine into the muscle cell, many sports scientists recommend that creatine supplements be taken with a meal or substantial carbohydrate-rich snack.

EFFECTS OF CREATINE SUPPLEMENTATION ON EXERCISE PERFORMANCE

Muscle creatine content will remain elevated for several weeks following creatine supplementation. If athletes are used as subjects, the increased training loads that seem to be possible after creatine supplementation make it difficult to interpret results of crossover studies where placebo is administered as the second treatment. For these reasons, most of the reported studies have used matched groups of subjects. The past decade has seen the publication of a large number of studies that have investigated the effects of creatine supplementation on the performance of a variety of modes and types of exercise. This literature shows that there appears to be no significant benefit to the peak power output that can be achieved in a single high-intensity exercise bout, but the balance of the available evidence suggests that performance is improved in tasks involving repeated high-intensity exercise with short recovery intervals. In fact, some very recent studies have shown that these benefits are seen in well-trained subjects undertaking field tests or laboratory protocols that simulate competitive events such as team sports. On this basis, creatine supplementation may be a useful adjunct to the training programs of athletes that involve interval or resistance training and to the competition performance of field and court sports involving intermittent high-intensity bursts of play.

There is little information on the effects of creatine supplementation on the performance of more prolonged exercise. In an incremental treadmill running test there was no effect of creatine supplementation on the cardiorespiratory or metabolic response to submaximal exercise, but exercise performance was not measured in this study. However, another study has reported no beneficial effect of creatine supplementation on performance in an endurance running test. In fact, the performance was impaired, perhaps as a result of the small weight gain (~ 1 kg) that is usually associated with acute supplementation with creatine.

The mechanism by which creatine supplementation might improve performance is not entirely clear, although it seems clear that this effect is related to the increased muscle CP content. Recent results indicate that the rate of CP resynthesis after intense exercise is enhanced after high-dose creatine supplementation. This allows faster recovery after sprints as well as allowing more work to be done during each subsequent high-intensity effort.

Creatine and muscle strength

Although there have been numerous investigations into the effects of creatine supplementation on the ability to generate high levels of muscle power, few studies have looked for possible effects on muscle strength. This seems surprising in view of the importance of a high force-generating capacity for the development of power. In an early study, subjects were required to perform five sets of 30 maximal voluntary isokinetic contractions before and after supplementation with creatine or placebo. No effect was seen in the placebo group, and an increase in muscle peak torque production was seen in the creatine group only in the later stages of some of the sets. No effect of creatine supplementation on peak torque was seen, but this experimental model might not allow subjects to generate maximum forces because of the large number of contractions to be performed.

More recently, it has been shown that 5 days of creatine supplementation was effective in increasing maximum voluntary isometric strength of the knee extensor muscles in individuals engaged in a strength training program. This gain was maintained in a subsequent test after a period during which a placebo was administered. In a second group of subjects, the treatment order was reversed: no gain in strength was seen after the first period of placebo administration, but an increase was observed in the third test, after the creatine supplementation period. Isometric endurance capacity at various fractions of maximal voluntary contraction was also increased after creatine supplementation but was not affected by the placebo treatment. Other studies have also shown bigger improvements in strength gains in naïve subjects embarking on a strength training program.

Creatine and body mass

Many studies and anecdotal reports support the suggestion that acute supplementation with creatine is associated with a prompt gain in body mass. This typically seems to amount to about 1-2 kg over a supplementation period of 4-5 days, but may be more than this. Because of the rapid increases in body mass, it must be assumed that this is mostly accounted for by water retention. Increasing the creatine content of muscle by 80-100 $mmol \cdot kg^{-1}$ will increase intracellular osmolality, leading to water retention.

There is some preliminary evidence for a stimulation of protein synthesis*a*perhaps secondary to this osmotically induced swelling of the cells*a*in response to creatine supplementation, but further experimentation is required. It seems unlikely that major effects on muscle protein content can be achieved within 4-5 days. It must be conceded, however, that the reported gains in muscle strength within the same timescale are difficult to explain.

Health concerns of creatine supplementation

Many concerns have been raised that the effects of long-term use of large doses of creatine are unknown and that its use may pose a health risk. Concerns seem to focus primarily on the possible effects on renal function, in particular in individuals with impaired renal capacity. Studies on the response to long-term creatine use are in progress at this time, but results are not yet available. There have, however, been no reports of adverse effects in any of the studies published in the literature, and the few reports of medical problems that have received attention in medical journals have concerned a few individuals who have had pre-existing renal problems prior to taking creatine. One study that specifically examined renal function in individuals supplementing with creatine found no reason to believe that renal complications were likely. Anecdotal reports of an increased prevalence of muscle cramps in athletes taking creatine supplements have been circulating for some time, but there seems to be no substance to any of these stories. It seems likely that any injury suffered by an athlete will be ascribed to an easily identifiable change in habit, such as the introduction of a new supplement.

Uninformed comment blamed the deaths of three American collegiate wrestlers on creatine use, but this was not substantiated at the formal inquiries conducted. Given the increase in body mass that often accompanies supplementation, it does seem possible that athletes who must acutely reduce body mass to qualify for a particular weight category might face problems. It is not unusual in some sports for body mass to be reduced by as much as 10% in the few days before competition: if the mass loss necessary to make the qualifying weight is 1-2 kg more than anticipated due to the weight gain associated with creatine use, the measures required to achieve the target mass will be unusually severe and may provoke problems related to dehydration and hyperthermia.

The concern over possible adverse effects is entirely justified. It is usually recommended that athletes take 20 g of creatine per day for 4-5 days (a loading dose) followed by 1-2 g per day (maintenance dose). Many athletes, however, work on the principle that more is better and may greatly exceed these amounts. Even with very large doses, however, the possibility of adverse effects seems remote. Creatine is a small water-soluble molecule easily cleared by the kidney, and the additional nitrogen load resulting from supplementation is small. The same concerns over renal damage have been raised in the context of protein supplementation among strength athletes and body builders. These athletes may consume up to 400 g of protein per day over very long periods, but there is no evidence that the theoretical problems of clearance of the extra solute load are real.

Carnitine

Depletion of the intramuscular glycogen stores is recognized as one of the primary factors involved in the fatigue that accompanies prolonged exercise. The importance of carbohydrate as a fuel for the working muscles is confirmed by the close relationship between the pre-exercise glycogen concentration and the time for which exercise can be sustained. Further evidence comes from studies that show that increasing the combustion of fat during prolonged exercise, and thus sparing the limited carbohydrate stores, can improve endurance capacity. Increasing fatty acid mobilization by heparin administration has been shown to be effective in improving performance, even though this method is not practical for competitive sport.

Although the supply of plasma free fatty acids to the exercising muscle is an important factor in determining the relative contributions of fat and carbohydrate to oxidative metabolism, a number of other steps are recognized as being involved in fat oxidation. Fatty acid uptake into the cell and translocation across the mitochondrial membrane are also key steps and carnitine is involved in this process, allowing fatty acids to enter the mitochondrion. Within the mitochondrion, carnitine also functions to regulate the acetyl-CoA concentration and the concentration of free CoA. It has been proposed that an increased availability of carnitine within the mitochondrion might allow the cell to maintain a higher free CoA concentration, resulting in a stimulatory effect on oxidative metabolism.

Because of the key role of carnitine in the oxidation of both fat and carbohydrate, it has been proposed that carnitine supplementation may improve exercise performance and also that it may help promote loss of body fat. On the basis of this logic, carnitine is widely sold in sports shops as a supplement for endurance athletes and for those seeking to lose weight. There is, however, no good evidence that carnitine deficiency occurs in the general population or in athletes. Carnitine is present in the diet in red meat and dairy products, so it might be thought that individuals who follow a vegan lifestyle might be at increased risk of deficiency, but it can also be synthesized from lysine and methionine in liver and kidney. Studies have failed to find clear evidence that carnitine supplementation enhances exercise performance. Surprisingly, only a few studies have examined the effect of carnitine on fat oxidation or on success in reducing body fat levels. However, studies of carnitine supplementation have failed to find evidence that it causes an increase in muscle carnitine levels; this would be a necessary starting point for expecting a change in muscle function in response to the supplementation.

It must be concluded from the studies published in the scientific literature that, although there is a theoretical basis for an ergogenic effect of carnitine on performance of both high-intensity and prolonged exercise, this is not supported by the experimental evidence. Supplementation of the diet with carnitine is unlikely to be beneficial for athletes.

Bicarbonate

In exercise that causes fatigue within a few minutes, anaerobic glycolysis makes a major contribution to energy metabolism. Although glycolysis allows higher rates of ATP resynthesis than can be achieved by aerobic metabolism, the capacity of the system is limited, and fatigue is inevitable when high rates of anaerobic glycolysis occur. The metabolic acidosis that accompanies glycolysis has been implicated in the fatigue process, either by inhibition of key glycolytic enzymes, by interfering with calcium transport and binding, or by a direct effect on the actin-myosin interaction. Because of these effects of acidosis on the muscle, it is intuitively attractive to believe that induction of alkalosis prior to exercise, an increase in the muscle buffering capacity, or an increased rate of efflux of hydrogen ions from the active muscles will all have the potential to delay fatigue and improve exercise performance.

Several investigators have reported a decrease in perceived exertion or an increase in performance during high-intensity exercise after bicarbonate administration. Others, however, have shown no benefit of an induced metabolic alkalosis on perceived exertion or performance. In one study designed to simulate athletic competition, trained non-elite (best 800 m time about 2 min 5 s) middle-distance runners were used as subjects and the exercise consisted of a simulated 800-m race: in the alkalotic condition, subjects ran almost 3 s faster than in the placebo or control trials. A more recent report has indicated similar improvements (3-4 s) over a distance of 1500 m in runners who completed simulated races in about 4 min 15 s.

Although these effects on performance might seem small, they are of considerable significance to the athlete: an improvement of even a fraction of a second in these events is considered to be a major achievement. The reason for the conflicting effects reported in the published literature is not altogether clear, but some at least is probably due in part to variations in the intensity and duration of the exercise tests used, in the nature of the exercise task, in the dosage of sodium bicarbonate administered, and in the time delay between bicarbonate administration and the beginning of the exercise test (i.e. in the degree of metabolic alkalosis induced).

There are, of course, potential problems associated with the use of increased doses of bicarbonate. Vomiting and diarrhea are not infrequently reported as a result of ingestion of even relatively small doses of bicarbonate, and this may limit any attempt to improve athletic performance by this method, certainly among those individuals susceptible to gastrointestinal problems. There have been reports of athletes using this intervention, which is not prohibited by the rules of sport, being unable to compete because of the severity of these symptoms. Although unpleasant and to some extent debilitating, these effects are not serious and there are no long-term adverse consequences of occasional use. Sodium citrate administration, which also results in an alkaline shift in the extracellular fluid, has also been reported to improve peak power and total work output in a 60-s exercise test, but without any adverse gastrointestinal symptoms.

Where an increase in performance after bicarbonate ingestion has been observed, it has been ascribed to an increased rate of hydrogen ion efflux from the exercising muscles, reducing the rate of fall of intracellular pH, and relieving the pH-medi-ated inhibition of phosphofructokinase. The higher blood lactate levels after exercise associated with metabolic alkalosis, even when the exercise duration is the same, may therefore be indicative not only of a higher rate of lactate efflux, but also of an increased contribution of anaerobic glycolysis to energy production. There is also a loss of adenine nucleotides from muscle when the exercise intensity is very high, and this loss may be reduced by ingestion of bicarbonate before exercise. Whatever the mechanism, however, it seems reasonable to suggest that bicarbonate administration prior to high-intensity exercise will only enhance performance when the intensity and duration of the exercise are sufficient to result in significant muscle acidosis and adenine nucleotide loss.

CAFFEINE

Caffeine is a drug that, because of its longstanding and widespread use, is considered socially acceptable. Caffeine and the related compounds theo-phylline and theobromine are naturally occurring food components. For many people, these substances are part of the normal daily diet and caffeine is probably the most widely used stimulant drug in the world. Caffeine is included among the list of prohibited (banned) stimulants in the Olympic Movement Anti-Doping Code (1 September 2001), with the comment that "the definition of a positive test is a concentration in urine greater than 12 |ag/ml". This wording is ambiguous since it can be interpreted to mean that either:

1. caffeine intake is banned at all times, with the reporting level being 12 |ag ml^{-1}; or
2. caffeine intake is permitted up to the level that causes a urinary concentration above 12 |ag ml^{-1}.

Actions of caffeine

Caffeine achieves a complex array of effects within the body, including stimulation of the central nervous system, cardiac muscle and epinephrine release and activity. Caffeine has several effects on skeletal muscle involving calcium handling, sodium-potassium pump activity, elevation of cyclic AMP, and direct action on enzymes such as glycogen phos-phorylase. Increased catecholamine action, and the direct effect of caffeine on cyclic AMP, may both act to increase lipolysis in adipose and muscle tissue, causing an increase in plasma free fatty acid concentrations and increased availability of intramuscular triglyceride.

It has been proposed that an increased potential for fat oxidation during moderate-intensity exercise promotes glycogen "sparing"; indeed the early studies of caffeine ingestion and endurance performance identified this as the most likely mechanism to explain the beneficial outcomes. However, more recent studies have provided considerable evidence that the ergogenic benefits of caffeine on exercise performance are not limited to, or always explained by, the so-called "metabolic theory". Several studies have reported an enhancement of performance following caffeine intake in the absence of any change to substrate oxidation, or have found that glycogen sparing is limited to the first 15-20 min of exercise. Others have found individual variability in the metabolic response to caffeine: half of a group of subjects was shown to "spare" glycogen during the first 15 min of exercise following caffeine intake compared with a placebo treatment, while glycogen utilization was unaffected in the other half of the group following caffeine treatment.

Other popular explanations for performance enhancement with caffeine ingestion include effects on the central nervous system (CNS) or a direct effect of caffeine on skeletal muscle. Caffeine ingestion has been shown to elicit greater motor unit recruitment and alter neurotransmitter function in the muscle. It also affects the CNS in ways that cause it to override fatigue signals during exercise. Breakdown products of caffeine such as paraxanthine and theophylline may also have actions within the body. Caffeine supplementation is complex to investigate due to the difficulty in isolating individual effects of caffeine and the potential for variability between subjects.

Effects of caffeine on performance

There are a number of studies showing beneficial effects of caffeine ingestion in a variety of laboratory tests, and a smaller number showing improvements in field tests. Caffeine is unusual in that it appears to provide ergogenic effects across a range of exercise protocols, from shorter efforts of high-intensity exercise to prolonged submaximal exercise. Different mechanisms may be involved to explain the observed performance outcomes. Early studies focused on the effects of caffeine intake on the performance of endurance exercise protocols, with subjects ingesting caffeine doses of 6 mg·kg body mass^{-1}, 1 h before the start of exercise. An increased time to exhaustion was observed in a number of these studies, but performance in simulated race situations, where a fixed amount of work has to be done in the shortest possible time, is also improved.

More recent studies have focused on exercise of shorter duration, and a number of studies have shown beneficial effects on the performance of higher-intensity exercise lasting 4-6 min (e.g. track cycling events, 1500-m running) or 20-60 min (e.g. 1500-m swimming, 40-km cycling). There is little information on performance in sprint tasks, and what is reported is conflicting. There appears to be considerable individual variability in the response to caffeine, for reasons that are unclear, but, surprisingly, seem unrelated to habitual caffeine use.

Whereas the traditional protocol for caffeine ingestion was a 5-6 mg $\cdot kg^{-1}$ dose, consumed 1 h prior to the start of exercise, recent studies have shown performance benefits when caffeine is consumed throughout the exercise bout, or even just towards the end of the protocol. Furthermore, performance enhancement is seen with lower doses of caffeine (i.e. 1-3 mg $\cdot kg^{-1}$). There does not seem to be a dose related effect of caffeine intake; when benefits are seen with a low dose, there are no further improvements with consumption of larger amounts of caffeine.

There is some variability in urinary caffeine excretion between individuals, but in general a caffeine intake of < 6 mg $\cdot kg^{-1}$ is unlikely to cause the urinary caffeine concentration to exceed 12 Hg $\cdot ml^{-1}$. Indeed, such concentrations are typically not reached until caffeine intakes reach 9 mg $\cdot kg^{-1}$ or more. It is therefore clear that positive effects of caffeine can be obtained in a variety of exercise situations with caffeine doses that are far below those necessary to produce a "reportable" sign of caffeine usage. Although some people feel that caffeine is technically a drug that enhances performance and is therefore against the ethics of sport, others feel that the widespread intake of caffeine-containing foods and drinks prevents a meaningful ban from being practical. It is also important for athletes to remember that caffeine is not tested for in out-of-competition samples. Clarification of the present status of caffeine in relation to doping is needed.

Other effects of caffeine

Caffeine has a number of unwanted side-effects that may limit its use in some sports or by sensitive individuals: these effects include insomnia, headache, gastrointestinal irritation and bleeding, and a stimulation of diuresis. There are also some suggestions that high levels of caffeine intake may be a risk factor for bladder cancer. This is unlikely to be modified by occasional use of modest doses prior to competition, but the athlete who may contemplate using high doses of caffeine prior to training on a daily basis should consider this. In the very high doses that were sometimes used by athletes, noticeable muscle tremor and impairment of coordination have been noted.

The diuretic action of caffeine is often stressed, particularly in situations where dehydration is a major issue. This affects particularly competitions held in hot, humid climates where the risk of dehydration is high, and is more important for all athletes whose performance might be negatively affected by dehydration. Athletes competing in these conditions are advised to increase their intake of fluid, but are usually also advised to avoid tea and coffee because of their diuretic effect. It seems likely, however, that this effect is small for those habituated to caffeine use and the negative effects caused by the symptoms of caffeine withdrawal may be more damaging.

Protein and amino acid supplements

Chapter 3 provided a summary of protein metabolism and requirements for training and competition. This chapter concluded that protein supplements are expensive and are unnecessary for achieving an increase in muscle mass or strength. However, as we will discuss in the following section in this chapter on sports foods, products like liquid meal supplements, which provide a compact source of carbohydrate, protein, and micronutrients, are often useful in helping athletes to meet their sports nutrition goals. Typical scenarios include meeting the high-energy needs involved in heavy training, a growth spurt, or a muscle hypertrophy program, or providing a postexercise recovery meal which can simultaneously promote a positive protein balance and glycogen restoration. In both situations a liquid meal supplement might provide a practical alternative or adjunct to everyday foods. The cost of this sports food is usually considerably less than high-protein, or all-protein supplements, but is typically higher than that of normal foods. Nevertheless, this expense may be justified when convenience is an important issue in achieving nutrient intake goals. Several individual amino acids, or amino acid groups, have been singled out for special attention in sports nutrition. During the 1980s, preparations of individual amino acids were the most successfully marketed "designer" supplement, despite a lack of evidence that "free-form" preparations of amino acids were superior in digestion or absorption to amino acids found in intact proteins (i.e. in everyday foods). Today it is possible to purchase a range of tablets or powders containing individual amino acids as the sole ingredients, as well as general sports supplements (sports drinks, liquid meal powders, bars) fortified with additional amino acids. Many of these specialized products provide amino acid intakes that can easily be consumed from everyday foods, but at highly elevated prices. There is currently no good evidence that amino acid supplements enhance sports performance. Special commentaries have been provided in this chapter to address the case for branched-chain amino acids (BCAAs) and glutamine.

Chromium picolinate

Chromium is an essential trace element that has a number of functions in the body, and it has been reported to potentiate the effects of insulin. Because of the anabolic effects of insulin, it might be expected that amino acid incorporation into muscle protein would be stimulated, enhancing the adaptive response to training. There is also some evidence to suggest an increased urinary chromium loss after exercise, further supporting the idea that athletes in training may have higher requirements than sedentary individuals. Chromium is widely used as a supplement by strength athletes, and is usually sold as a conjugate of picolinic acid: this form is reported to enhance chromium uptake.

Supplementation of the diet with chromium picolinate was reported to enhance the adaptive response to a strength training program, with an increase in lean body mass. No direct measures of muscle mass were made in this study, however, and the results must be viewed with caution. A number of subsequent studies, mostly using more appropriate methodology, have failed to reproduce these results, with no effect on lean tissue accretion or on muscle performance being seen. Nonetheless, chromium supplementation remains popular.

Coenzyme Q10

Coenzyme Q10, also known as ubiquinone, is a non-essential lipid-soluble nutrient found predominantly in animal foods and in low levels in plant foods. In the body it is located primarily in the mitochondria, especially in skeletal and cardiac muscle. One of its well-known functions is as a link in the electron transport chain within the mitochondria, thus playing a role in the final production of ATP. It is also believed to have an antioxidant function, mopping up free oxygen radicals in the mitochondrial antioxidant defense system and preventing damage to DNA and cell membranes. It has been suggested that some cardiac and neuro-muscular dysfunction is due to coenzyme Q10 deficiency; indeed patients with ischemic heart disease have been shown to have lower plasma Q10 concentrations. Some studies have shown that these patients respond to coenzyme Q10 supplementation with increased exercise capacity.

Coenzyme Q10 supplements have recently emerged as new products marketed in the general community to promote vigor. For athletes, they are claimed to enhance energy production through the electron transport chain, and to reduce the oxidative damage of exercise. However, a summary of studies which have examined the effects of coenzyme Q10 supplementation on exercise metabolism and performance and on oxidative damage caused by exercise, has failed to find convincing evidence of positive effects. In fact, there are a number of studies that show that coenzyme Q10 has an ergolytic (negative) effect on high-intensity performance and training adaptations. A series of studies undertaken at the Karolinska Institute in Sweden has produced consistent evidence that Q10 supplementation *increases* the oxidative damage and reduces the training re-sponse in previously untrained subjects who undertake a high-intensity exercise program. Clearly, further work is required to investigate the effects of coenzyme Q10 supplementation on exercise performance and training. However, at present there is little to recommend Q10 supplementation to athletes undertaking high-intensity training, and we are reminded that the issue of antioxidant supplementation is complex and as yet unsolved.

Beta-hydroxy beta-methyl butyrate (HMB)

Beta-hydroxy beta-methyl butyrate (HMB) is a metabolite of the amino acid leucine, and is currently one of the most popular dietary supplements. It is claimed to enhance gains in strength and body mass associated with resistance training, to enhance loss of body fat, and to enhance recovery from exercise. These effects are said to occur because of its role as an anticatabolic agent, minimizing protein breakdown and the cellular damage that occurs with high-intensity exercise. Leucine administration is known to influence protein metabolism, specifically to reduce protein degradation during periods of stress or trauma that are associated with elevated protein catabolism. It has been proposed that it is the increase in leucine metabolites such as HMB that mediates this effect. To date, only a few studies of HMB supplementation in humans have appeared in the peer-reviewed literature.

In one study involving healthy but untrained males, daily HMB supplementation was found to reduce urinary 3-methyl histidine excretion (a marker of muscle protein degradation) and plasma creatine kinase concentrations (a crude indicator of cellular damage) when a training program was undertaken. HMB supplementation was associated with a dose-responsive increase in weight lifted during training (particularly in lower body strength), and there was a trend for increased gain in lean body mass with the increase in HMB dose. A second investigation of HMB supplementation (3 mg$\cdot$day^{-1}) and resistance training in previously trained subjects reported trends for greater increases in fat-free mass (assessed by total body electrical conductivity) in the HMB group and increases in muscle strength measurements that were greater for some (upper body) but not all (lower body) lifts. Although these results support the possibility of benefits from HMB supplementation, there are several methodological concerns with these investigations such as the lack of dietary control and the failure to equally match groups for their baseline values.

It is possible to explain the increased gains in the HMB group as the outcome of lower initial levels and a greater potential for change with training. Two other studies of HMB supplementation in trained individuals have failed to find any difference in gains in body mass, strength, and markers of muscle damage when undertaking a matched training program. Therefore, until further studies of HMB supplementation are conducted and reported in full, it is impossible to make a decision on the potential of this supplement, particularly when it is used in well-trained subjects.

Other compounds

Athletes use a wide range of nutritional supplements in their quest for improved performance. Even a cursory inspection of sports shops and magazines reveals the scale and diversity of supplement use. Most of the exotic supplements make extravagant claims and are sold at inflated prices. The market, however, is largely unregulated and few of the claims made for these products are supported by any evidence; instead, they rely on endorsement by top athletes (who are paid handsomely for doing so) and on the gullibility of the consumer.

Sales figures for exotic supplements such as ginseng, inosine, colostrum, bee pollen, royal jelly, and pangamic acid, together with a wide range of vitamins and minerals (including boron, vanadium, zinc, magnesium, and manganese), demonstrate that many athletes remain convinced of their effectiveness. In spite of the limited and conflicting evidence, however, the balance of the available information suggests that there is no benefit from these substances for healthy individuals consuming a normal diet. Some supplements are potentially harmful in large doses and their use should be actively discouraged. Many studies that purport to show beneficial effects are poorly designed, often with inadequate subject numbers and no control group, and few are published in reputable journals. The power of the placebo effect is well recognized, and athletes seem to be particularly susceptible.

Athletes should consider several factors before deciding to use a supplement. The likely benefits should be considered carefully, and weighed against the cost of a supplement program and the risk of negative outcomes. Supplement use, even when it provides a performance advantage, is an expense that athletes must acknowledge and prioritize appropriately within their total budget.

The other disadvantages of supplement use include the potential for side-effects and the possibility of an inadvertent doping outcome. There has been much recent publicity about doping infringements by leading athletes involving alleged use of nandrolone (an anabolic steroid) that has been attributed to their inadvertent intake of prohormones from the use of dietary supplements. Although these prohormones (e.g. 19-norandrostenedione, DHEA, androstenedione, and others) are also banned by antidoping codes, they are often found in dietary supplements both as stated ingredients and as an undeclared ingredient or contaminant.

Other supplements may contain banned stimulants including ephedrine and large amounts of caffeine. Antidoping education messages warn athletes to carefully read the labels of supplements and avoid using products that contain ingredients that are banned in sport. However, several recent reports from independent analyses of dietary supplements have found that a large percentage of products contain banned substances without declaring their presence on labels. Reports from the IOC accredited laboratories in Cologne and Vienna suggest that up to 25% of supplements may contain low levels of unlisted steroids. Therefore, the use of dietary supplements carries a small but real risk of causing high-level athletes who compete in competitions governed by antidoping codes to infringe these rules. Strict liability means that the governing bodies of sport will not accept ignorance as a valid excuse in the case of the athlete who inadvertently consumes a prohibited substance. The cost may be a ban from sport, and the loss of money and prestige.

SUMMARY

Athletes are forever searching for nutritional supplements that will give them a significant advantage over their competitors. This accounts in part for the reports of widespread use of illegal drugs in sport. The difficulty lies in finding something that is effective in improving performance but is not against the rules. It is also important that any chemical substance to be used in this way should not have harmful side-effects. All essential dietary components, including protein, essential fatty acids, vitamins, and minerals, might be considered to come into the category of ergogenic aids, since they indirectly assist performance by maintaining normal health and physiological function. However, supplementation above the level required for maintenance of health is not likely to improve exercise performance. While research supports direct benefits from compounds such as creatine, bicarbonate, and caffeine, the majority of the compounds and products targeted to athletes have not been shown to provide performance enhancements. A promise of instant and dramatic results is alluring to all athletes, regardless of their level of achievement, and the supplement industry that provides these ingredients in pills and powder (non-food form) is a multibillion dollar concern. Many athletes do not understand that the claims made for many supplements and their individual ingredients result from lack of regulation rather than the results of rigorous research. As a result, athletes can be drawn to products that are insubstantial and faddish rather than strategies that provide a worthwhile and lasting contribution to sports performance.

Sports foods that address real nutritional needs of athletes can provide a valuable, although often more expensive, way for the athlete to meet their sports nutrition goals. The most obvious examples of valuable sports foods are liquid meal supplements and sports drinks. However, if the manufacture of these products becomes driven by the inclusion of unsupported "ergogenic" compounds rather than addressing true goals of sports nutrition, there is a risk that these products will become of less value to the athlete. The use of all sports foods and supplements needs to be balanced against expense, the risk of side-effects from some ingredients, and the possibility of an inadvertent doping outcome.

Bibliography

Caswell, Lucy Shelton: *Guide to Sources in Sports History,* New York, Greenwood Press, 1989.

Crowley, David. J. and Paul Heyer: *Sports Chronology,* Boston, Allyn and Bacon, 2003.

Ehrlich, Matthew C.: *Sports in the Movies.* Urbana: University of Illinois Press, 2004.

Andrew, N; Flanagan, S & Ruddy, J: *Sports Tourism Destination Planning,* Dublin, Dublin Institute of Technology, 2002.

Edgell, David L: *International Tourism Policy and Sports, New York,* Van Nostrand and Reinhold, 1990.

Elliott, James: *Sports: Politics and Public Sector Management,* London, Retailed, 1997.

Goeldner, C. R: *The Evaluation of Sports as an Industry and a Discipline, Paper Presented to,* International Conference for Tourism Educators, Guildford, University of Surrey, 1988.

Hall, C Michael *Sports Planning: Policies, Processes and relationships,* Harlow, Prentice Hall, 2000.

Jennings, Gayle: *Sports Economics: Research and Development,* Chichester, Wiley, 2001.

Machin, Alan: *Retracing the Steps: Tourism as Education, Janus,* Fin, ATLAS / FUNTS, 2001.

Schwaninger, M: *Trends in Leisure and Tourism for 2000 - 2010,* Prentice Hall, 1989.

Stevens, Terry: *Island Tourism*: Malta, , WTO, 1993.

Index

□□□